KALLIS' iBT TOEFL® PATTERN

Reading 2

KALLIS' iBT TOEFL® Pattern Reading 2

KALLIS EDU, INC.
7490 Opportunity Road, Suite 203
San Diego, CA 92111
(858) 277-8600
info@kallisedu.com
www.kallisedu.com

ISBN-10: 1-4953-1760-9
ISBN-13: 978-1-4953-1760-6

iBT TOEFL® Pattern - Reading II is the second of our three-level iBT TOEFL® Reading Exam preparation book series.

Our **iBT TOEFL® Pattern Reading** series helps students understand the *context* of each question and provides numerous types of *practice* to master test-taking skills. **Hacking Strategies** and **Quick Looks** break down each question type seen on the official exam so that students have a better understanding of what they are asked to look for in each question. *Practice* includes **Warm Up** questions, **Quick Practice** for focusing on particular question types, and an **Actual Test** that combines all question types.

KALLIS

KALLIS'

TOEFL® iBT

PATTERN

READING 2

ANALYST

Getting Started

A study guide should familiarize the reader with the material found on the test, develop unique methods that can be used to solve various question types, and provide practice questions to challenge future test-takers. *KALLIS' iBT TOEFL® Pattern Series* aims to accomplish all these study tasks by presenting iBT TOEFL® test material in an organized, comprehensive, and easy-to-understand way.

   KALLIS' iBT TOEFL® Pattern Reading Series presents the ten different types of questions that you can expect to encounter on the reading component of the iBT TOEFL test. An entire chapter is devoted to each type of question, allowing you to easily discover which question types you find most challenging and then develop an individual strategy for each type of question. Each chapter uses unique techniques of presenting the reading test material in order to make the practice questions as easy to understand as possible.

Putting the Question into Context

▶ The beginning of each chapter provides a definition of the type of questions that you will learn to master throughout the chapter.

▶ The *Question Model* section located below the definition provides an example question that is then solved in a step-by-step process using the **Hacking Strategy**.

▶ The *Question Formats* section presents the specific wording used to ask each question.

▶ The *Tips* section provides helpful hints so that you know the features of a correct answer and how to identify incorrect answers.

Hacking Strategy

● **Hacking Strategy** provides a step-by-step visualization of how to approach each question.

● Because dealing with so many different types of questions can be confusing, the **Example Breakdown** that follows the **Hacking Strategy** develops a common process to assist you in properly analyzing the text and selecting the most logical answer.

Quick Look

● **Quick Look** provides necessary information to understand how to solve the practice questions.

● The hints given in **Quick Look** can be utilized to learn new aspects of English grammar, and they can be used to brush up on concepts that may already be familiar to you.

● For the more difficult types of questions that are presented in later chapters, **Quick Look** combines visual representations and written descriptions to illuminate what you need to find within each question.

Enhancing Test-Taking Skills with Numerous Practice Questions

Though understanding test-taking strategies will greatly improve your success on the reading test, the best way to improve your skills is through practice. Thus, *KALLIS' iBT TOEFL® Pattern Reading Series* includes a variety of practice questions with varying levels of difficulty.

Warm Up

- The **Warm Up** provides practice questions that are simplified versions of the problem types that you will spend much of your time solving on the actual iBT TOEFL test.

Quick Practice

- Each chapter contains **Quick Practice**, which is composed of ten practice passages with questions that elaborate on the skills developed during the **Quick Look** and **Warm Up**.
- At the end of each chapter, you will be challenged with a **Pop Quiz** that tests your vocabulary skills using words found throughout the passages in the corresponding chapter.

Exercises

- At the end of every two chapters, **Exercises** provides a mini-test that requires you to distinguish one type of question from another and use multiple strategies within the same reading passage.

Actual Practice

- Located in Chapter 11, the **Actual Practice** provides passages with multiple question types that require the reader to combine skills developed throughout the book.
- This section is meant to be more challenging and should be attempted only after you understand the types of questions presented in Chapters 1 through 10.

Actual Test

- The **Actual Test** will familiarize you with the format of the official TOEFL reading test and includes types of questions from each chapter.
- A scaled scoring chart is located at the beginning of the test so that you can grade yourself and get an idea of how you might score on the official TOEFL reading test.
- After the **Actual Test**, you will find **Actual TOEFL Vocabulary**, which contains hundreds of the most commonly employed vocabulary words from TOEFL reading tests.

In Case You Need Help

- ▶ Toward the back of this book, you will find the **Answer Key**, which provides the correct answer to each question and includes explanations.
- ▶ If you do not want to repeatedly flip to the back of the book for answers, simply cut out the **Simple Answers** at the very back of the book. **Simple Answers** provides a quick reference so you can confirm that all your answers are correct.

Now it is time for you to analyze.

Table of Contents

Reading 2
Analyst

I. What Is a Vocabulary Question?

Vocabulary in Context

The vocabulary question asks you to define a vocabulary word or a phrase as it is used within a sentence. Everything surrounding the vocabulary word is called its *context*. Since many English words can have several meanings, the definition of the vocabulary word or the phrase is determined by its context.

A. VOCABULARY QUESTION MODEL

The Republican Party and the Democratic Party are the two main political factions in the United States. The parties have conflicting views on many issues, such as taxes. Democrats generally **favor** increased taxes for the wealthy while Republicans oppose this.

1. The word "**favor**" is closest in meaning to
   (A) want
   (B) discourage
   (C) give
   (D) plan

B. VOCABULARY QUESTION FORMATS

The word/phrase is closest in meaning to _____.

The word/phrase means _____.

The word/phrase _____ probably means _____.

What does the word/phrase _____ mean?

In stating _____, the author means that _____.

C. TIPS

1. To identify the correct meaning of the word in context, take a close look at the sentence and grammatical structure, the usage of punctuation marks, and the meanings of surrounding words.
2. In some cases, you can figure out the meaning of a word simply based on your understanding of the passage's main idea.
3. On the official TOEFL test, some unusual or technical terms have hyperlinked definitions. In this book, such terms are defined at the end of the passage. Because the definition is provided, these words will not appear as questions.

II. Hacking Strategy

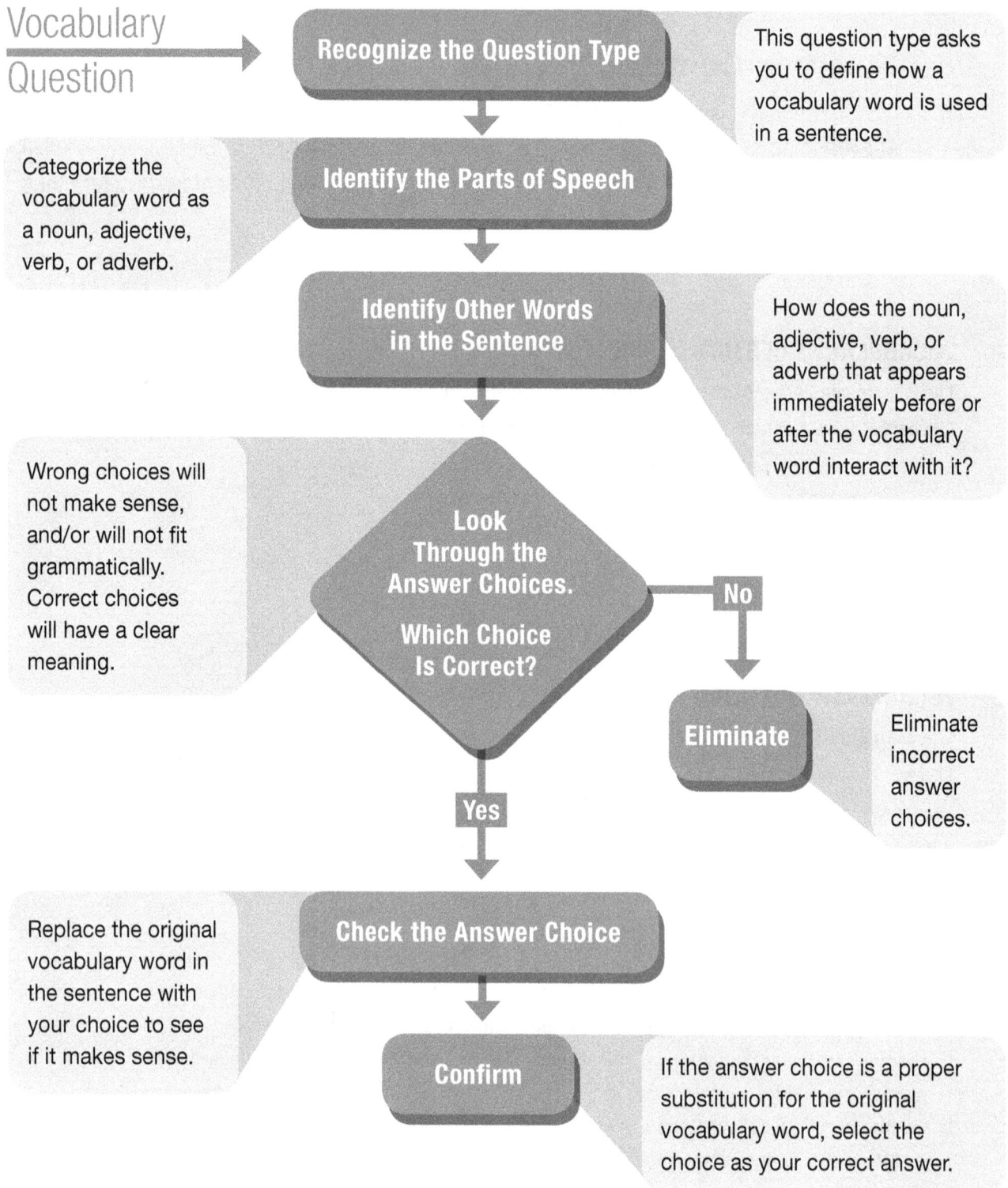

Vocabulary
Question →

Recognize the Question Type

This question type asks you to define how a vocabulary word is used in a sentence.

Categorize the vocabulary word as a noun, adjective, verb, or adverb.

Identify the Parts of Speech

Identify Other Words in the Sentence

How does the noun, adjective, verb, or adverb that appears immediately before or after the vocabulary word interact with it?

Wrong choices will not make sense, and/or will not fit grammatically. Correct choices will have a clear meaning.

Look Through the Answer Choices.

Which Choice Is Correct?

No

Eliminate

Eliminate incorrect answer choices.

Yes

Replace the original vocabulary word in the sentence with your choice to see if it makes sense.

Check the Answer Choice

Confirm

If the answer choice is a proper substitution for the original vocabulary word, select the choice as your correct answer.

EXAMPLE

Recognize the Question Type

The Republican Party and the Democratic Party are the two main political factions in the United States. The parties have conflicting views on many issues, such as taxes. Democrats generally **favor** increased taxes for the wealthy while Republicans oppose this.

The word "**favor**" is closest in meaning to
(A) want
(B) discourage
(C) give
(D) plan

Identify the Parts of Speech

Favor is a verb describing the attitude of Democrats toward increased taxes.

Identify Other Words in the Passage

Democrats generally **favor** increased taxes for the wealthy *while* Republicans oppose this.

We see that the transition word *while* is at the beginning of the second clause. This suggests a contrast between the first clause and second clause.

The second clause uses the verb *oppose* to describe the Republicans' opinion. We can infer from this that **favor** means the opposite of *oppose*, which is a big clue.

Look Through the Answer Choices. Which Choice Is Correct?

(A) want
(B) discourage
(C) give
(D) plan

The correct choice will be a verb, and its meaning will be the opposite of *oppose*.

Eliminate Incorrect Choices

- Eliminate **Choices C** and **D** because they do not mean the opposite of *oppose*.
- Eliminate **Choice B** because *discourage* is similar in meaning to *oppose*, and we are looking for the opposite of *oppose*.

Check the Answer Choice

Democrats generally *want* increased taxes for the wealthy while Republicans oppose this.

This makes sense because *wanting* something is the opposite of *opposing* something.

Confirm

Select the correct answer — **Choice A**.

III. Quick Look

Word Prefixes, Suffixes, Roots

Prefix, Suffix or Root	Meaning	Example and Definition
ab, abs	away from, off	**ab**solve: ab (from) + solve (loosen) = *to free from blame* **ab**duct: ab (away) + duct (draw) = *carry away by force*
ac, acu	sharp	**acu**ity: acu (sharp) + ity (state of) = *sharpness of thought, vision, or hearing* **ac**curate: ac (sharp) + cur (care) + ate (state of) = *precise*
ant, anti	against, opposite	**anti**violence: anti (opposite) + violence = *opposed to violence* **anti**slavery: anti (against) + slavery = *opposed to slavery*
ben, bene	good, well	**bene**factor: bene (well) + factor (to do) = *supporter* **bene**diction: bene (well) + diction (to speak) = *an utterance of good wishes*
cent	one hundred (100)	**cent**ennial: cent (100) + ennial (a period of years) = *pertaining to 100 years* **centi**pede: cent (100) + pede (foot) = *a kind of of insect with numerous legs*
cide, cis, cise	to kill, to cut, cut down, slay	pest**icide**: pest + cide (to kill) = *a chemical used to kill pests such as insects* hom**icide**: hom (human) + cide (to slay) = *the killing of one person by another*
dec, deca	ten, ten times	**deca**thlon: deca (ten) + thlon (contest, prize) = *an athletic contest comprising ten different track and field events* **deca**logue: deca (ten) + logue (words) = *ten commandments*
dent, dont, odont	tooth	ortho**dont**ist: ortho (straight) + dont (tooth) + ist (a person) = *a dentist concerned with preventing or correcting irregularities of the teeth* peri**odont**al: peri (around) + odont (tooth) + al (relating to) = *affecting the gums and other tissues around the teeth*
e, ef, el, em, ex	beyond, out	**e**motion: e (out) + mot (move) + ion (suffix) = *feelings* **ex**pend: ex (out) + pend (pay) = *use up*
equi	equal	**equi**distant: equi (equal) + distant = *equally distant* **equi**nox: equi (equal) + nox (night) = *time when day and night are about equal in length*
exter, extra, extro	outside of, beyond	**extra**ordinary: extra (beyond) + ordinary (common) = *phenomenal* **extro**vert: extro (outside of) + vert (to turn) = *an outgoing person*

Prefix, Suffix or Root	Meaning	Example and Definition
homo	same	**homo**genize: homo (same) + gen (kind) + ize (become) = *to make uniform* **homo**nym: homo (same) + nym (name) = *a word of the same sound or written form*
ia	names, diseases	**phob***ia*: phob (fearing) + ia (disease) = *irrational fear of something* **anem***ia*: anem (want of blood) + ia (disease) = *a disorder that causes a deficiency of red blood cells*
im, in	into, on, near, towards, in	**in**stead: in + stead (place) = *substitute, in place of* **im**port: im (towards) + port (carry) = *to bring in from a foreign country*
inter	between, among	**inter**national: inter (between) + nation (country) + al (relating to) = *worldwide* **inter**cept: inter (between) +cept (to take) = *to take, stop; to see or overhear*
join, junct	join	ad**join**ing: ad (toward) + join + ing = *located next to another* en**join**: en (make) + join = *to direct or order*
luc, lucent, lucid	light, shine	e**lucid**ate: e (out) + lucid (light) + ate (state of) = *clarify* trans**lucent**: trans (through) + lucent (shine) = *transparent*
man, mani manu	hand, make, do	**manu**facture: manu (hand) + facture (make) = *build* **mani**cure: mani (hand) + cure (care) = *cosmetic care of hands and fingernails*
mega	great, million, loud	**mega**phone: mega (loud) + phone (sound) = *a cone-shaped device for magnifying the voice* **mega**ton: mega (million) + ton = *an explosive force equal to one million tons of dynamite*
min, minu	little, small	**minu**te: minu (small) + te (suffix) = *brief time period* **min**or: min (little) + or (condition) = *unimportant; secondary*
mono	one	**mono**poly: mono (one) + pol (sell) + y (characterized by) = *exclusive control of something* **mono**type: mono (one) + type = *the only print of a design made in metal*
multi	many, much	**multi**fold: multi (many)+ fold (so many parts) = *varied and numbered* **multi**lingual: multi (many) + lingual (spoken language) = *able to speak more than two languages*
numer, numera	number	e**numer**ate: e + numer (count) + ate (state of) = *recount* in**numera**ble: in (not) + numerable (countable) = *too many to be numbered*
phon, phone	sound	tele**phone**: tele (distant) + phone (sound) = *a system for transmission of sound* **phon**ics: phon (sound) + ics (pertaining to) = *a method of teaching and reading*
poli	city	necro**polis**: necro (dead) + polis (city) = *a large cemetery* metro**polis**: metro (large) + polis (city) = *a large city*

Prefix, Suffix or Root	Meaning	Example and Definition
pro	for, forward	**pro**pel: pro (forward) + pel (drive) = push; get something going **pro**voke: pro (forward) + vok (call) = to anger or stir up
quad, quadru	four	**quad**rangle: quad (four) + angle = a plane figure having four angles **quadru**plet: quadru (four) + plet (suffix) = any group of four
sat, satis, satur	enough	**satur**ate: satur (full) + ate (state of) = to fill up or soak through **satis**fy: satis (enough) + fy (cause) = gratify
scope	see, watch	tele**scope**: tele (far) + scope (seeing) = instrument used to see distant objects micro**scope**: micro (small) + scope (seeing) = instrument used to view small objects
simil, simul	like, resemble	as**simil**ate: as (make) + simil (like) + ate (state of) = become similar **simul**acrum: simul (like) + lacrum (Latin suffix) = representation
sol, soli solus	alone	**soli**loquy: soli (alone) + loqu (speaking) + y = the act of talking alone **soli**tude: soli (alone) + tude (state) = isolation
sub, sug, sus	under, beneath	**sug**gest: sug (under) + gest (gesture) = recommend **sub**alpine: sub (beneath) + alpine (Alps) = situated in or relating to the regions at the foot of mountains
super, supra	over, above	**super**vise: super (over) + vise (see) = manage **super**ior: super (above) + ior (pertaining to) = higher in rank or quality
therm, thermo	heat	**thermo**meter: thermo (heat) + meter (measure) = an instrument for measuring temperature **thermo**stat: thermo (heat) + stat (standing) = a device that maintains a system at a constant temperature
tox, toxin	poison	**tox**ic: tox (poison) + ic (pertaining to) = harmful to health anti**toxin**: anti (opposite of) + toxin (poison) = substance that neutralizes a specific toxin or poison
tri	three	**tri**pod: tri (three) + pod (foot) = a stand with three legs **tri**angle: tri (three) + angle = any three-sided figure
uni	one	**uni**form: uni (one) + form (shape) = identical **uni**corn: uni (one) + corn (horn) = an imaginary creature with one horn
vid, vis	see	pro**vid**e: pro (before) + vid (see) + e = give **vis**ible: vis (see) + ible (able) = can be seen
zo, zoo	animal	**zoo**nosis: zoo (animal) + nosis (sickness) = any disease of animals communicable to humans under natural conditions **zoo**logy: zoo (animal) + logy (study) = the study of animals

IV. Warm Up

Circle the vocabulary word that correctly completes each sentence.

1. New York City is a well-known (**metropolis** / **necropolis**).

2. When Richard sat in (**soliloquy** / **solitude**), he was able to think more carefully about his decision.

3. The spy was able to (**intercept** / **interject**) only part of the message on the radio.

4. The excellent service from the hotel provided the most (**satisfying** / **saturating**) experience for the travelers.

5. Maria decided to (**absolve** / **abstain**) from eating desserts so that she could fit into her favorite holiday dress.

6. The woman had an (**extraordinary** / **extroverted**) ability to read people's minds.

7. The audience listened with great interest to the actor's (**monologue** / **monotype**).

8. In the novel *Daddy Long-Legs*, main character Judy Abbott is supported by her (**benefactor** / **benediction**).

9. My house is (**equivalent** / **equidistant**) from both John's house and Kevin's house.

10. The students used the (**microscope** / **telescope**) to observe bacterial DNA.

11. The boy felt ill, so his mother used a (**thermometer** / **thermostat**) to check for a fever.

12. President Abraham Lincoln is well known for his contributions to the (**antiviolence** / **antislavery**) movement.

13. Please (**supervise** / **superimpose**) the children while they do their math homework this afternoon.

14. I (**suggest** / **suspend**) that you check the weather report before leaving home this morning.

15. Sharks (**provoke** / **propel**) themselves through the sea with their fins.

16. Living in several different countries enabled Charlie to become (**multifold** / **multilingual**).

17. The airplane experienced a (**minor** / **minted**) delay in landing due to bad weather.

18. Tina sent the publisher a (**manuscript** / **manicure**).

19. The children prepared their school (**uniforms** / **unicorns**) the night before.

20. "Please step forward!" the man called to the crowd through a (**megaphone** / **megaton**).

V. Quick Practice

Practice #1

Read the passage. Then answer the questions that follow.

Model railroading became a well-known hobby when model railroads were first displayed at the Century of Progress **Exposition** in Chicago during 1933 and 1934. Public interest in these models **spurred** manufacturers to produce model railroad **kits** and parts. In 1935, model railroad businesses and hobbyists organized the National Model Railroad Association to establish **uniform** standards for model railroad equipment.

1) The word "**Exposition**" in the passage means
   (A) exhibition
   (B) description
   (C) celebration
   (D) selection

2) The word "**spurred**" in the passage means
   (A) invented
   (B) lengthened
   (C) encouraged
   (D) shortened

3) The word "**kits**" in the passage means
   (A) acts
   (B) sets
   (C) clothes
   (D) ideas

4) The word "**uniform**" in the passage means
   (A) attractive
   (B) frequent
   (C) consistent
   (D) hopeful

Practice #2

Read the passage. Then answer the questions that follow.

The Earth as a whole receives large amounts of rainfall. However, rain does not fall **evenly** on the Earth's surface. For example, rain often **drenches** forests and mountain ranges while it rarely **descends** on desert areas. **Uneven** rainfall causes a lack of water on some parts of the Earth while providing an abundance in other parts.

5) The word "**evenly**" in the passage means
   (A) officially
   (B) slowly
   (C) reasonably
   (D) equally

6) The word "**drenches**" in the passage means
   (A) rapidly cleans
   (B) excessively wets
   (C) slowly changes
   (D) wildly destroys

7) The word "**descends**" in the passage means
   (A) falls
   (B) appears
   (C) advances
   (D) decreases

8) The word "**Uneven**" in the passage means
   (A) brief
   (B) various
   (C) unbalanced
   (D) predictable

Practice #3

Read the passage. Then answer the questions that follow.

According to a Greek legend, the Greek messenger Pheidippides ran **swiftly** from the Greek city of Marathon to Athens, located 42 kilometers away. Once he arrived at the city of Athens, he **announced** the Greek victory over the invading Persian army. However, after his **declaration**, he dropped to the ground and died of exhaustion. Today, people often run in 42-kilometer footraces called "marathons," which **derive** from this ancient Greek legend.

9) The word "**swiftly**" in the passage means
(A) precisely
(B) rapidly
(C) carefully
(D) secretly

10) The word "**announced**" in the passage is closest in meaning to
(A) made historical
(B) made natural
(C) made known
(D) made unclear

11) The word "**declaration**" means
(A) frustration
(B) suppression
(C) notification
(D) calculation

12) The word "**derive**" in the passage is closest in meaning to
(A) originate
(B) finish
(C) direct
(D) harden

Practice #4

Read the passage. Then answer the questions that follow.

High Noon is an **exemplary** American Western motion picture released in 1952. Critics have praised *High Noon* for its vivid **depiction** of a **bleak**, empty landscape. In addition, the film **breaks with** the American cowboy stereotype of an uncomplicated character by showing the hero as an average man filled with fears and doubts.

13) The word "**exemplary**" in the passage means
(A) honest
(B) praiseworthy
(C) extreme
(D) creative

14) The word "**depiction**" in the passage means
(A) portrayal
(B) knowledge
(C) definition
(D) destruction

15) The word "**bleak**" in the passage is closest in meaning to
(A) quick
(B) curious
(C) bright
(D) bare

16) The phrase "**breaks with**" is closest in meaning to
(A) abandons
(B) cancels
(C) disturbs
(D) locates

Practice #5

Read the passage. Then answer the questions that follow.

Although much of Turkey is covered by rocky and **barren** mountains and hills, it has been at the center of two of the largest empires in history. The first was the Greek-speaking Byzantine Empire, which was originally established as part of the Roman Empire. In 330 CE, the Roman emperor Constantine I **appointed** Constantinople as the empire's capital. Although the Byzantine Empire experienced **astonishing** success, it started losing its power and many of its territories by the 1300s. As a result, the Turkish Ottoman Empire was able to **conquer** the Byzantine Empire in 1453.

17) The word "**barren**" in the passage means
   (A) unfortunate
   (B) strange
   (C) ancient
   (D) empty

18) The word "**appointed**" in the passage means
   (A) designed
   (B) celebrated
   (C) selected
   (D) honored

19) The word "**astonishing**" in the passage means
   (A) amazing
   (B) challenging
   (C) unnatural
   (D) boring

20) The word "**conquer**" in the passage means
   (A) exist in
   (B) take over
   (C) take part in
   (D) rely on

Practice #6

Read the passage. Then answer the questions that follow.

An instinctive behavior is a behavior that an organism is born with. For example, after hatching out of its egg on a sandy beach, a sea turtle will **intuitively** crawl toward ocean waves, where it will be safer. This type of behavior is **generated** by a *stimulus*, something that **cues** an animal to act as it does. Another example would be the male stickleback, a type of fish found mainly in the ocean. During the mating season, the male stickleback instinctively becomes **belligerent** and attacks anything red because other male sticklebacks have red bellies.

21) The word "**intuitively**" in the passage is closest in meaning to
   (A) certainly
   (B) continually
   (C) indefinitely
   (D) naturally

22) The word "**generated**" in the passage means
   (A) fixed
   (B) crushed
   (C) produced
   (D) defeated

23) The word "**cues**" in the passage is closest in meaning to
   (A) maintains
   (B) signals
   (C) produces
   (D) leaves

24) The word "**belligerent**" in the passage means
   (A) aggressive
   (B) problematic
   (C) seasonal
   (D) desirable

Practice #7

Read the passage. Then answer the questions that follow.

Cuneiform was a system of writing that was used in the Middle East and became **widespread** long before the development of modern alphabets. Cuneiform started out as pictography* and eventually became more refined. Its characters included **copious** wedge-shaped marks that conveyed sounds and grammatical elements as well. Although cuneiform is considered the earliest known system of writing, people **ceased** using it by the second century CE as more **efficient** writing systems developed.

Pictograph: a picture or symbol standing for a word or group of words, as in written Chinese

25) The word "**widespread**" in the passage means
   (A) exciting
   (B) complete
   (C) knowledgeable
   (D) common

26) The word "**copious**" in the passage means
   (A) plentiful
   (B) copied
   (C) neat
   (D) organized

27) The word "**ceased**" in the passage means
   (A) evaded
   (B) continued
   (C) started
   (D) stopped

28) The word "**efficient**" in the passage means
   (A) experimental
   (B) troublesome
   (C) effective
   (D) interesting

Practice #8

Read the passage. Then answer the questions that follow.

Rube Goldberg was an American cartoonist best known for his crazy and funny cartoons about **intricate** devices designed to accomplish simple tasks. The term *Rube Goldberg* has entered the English **lexicon** as a synonym for "ridiculously complex." One of Goldberg's characters, Professor Gorgonzola Butts, an inventor, introduced the **gadgets** that made Goldberg famous, such as a "Self-Operating Napkin." Goldberg's cartoons were humorous because of their **absurd** subject matter.

29) The word "**intricate**" in the passage is closest meaning to
   (A) expensive
   (B) innovative
   (C) complex
   (D) successful

30) The word "**lexicon**" in the passage means
   (A) equipment
   (B) vocabulary
   (C) identity
   (D) life

31) The word "**gadgets**" in the passage is closest in meaning to
   (A) drawings
   (B) devices
   (C) instructions
   (D) problems

32) The word "**absurd**" in the passage is closest in meaning to
   (A) nonsensical
   (B) enjoyable
   (C) practical
   (D) outstanding

Practice #9

Read the passage. Then answer the questions that follow.

The history of parachutes begins with Leonardo da Vinci in the 15th century. Leonardo drew a sketch of a device that was the **predecessor** of the modern parachute. Although Leonardo never **proceeded** to make such a device, Fauste Veranizo **fabricated** something similar to what Leonardo had sketched and jumped off a building wearing one in 1617. Inventors made many attempts to create a functional parachute. The first parachute for emergency use was invented by Jean Pierre Blanchard in 1785. Blanchard had to **utilize** his parachute when a hot air balloon that he was riding in exploded while in operation.

33) The word "**predecessor**" in the passage means
(A) forecaster
(B) presence
(C) preface
(D) forerunner

34) The word "**proceeded**" in the passage means
(A) proclaimed
(B) continued
(C) succeeded
(D) stopped

35) The word "**fabricated**" in the passage means
(A) fought
(B) wanted
(C) lost
(D) made

36) The word "**utilize**" in the passage is closest in meaning to
(A) bring
(B) create
(C) use
(D) buy

Practice #10

Read the passage. Then answer the questions that follow.

People have **asserted** for decades that there is an **eerily** dangerous region of the Atlantic Ocean where ships and airplanes **inexplicably** disappear. This area is called the Bermuda Triangle because it lies between Bermuda, Puerto Rico, and Florida. The Bermuda Triangle **anomaly** is pseudoscientific* because the area and boundaries of the triangle vary between reports, and documented events of missing aircraft and ships are often questionable.

Pseudoscientific: describes a claim that lacks scientific credibility

37) The word "**asserted**" in the passage is closest in meaning to
(A) claimed
(B) denied
(C) questioned
(D) checked

38) The word "**eerily**" in the passage means
(A) undeniably
(B) frighteningly
(C) reportedly
(D) attractively

39) The word "**inexplicably**" in the passage is closest in meaning to
(A) significantly
(B) mysteriously
(C) arguably
(D) carelessly

40) The word "**anomaly**" in the passage means
(A) trend
(B) pattern
(C) irregularity
(D) attraction

Select the vocabulary word or phrase that has the closest meaning.

7. propel
   A. keep
   B. hold
   C. work
   D. move

8. provoke
   A. raise
   B. anger
   C. please
   D. delight

1. benefactor
   A. opposer
   B. supporter
   C. founder
   D. detractor

2. extraordinary
   A. common
   B. normal
   C. amazing
   D. familiar

3. intercept
   A. interrupt
   B. forward
   C. permit
   D. continue

4. minor
   A. medium
   B. huge
   C. small
   D. major

5. multifold
   A. single
   B. unique
   C. various
   D. general

6. metropolis
   A. dense jungle
   B. major city
   C. main focus
   D. exact center

9. saturate
   A. parch
   B. empty
   C. reduce
   D. drench

10. suggest
    A. hesitate
    B. recommend
    C. alternate
    D. pretend

11. supervise
    A. follow
    B. resign
    C. serve
    D. oversee

12. solitude
    A. desert
    B. waste
    C. attitude
    D. isolation

13. satisfying
    A. failed
    B. offensive
    C. enjoyable
    D. hopeless

14. abstain
    A. decline
    B. indulge
    C. assist
    D. embrace

15. monologue
    A. silence
    B. piece
    C. voice
    D. speech

16. equivalent
    A. similar
    B. distinct
    C. mismatched
    D. different

17. manuscript
    A. text
    B. word
    C. poll
    D. survey

18. manufacture
    A. obtain
    B. produce
    C. transport
    D. authorize

19. lengthen
    A. shorten
    B. finish
    C. hasten
    D. extend

20. consistent
    A. varying
    B. erratic
    C. irrational
    D. regular

21. officially
    A. formally
    B. vaguely
    C. doubtfully
    D. unlikely

22. empty
    A. filled
    B. earthy
    C. bare
    D. final

23. amazing
    A. incredible
    B. boring
    C. expected
    D. terrible

24. ancient
    A. modern
    B. young
    C. antique
    D. unripe

25. naturally
    A. virtually
    B. fairly
    C. ordinarily
    D. uncommonly

26. aggressive
    A. quiet
    B. passive
    C. hostile
    D. tiresome

27. cancel
    A. permit
    B. allow
    C. establish
    D. revoke

28. create
    A. destroy
    B. finish
    C. complete
    D. invent

29. fought
    A. agreed
    B. battled
    C. retreated
    D. upheld

30. attractive
    A. appealing
    B. repellent
    C. cursed
    D. repulsive

1B 2C 3A 4C 5C 6B 7D 8B 9D 10B 11D 12D 13C 14A 15D 16A
17A 18B 19D 20D 21A 22C 23A 24C 25C 26C 27D 28D 29B 30A

I. What Is a Referent Question?

Referent

The referent question asks you to locate a referent, which is a noun or a noun phrase that another word, usually a pronoun, refers. A correct referent should be able to replace the pronoun in the paragraph or passage. It must also agree with the pronoun in number and gender (examples: vehicle → it ; people → they).

A. REFERENT QUESTION MODEL

Although the Dutch artist Vincent van Gogh is celebrated today, his short life was marked by poverty and mental illness. Even during periods of illness, however, van Gogh studied other artists, drew, and painted. In only 10 years, he produced around 900 paintings. **They** depicted everything that he saw. Subjects included flowers, fields, people working, and even hospital wards.

2. The word "**They**" in the passage refers to
   (A) other artists
   (B) ten years
   (C) around 900 paintings
   (D) subjects

B. REFERENT QUESTION FORMATS

The word/phrase _____ refers to _____.
The word/phrase _____ in the passage refers to _____.
What does the word/phrase _____ refer to?
Which of the following does the word/phrase _____ refer to?

C. TIPS

1. A pronoun's referent normally appears before the pronoun, but occasionally the referent will appear after the pronoun.
2. The referent can show up within the same sentence of the pronoun or in a different sentence.
3. In some cases, you may have to locate the referent of a term or phrase instead of a pronoun.
4. Understanding the meaning of the sentence and the role of the pronoun within the sentence can lead you to the referent.
5. Unless a specific gender is indicated, an animal is usually referred to as "it."

II. Hacking Strategy

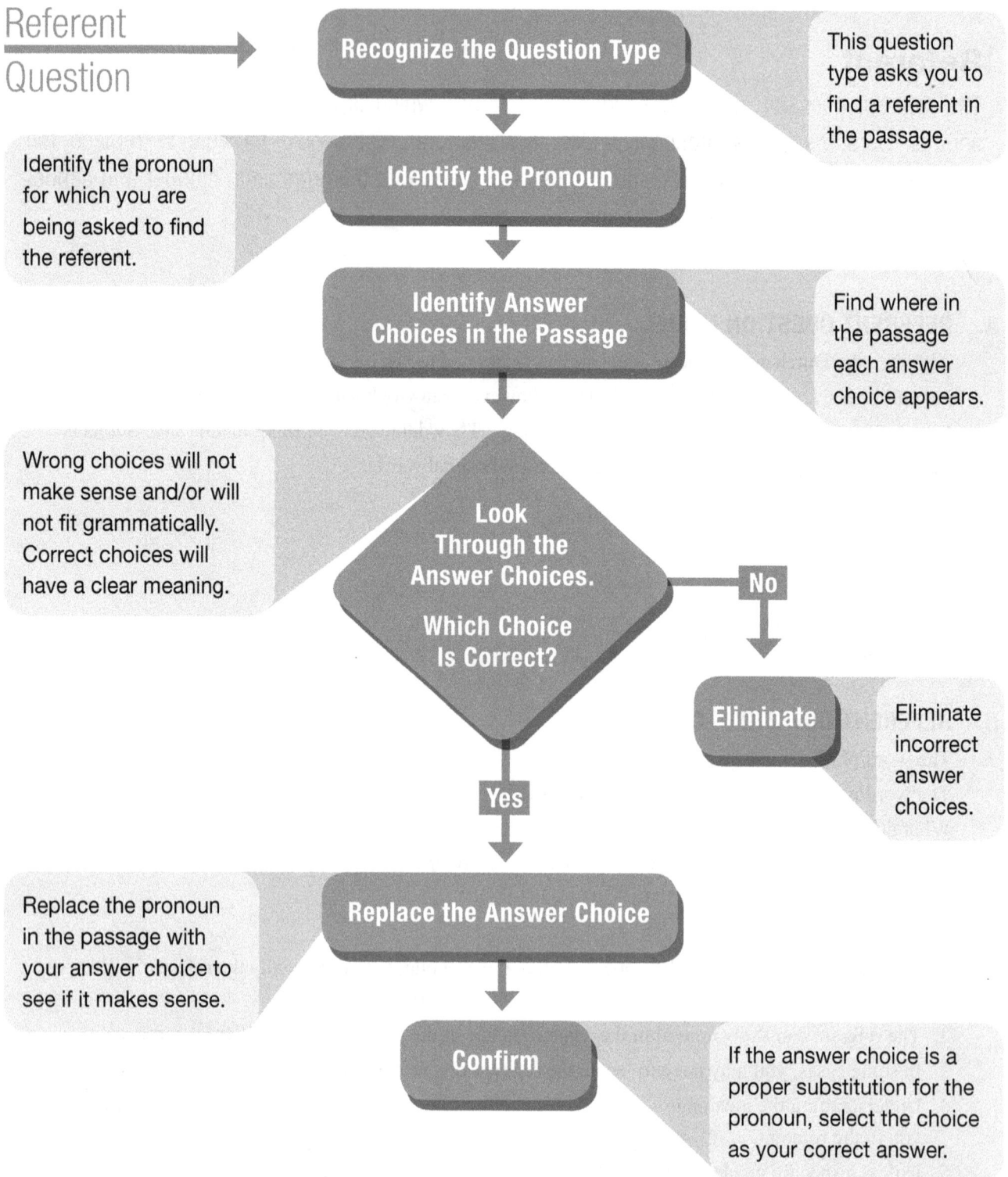

Referent Question

Recognize the Question Type

This question type asks you to find a referent in the passage.

Identify the Pronoun

Identify the pronoun for which you are being asked to find the referent.

Identify Answer Choices in the Passage

Find where in the passage each answer choice appears.

Wrong choices will not make sense and/or will not fit grammatically. Correct choices will have a clear meaning.

Look Through the Answer Choices.

Which Choice Is Correct?

No

Eliminate

Eliminate incorrect answer choices.

Yes

Replace the pronoun in the passage with your answer choice to see if it makes sense.

Replace the Answer Choice

Confirm

If the answer choice is a proper substitution for the pronoun, select the choice as your correct answer.

Recognize the Question Type

Although the Dutch artist Vincent van Gogh is celebrated today, his short life was marked by poverty and mental illness. Even during periods of illness, however, van Gogh studied other artists, drew, and painted. In only 10 years, he produced around 900 paintings. **They** depicted everything that he saw. Subjects included flowers, fields, people working, and even hospital wards.

The word "**They**" in the passage refers to
(A) other artists
(B) 10 years
(C) around 900 paintings
(D) subjects

Identify the Pronoun

They is the pronoun that you are being asked to find the referent for. Notice that **They** is a plural pronoun.

Identify Answer Choices in the Passage

Although the Dutch artist Vincent van Gogh is celebrated today, his short life was marked by poverty and mental illness. Even during periods of illness, however, van Gogh studied <u>other artists</u>, drew, and painted. In only <u>10 years</u>, he produced <u>around 900 paintings</u>. **They** depicted everything he saw. <u>Subjects</u> included flowers, fields, people working, and even hospital wards.

Look Through the Answer Choices. Which Choice Is Correct

(A) other artists
(B) 10 years
(C) around 900 paintings
(D) subjects

Check the choices for grammatical fit and logical meaning.

Eliminate Incorrect Choices

Determine which choices to eliminate by replacing the pronoun with each answer choice:
• Eliminate **Choice A** because "*Other artists* depicted everything that he saw" does not make sense, as van Gogh did not have other people depict what he saw.
• Eliminate **Choice B** because "*10 years* depicted everything that he saw" does not make sense since a period of time cannot depict anything.
• Eliminate **Choice D** because "*Subjects* depicted everything that he saw" does not make sense, as *subjects* refers to "everything that he saw," so it is repetitive in context.

Replace the Answer Choice

Replace the pronoun with the answer choice you think is correct:
• Select **Choice C** because "*Around 900 paintings* depicted everything that he saw" makes sense both grammatically and logically.

Confirm

Select the correct answer — **Choice C**.

III. Quick Look

Pronouns Used in Referent Questions						
Subject Pronouns	he	she	you	it	they	we	one
Object Pronouns	him	her	you	it	them	us	one
Possessive Pronouns	his	her	your	its	their	our	one's
Demonstrative Pronouns	this	these	that	those			
Relative Pronouns	who	whom	which/that	whose			
Other Pronouns	some	most	many	any	one(s)	another	(a) few
	the other	(the) others	all	both	none	several	(a) little
	either	neither	each	the first	the last	the former	the latter

Example   There are two roads. Which route will get you to your destination?

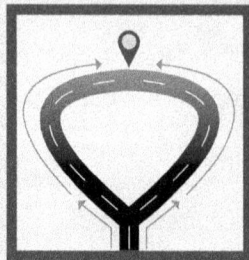

Either will get you there.

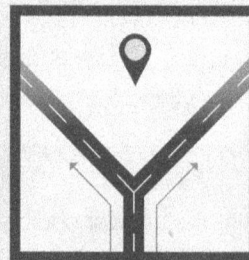

Neither will get you there.

IV. Warm Up

Circle the noun or pronoun that correctly completes each sentence.

1. Although Bart and Lisa agreed to attend the party, (**some / neither**) of them showed up.

2. Timothy wanted to explore the forest, but (**it / he**) looked much too dark within.

3. All of the ducklings followed the mother duck to the lake except (**either / one**) of them.

4. Several people gave Susie different advice about the new job offer, and most of them told her to take (**them / it**).

5. There were two dogs in the competition, and (**most / both**) of them proved that they could perform the tricks.

6. Of the eight major planets in the solar system, Jupiter is the largest and is known for (**its / their**) big red dot.

7. The most common eye color among people is brown; more than half of the world's population has (**it / them**).

8. Bryan saw many fish while scuba diving, but he thought that only (**many / a few**) of them were pretty.

9. Chelsea's favorite place to go is the beach, and many of her friends would agree that (**it / there**) is also their favorite place.

10. Barney and Robin have been good friends for many years, and (**her / their**) mothers get along well, too.

11. We opened (**one's / our**) refrigerator to see what we could prepare for tonight's dinner.

12. If you do not understand the directions, it is (**your / his**) responsibility to ask the teacher.

13. When asked if she preferred vanilla or chocolate ice cream, the girl chose (**the first / the other**).

14. Michael, the only (**one / some**) with a driver's license, is driving us to the movie.

15. The class was divided on which United States president they should write an essay on; some wanted to write an essay on Andrew Jackson while (**others / all**) preferred writing on James Madison.

16. The girl had heard that it was going to rain today, so she made sure to take (**its / her**) umbrella when she left the house.

17. While both dogs and cats make great pets, I prefer (**the latter / the last**) because I have always owned one.

18. Thomas called his boss to let her know that (**he / she**) would be late for work because his dog was sick.

19. The members of Congress regretted (**its / their**) decision to pass the bill.

20. "I prefer not to have a lot of ice cream, just (**a little / a few**), please," Stacy said during dinner.

V. Quick Practice

Practice #1

Read the passage. Then answer the questions that follow.

There are numerous stories about George Washington, the first president of the United States, but many of them are not true. One famous but fictional story tells of a young Washington cutting down a cherry tree that belonged to his father. When confronted by **him**, Washington is believed to have confessed, saying, "I cannot tell a lie." Although this story is untrue, people often use **it** to illustrate Washington's character.

1) The word "**him**" in the passage refers to
   (A) the first president of the United States
   (B) young Washington
   (C) a cherry tree
   (D) his father

2) The word "**it**" in the passage refers to
   (A) a cherry tree
   (B) Washington
   (C) this story
   (D) Washington's character

Practice #2

Read the passage. Then answer the questions that follow.

The tradition of literati painting in China was distinct from professional art. Literati painting was a means of self-expression by amateur painters. They were usually educated government employees who had acquired great skills in calligraphy. They used **these** to create simple black brushstrokes to express their unique perspectives. Most often, literati painters produced scenes of peaceful wilderness. But beyond that, they loved to experiment, leading to highly diverse works. **Some** consist of older men or travelers appreciating natural beauty. Many include a poem written by the painter or a friend.

3) The word "**these**" in the passage refers to
   (A) amateur painters
   (B) educated government employees
   (C) great skills in calligraphy
   (D) simple black brushstrokes

4) The word "**Some**" in the passage refers to
   (A) unique perspectives
   (B) literati painters
   (C) scenes of peaceful wilderness
   (D) highly diverse works

Practice #3

Read the passage. Then answer the questions that follow.

Located in South Asia, Nepal is a small country with a unique and tremendously diverse geography that includes both low and high elevations. Three main geographical regions make up Nepal. **These** are the Terai plains, the mid-level hills, and the Himalaya mountains. The snow-capped Himalayas provide a sharp contrast to Nepal's lower terrain. Tallest among **them** is Mount Everest. At 8,848 meters in height, it is the tallest mountain in the world.

5) The word "**These**" in the passage refers to
(A) low and high elevations
(B) three main geographical regions
(C) the Terai plains
(D) the Himalaya mountains

6) The word "**them**" in the passage refers to
(A) three main geographical regions
(B) the Terai plains
(C) the mid-level hills
(D) Himalayas

Practice #4

Read the passage. Then answer the questions that follow.

Besides heredity, many factors can influence a person's reaction to allergens. Factors such as changes in weather, certain diseases, and fatigue can affect how an individual reacts to **them**. Another that is often overlooked is one's emotional state. For example, stress can weaken the body's defenses and lead **one** to develop asthma when exposed to pollen.

7) The word "**them**" in the passage refers to
(A) factors
(B) changes in weather
(C) certain diseases
(D) allergens

8) The word "**one**" in the passage refers to
(A) an individual
(B) emotional state
(C) stress
(D) pollen

Practice #5

Read the passage. Then answer the questions that follow.

Aspirin is one of the most widely used medications in the world. It is used both as a fever reducer and as an anti-inflammatory* for minor aches. United States doctors commonly recommend that some of their patients use aspirin daily. **They** claim that for some patients, daily use of aspirin may prevent some of the leading causes of deaths in the U.S., such as heart attacks and strokes. While having certain benefits, aspirin does have side effects. Some common examples of **these** are heartburn and stomach irritation.

*Anti-inflammatory: medicine used to ease swelling, fever, and pain

9) The word "**They**" in the passage refers to
(A) medications
(B) minor aches
(C) U.S. doctors
(D) patients

10) The word "**these**" in the passage refers to
(A) leading causes of deaths
(B) certain benefits
(C) side effects
(D) heartburn and stomach irritation

Practice #6

Read the passage. Then answer the questions that follow.

Greek poet Theocritus has been called the creator of pastoral poetry. He left such an impression in the field of poetry that centuries later, the famous Roman poet Virgil drew from Theocritus' ideas for one of **his** famous works, the *Eclogues*. However, little is known about Theocritus' life except for what he himself wrote about in the *Idylls*, which remains the most famous ancient pastoral poetry in history. **It** includes characters and scenes from nature that were reflections of his life in Greece. Examples of these characters are rural people, fishermen, and southern Greek shepherds.

11) The word "**his**" refers to
 (A) Theocritus
 (B) the creator of pastoral poetry
 (C) Virgil
 (D) *Eclogues*

12) The word "**It**" in the passage refers to
 (A) the *Eclogues*
 (B) Theocritus
 (C) the *Idylls*
 (D) history

Practice #7

Read the passage. Then answer the questions that follow.

Industrial designers try to create or improve products that are useful, comfortable, and attractive. During the late 1800s and early 1900s, manufacturers began to produce various machines and gadgets, but **they** often lacked appeal. Gradually, traditional crafters and artists lent their help to businesses so that **their** products looked more appealing. By the 1930s, many everyday objects such as pencil sharpeners and sewing machines became more visually attractive.

13) The word "**they**" in the passage refers to
 (A) industrial designers
 (B) products
 (C) manufacturers
 (D) machines and gadgets

14) The word "**their**" in the passage refers to
 (A) machines and gadgets
 (B) crafters and artists
 (C) businesses
 (D) everyday objects

Practice #8

Read the passage. Then answer the questions that follow.

The Mexican-American War, which lasted from 1846 to 1848, arose from border conflicts. Texas had declared independence from Mexico, and the United States was planning to include the territory in **its** borders. Ultimately, the Mexican-American War broke out because Mexico refused to give up Texas. However, by the end of the war, **it** was forced to surrender a vast territory including Texas, New Mexico, Arizona, and California.

15) The word "**its**" in the passage refers to
 (A) Texas
 (B) independence
 (C) Mexico
 (D) the United States

16) The word "**it**" in the passage refers to
 (A) the United States
 (B) the Mexican-American War
 (C) Mexico
 (D) Texas

Practice #9

Read the passage. Then answer the questions that follow.

Fuel gases are very combustible and can easily explode. Explosions can occur when a gas leaks from its container and reaches an ignition source, such as an open flame or spark. In the United States, many changes have been made to prevent gas explosions. The addition of odorizers to fuel gases is one of **them**. An odorizer adds a strong *odor*, or smell, to a fuel gas. Therefore, when a gas leak happens, the strong odor helps individuals in the area detect **it** in time to prevent an explosion.

17) The word "**them**" in the passage refers to
   (A) many changes
   (B) gas explosions
   (C) odorizers
   (D) fuel gases

18) The word "**it**" in the passage refers to
   (A) an odorizer
   (B) a fuel gas
   (C) a gas leak
   (D) an explosion

Practice #10

Read the passage. Then answer the questions that follow.

Many people associate hearts with feelings, though they know that hearts are actually muscles. One reason that **they** do not literally "get broken" is that the heart sits in the pericardium, a kind of cone-shaped bag of fluid. The pericardium is multilayered, and has fluid between the layers that acts as a cushion. **It** also holds the heart just tightly enough so that it cannot over-expand or move around.

19) The word "**they**" in the passage refers to
   (A) people
   (B) feelings
   (C) hearts
   (D) muscles

20) The word "**It**" in the passage refers to
   (A) heart
   (B) pericardium
   (C) fluid
   (D) cushion

Select the vocabulary word or phrase that has the closest meaning.

7. consist of
A. contain
B. create
C. comfort
D. conceal

8. tremendously
A. enormously
B. interestingly
C. lovingly
D. thoughtfully

1. explode
A. erupt
B. snap
C. crackle
D. shiver

2. ignition
A. evaporation
B. condensation
C. precipitation
D. combustion

3. source
A. effect
B. finish
C. result
D. start

4. acquire
A. obtain
B. demand
C. provide
D. spend

5. unique
A. uncommon
B. hidden
C. explosive
D. uniform

6. perspectives
A. individuals
B. performances
C. areas
D. outlooks

9. region
A. yard
B. area
C. forest
D. sphere

10. heredity
A. attendance
B. genetics
C. acquirement
D. residence

11. allergens
A. irritants
B. allotments
C. fears
D. changes

12. overlook
A. conquer
B. scrutinize
C. magnify
D. ignore

13. weaken
A. sharpen
B. rescue
C. ripen
D. debilitate

14. ache
A. comfort
B. pain
C. relief
D. thought

15. irritation
A. calmness
B. enjoyment
C. annoyance
D. happiness

16. benefit
A. advantage
B. handicap
C. obstruction
D. prevention

17. pastoral
A. fierce
B. peaceful
C. stormy
D. violent

18. reflections
A. lamentations
B. representations
C. exclamations
D. revelations

19. useful
A. efficient
B. important
C. practical
D. appropriate

20. gadget
A. point
B. stone
C. device
D. concept

21. appeal
A. charm
B. petition
C. claim
D. application

22. arose
A. departed
B. fought
C. emerged
D. delayed

23. vast
A. beneficial
B. expensive
C. significant
D. enormous

24. fictional
A. concocted
B. true
C. apparent
D. tedious

25. confront
A. soothe
B. challenge
C. placate
D. answer

26. confess
A. conceal
B. disapprove
C. admit
D. refuse

27. illustrate
A. draw
B. represent
C. criticize
D. demonstrate

28. feeling
A. numbness
B. disregard
C. neglect
D. sensation

29. literally
A. longingly
B. figuratively
C. forcefully
D. actually

30. fluid
A. solid
B. liquid
C. motion
D. fixation

17B 18B 19C 20C 21A 22C 23D 24A 25B 26C 27D 28D 29D 30B
1A 2D 3D 4A 5A 6D 7A 8A 9B 10B 11A 12D 13D 14B 15C 16A

Exercises

Exercise #1 Read the passage. Then answer the questions that follow.

From the early 1940s to the late 1950s, Hollywood studios produced many movies in the *film noir* style, such as *Double Indemnity* and *The Maltese Falcon*. **These** typically portray a world of moral corruption and crime. The main character is often a detective who is smart and **solitary**, and there is almost always a beautiful woman who **lures** him into a **grim** situation. The action usually takes place in a city at night. **It** is sometimes in **dingy** settings, such as **rundown** offices or hotel rooms. There is often a sense of **anxiety** that the characters will not be able to escape their fate, even if the crime is solved. **This** is further emphasized by **edgy** music and deep shadows.

1) The word "**These**" in the passage refers to
   (A) early 1940s to late 1950s
   (B) Hollywood studios
   (C) many movies in the *film noir* style
   (D) *Double Indemnity* or *The Maltese Falcon*

2) The word "**solitary**" in the passage means
   (A) alone
   (B) creative
   (C) lonely
   (D) solid

3) The word "**lures**" in the passage means
   (A) entices
   (B) relates
   (C) trims
   (D) washes

4) The word "**grim**" in the passage means
   (A) radical
   (B) hopeless
   (C) unusual
   (D) decisive

5) The word "**It**" in the passage refers to
   (A) a world of moral corruption and crime
   (B) a grim situation
   (C) the action
   (D) a city

6) The word "**dingy**" in the passage means
   (A) cool
   (B) uncertain
   (C) dreary
   (D) dangerous

7) The word "**rundown**" in the passage means
   (A) isolated
   (B) distinguished
   (C) imaginary
   (D) deteriorating

8) The word "**anxiety**" in the passage means
   (A) certainty
   (B) uneasiness
   (C) hysteria
   (D) misery

9) The word "**This**" in the passage refers to
   (A) a sense of anxiety
   (B) their fate
   (C) the crime
   (D) edgy music

10) The word "**edgy**" in the passage means
   (A) thoughtful
   (B) confusing
   (C) calm
   (D) tense

Exercise #2 Read the passage. Then answer the questions that follow.

Among 16th- and 17th-century Europeans, buyers of fine art did not usually **deem** women to be **proficient**, let alone **brilliant**, painters. However, they made an exception for one Italian woman, Artemisia Gentileschi. Gentileschi had learned from her father, a successful painter who worked in the Baroque style of the era. This style often took its subject from a story already known to the audience, illustrating **its** most dramatic moment. To add to the intensity, Baroque artists used deep shadow contrasted with light. Gentileschi became so **adept** at Baroque painting that she was eventually **commissioned** to paint for powerful families and kings.

While the few women painters who did succeed in this period mainly painted portraits, Gentileschi's work depicts scenes from myth or religious scripture. Her subjects are almost always women who are strong though **they** may be suffering. In some of her paintings, she portrays violence. Her most **sensational** paintings focus on the Biblical figure Judith. In **them**, Judith and a woman servant **ruthlessly** behead a man in order to take revenge.

11) The word "**deem**" in Paragraph 1 means
   (A) name
   (B) make
   (C) consider
   (D) prove

12) The word "**proficient**" in Paragraph 1 means
   (A) capable
   (B) perfect
   (C) unable
   (D) professional

13) The word "**brilliant**" in Paragraph 1 means
   (A) hostile
   (B) anxious
   (C) exceptional
   (D) promising

14) The word "**its**" in Paragraph 1 refers to
   (A) the style
   (B) the subject
   (C) a story
   (D) the audience

15) The word "**adept**" in Paragraph 1 means
   (A) adapted
   (B) skilled
   (C) handy
   (D) natural

16) The word "**commissioned**" in Paragraph 1 means
   (A) trained
   (B) sold
   (C) allowed
   (D) hired

17) The word "**they**" in Paragraph 2 refers to
   (A) portraits
   (B) scenes
   (C) subjects
   (D) women

18) The word "**sensational**" in Paragraph 2 means
   (A) dramatic
   (B) visionary
   (C) believable
   (D) three-dimensional

19) The word "**them**" in Paragraph 2 refers to
   (A) her painting subjects
   (B) all of Gentileschi's paintings
   (C) Gentileschi's sensational paintings
   (D) Judith and a woman servant

20) The phrase "**ruthlessly**" in Paragraph 2 means
   (A) eventually
   (B) fearfully
   (C) brutally
   (D) reluctantly

Exercise #3 Read the passage. Then answer the questions that follow.

Water fowl such as ducks, geese, and swans have **undergone** many **adaptations** – including the development of special beaks and feet – that allow them to paddle about in water and find **edible** organisms. However, flamingos stand out the most among **these**, and not only for their bright pink color. Flamingos have evolved unique **characteristics** that are specific to their preferred habitats, which are deep coastal lagoons.

　　To help **them** walk in deeper water, flamingos developed the longest legs relative to body size of any bird. As a result, they had to develop long necks, so that they could also reach down when the water was **shallow**. Their long necks, in turn, may be why flamingos developed sharply bent beaks. When **foraging**, **they** bend their long necks downward, which allows them to gaze into the water while their curved beaks scoop up food. They can stay this way for quite a long time without **arduous** effort.

21) The word "**undergone**" in Paragraph 1 means
(A) experienced
(B) understood
(C) expected
(D) undervalued

22) The word "**adaptations**" in Paragraph 1 means
(A) adoptions
(B) emphases
(C) changes
(D) challenges

23) The word "**edible**" in Paragraph 1 means
(A) dangerous
(B) audible
(C) helpful
(D) ingestible

24) The word "**these**" in Paragraph 1 refers to
(A) water fowl
(B) adaptations
(C) special beaks and feet
(D) edible organisms

25) The word "**characteristics**" in Paragraph 1 is closest in meaning to
(A) features
(B) strategies
(C) genetics
(D) environments

26) The word "**them**" in Paragraph 2 refers to
(A) characteristics
(B) habitats
(C) lagoons
(D) flamingos

27) The word "**shallow**" in Paragraph 2 means
(A) not strong
(B) not salty
(C) not coastal
(D) not deep

28) The word "**foraging**" in Paragraph 2 is closest in meaning to
(A) sleeping
(B) searching
(C) harvesting
(D) fishing

29) The word "**they**" in Paragraph 2 refers to
(A) legs
(B) long necks
(C) flamingos
(D) sharply bent beaks

30) The word "**arduous**" in Paragraph 2 means
(A) effortless
(B) flexible
(C) difficult
(D) organized

Exercise #4 Read the passage. Then answer the questions that follow.

Anger can be one factor that helps humans and animals survive. When humans and animals **confront** a threat, a physical fight-or-flight response is **triggered** in the body. This mechanism also occurs when humans and animals are angered. Anger can also be a useful emotion in society if **it** motivates people to challenge wrongdoing.

However, if a person's anger is uncontrolled, damages his or her relationships, or results in **hostile** behavior, anger management classes can be helpful. In these classes, people learn to recognize their fears and frustrations and assert themselves calmly. Classes may **cover** relaxation techniques and communication **strategies**. **They** also may include **cognitive** restructuring, a technique to change a person's habit of **irrational** and negative thinking. **This**, in turn, leads to more positive "self-talk."

31) The word "**confront**" in Paragraph 1 means
(A) encounter
(B) conceal
(C) attain
(D) support

32) The word "**triggered**" in Paragraph 1 means
(A) pursued
(B) initiated
(C) hindered
(D) destroyed

33) The word "**it**" in Paragraph 1 refers to
(A) body
(B) anger
(C) society
(D) wrongdoing

34) The word "**hostile**" in Paragraph 2 means
(A) combative
(B) interesting
(C) exhausted
(D) shallow

35) The word "**cover**" in Paragraph 2 means
(A) comprise
(B) hide
(C) release
(D) close

36) The word "**strategies**" in Paragraph 2 means
(A) arrangements
(B) proposals
(C) units
(D) tactics

37) The word "**They**" in Paragraph 2 refers to
(A) anger management classes
(B) fears and frustrations
(C) relaxation techniques
(D) communication strategies

38) The word "**cognitive**" in Paragraph 2 means
(A) negative
(B) creative
(C) physical
(D) mental

39) The word "**irrational**" in Paragraph 2 means
(A) technical
(B) logical
(C) unreasonable
(D) conventional

40) The word "**This**" in Paragraph 2 refers to
(A) cognitive restructuring
(B) a person's habit
(C) negative thinking
(D) self-talk

I. What Is a Fact and Detail Question?

Fact and Detail

The fact and detail question asks you to identify a fact or detail from the passage.

- A **fact** is something that can be proven when it agrees with an experience or observation.
- A **detail** is a piece of information used to support the main idea of a passage.
- Facts and details are directly stated in the passage.

A. FACT AND DETAIL QUESTION MODEL

An *archetype* is a well-known symbol or representation of something or someone. Archetypes often appear in folklore* and universally popular stories. For example, in the story of *Romeo and Juliet*, the two main characters are an archetype for star-crossed lovers who are desperately in love with one another but are forbidden from pursuing their relationship for some reason.

Folklore: traditional stories and beliefs that belong to a certain culture or group

3. According to the passage, where do archetypes commonly appear?
    (A) In *Romeo and Juliet*
    (B) In symbols and representations
    (C) In star-crossed lovers
    (D) In folktales and world-famous stories

B. FACT AND DETAIL QUESTION FORMATS

What _____? Which _____? Why _____? Where _____? When _____? How _____?

Which statement BEST describes _____?   What does the author say about _____?

What is the main cause of _____?   Which of the following is an example of _____?

Which of the following is true?

C. TIPS

1. The correct answer may be a paraphrase* of the passage's information.
    Paraphrase: the restatement of information in a different form

2. Incorrect answers may:
    - restate information from the passage without correctly answering the question
    - state information from the passage incorrectly
    - be false according to the information from the passage
    - be unnecessary or not mentioned in the passage

II. Hacking Strategy

Fact and Detail
Question →

Recognize the Question Type

This question type asks you about the facts and details given in a passage.

Find where in the passage each answer choice appears.

Identify Key Words and Phrases in the Question, and Locate Them in the Passage

Wrong choices will either disagree with what the passage says or may not appear in the passage at all.

Look Through the Answer Choices.

Which Choice Is Correct?

No →

Eliminate

Eliminate incorrect answer choices.

Yes ↓

Confirm

Select the correct answer choice that is true to the passage's information.

(EXAMPLE

An *archetype* is a well-known symbol or representation of something or someone. Archetypes often appear in folklore and universally popular stories. For example, in the story of *Romeo and Juliet*, the two main characters are an archetype for star-crossed lovers who are desperately in love with one another but are forbidden from pursuing their relationship for some reason.

*Folklore: traditional stories and beliefs that belong to a certain culture or group

According to the passage, where do archetypes commonly appear?
(A) In *Romeo and Juliet*
(B) In symbols and representations
(C) In star-crossed lovers
(D) In folktales and world-famous stories

Identify Key Words and Phrases in the Question, and Locate Them in the Passage

According to the passage, where do **archetypes commonly appear**?

An *archetype* is a well-known symbol or representation of something or someone. Archetypes often *appear* in folklore and universally popular stories. For example, in the story of *Romeo and Juliet*, the two main characters are an archetype for star-crossed lovers who are desperately in love with one another but are forbidden from pursuing their relationship for some reason.

Look Through the Answer Choices. Which Choice Is Correct?

By looking at the key words and phrases, we see that our answer is in the second sentence. Even though we believe that we have found the right answer, it is still a good idea to look further in the passage to be sure. Check thoroughly.

• Select **Choice D** because the passage states that "Archetypes often appear in folklore and universally popular stories," or *in folktales and world-famous stories*.

Eliminate Incorrect Choices

• Eliminate **Choice A** because *Romeo and Juliet* contains archetypes, but it is not where archetypes are commonly found.
• Eliminate **Choice B** because *symbols and representations* define archetypes, but they are not where archetypes are commonly found.
• Eliminate **Choice C** because the phrase *star-crossed lovers* describes a story, not an archetype.

Confirm

Select the correct answer — **Choice D**.

III. Quick Look

Transitions Used to Introduce Facts and Details

Illustrating	*provides description*					
	For example	Next	Such	For instance	To illustrate	Such as
Explaining	*tells more to provide better understanding*					
	At this point	Furthermore	In fact	Because	How	In this case
Adding	*gives more supporting information*					
	Also	Finally	Moreover	Another	Furthermore	Too
Giving Reasons	*tells why something is*					
	As a result of	Because of	One reason is	Because	Due to	Since
Contrasting	*gives information that is different from what was said before*					
	Although	Instead	Rather	However	Nevertheless	Like / Unlike
Comparing	*notes how things are similar to or different from/than each other*					
	Both	Like	Similarly	Equally important	The same	Similar to
Showing Results	*tells the outcome*					
	Accordingly	Consequently	Therefore	Thus	Otherwise	As a result of
Limiting	*puts boundaries on the information's scope or reach*					
	Although	Except for	However	But	Even though	Yet
Emphasizing	*highlights important information*					
	Clearly	In fact	Surely	Certainly	Indeed	Most important

IV. Warm Up

Identify whether each sentence contains a fact (F) or an opinion (O).

1. Caffeine has been confirmed by research _____ to have a stimulating effect on the human nervous system.

2. According to several sources, the first _____ modern Olympic Games were held in Athens, Greece, in 1896.

3. France is the most enjoyable country in _____ the world to visit because of its historical attractions.

4. Only the intelligent space aliens would _____ be able to travel to Earth.

5. China is the most populated country in _____ the world.

6. Most people enjoy spices in their foods _____ and cuisines.

7. Crocodiles are much scarier at night than _____ during the day.

8. Confucius was an ancient Chinese _____ philosopher who emphasized that people should treat others as they wish to be treated.

9. Drinking fruit juice is the only way that _____ you can get a great start on your day.

10. Children who participate in sports are _____ the only ones with high self-esteem.

11. Machu Picchu, a 15th-century site of the _____ Inca Empire in Peru, sits approximately 2,400 meters above sea level.

12. An individual must have a sense of _____ humor to become a great and influential leader.

13. Pyramid of Giza in Egypt is one of the _____ Seven Wonders of the Ancient World.

14. Native Americans inhabited America for thousands of years before Europeans _____ colonized it.

15. Before the Internet, one way that people communicated with each other was by _____ telephone.

16. Bell peppers taste better if they are first steamed for a short time. _____

17. It appears that women generally talk more than men during a conversation. _____

18. The most important teacher in a child's life is his or her mother. _____

19. Studies have shown that getting seven to eight hours of sleep each night can help _____ the body fight against diseases.

20. At one time, Czechoslovakia was one country, but now it is divided into _____ Slovakia and the Czech Republic.

V. Quick Practice

Practice #1   **Read the passage. Then answer the questions that follow.**

During Europe's High Middle Ages, members of the land-owning noble class engaged in a great deal of hunting. Generally, the wealthy claimed not only their inherited large farming estates but also private forests. Some vast forests were also claimed by kings; hunting in these royal forests required a royal license. For the most part, the peasants who lived and worked on a lord's estate could not expect to be granted such a license. A lower-class person who was caught with game from a restricted forest could be punished with death. The law may have preserved forests, but it caused great public resentment.

Hunting benefited nobles by relieving boredom and providing meat for their tables. It also helped them maintain war-related skills, as they had to track prey, ride horses, and shoot arrows at targets. To help in the hunt, nobles began training specialized breeds of dogs as well as birds, such as falcons and hawks.

1) According to Paragraph 1, what point does the author make about royal licenses?
   (A) Hunters given permission to enter royal forests were not peasants.
   (B) Licenses issued by the king or queen gave people the right to inherit estates.
   (C) Only royals were prohibited from hunting in selected forests.
   (D) Poor people could not play games in royal forests without licenses.

2) According to Paragraph 1, what was one outcome of nobles claiming private forests?
   (A) Kings inherited nobles' estates.
   (B) Many people thought that hunting rules were unfair.
   (C) Many peasants were illegally hunting in the forest.
   (D) People got in the habit of applying for hunting licenses.

3) According to Paragraph 2, what was one benefit of noble hunting?
   (A) Peasants were able to access more animal protein.
   (B) Nobles had something to do with their colleagues.
   (C) Nobles sharpened their skills for armed battle.
   (D) Social classes were organized into different zones.

4) According to Paragraph 2, what was TRUE about hunting in the High Middle Ages?
   (A) Nobles preferred only one type of animal for their hunts.
   (B) Hunting parties used large targets to encourage more sociability.
   (C) Hunting was often boring and mostly for practicing militarily.
   (D) Birds of prey were trained to help hunters acquire meat.

Practice #2

Read the passage. Then answer the questions that follow.

A solvent dissolving a solute creates a solution. For example, when a person dissolves a cube of sugar in a cup of hot tea, the sugar cube is a *solute*, and the water in the tea is a *solvent*. The two together make a *solution*, which indicates that the molecules of the tea water are attached to the molecules of sugar. The two types of molecules have attached to each other because they are attracted to areas of negative and positive charges in each other's structures. As a solution, they are evenly distributed throughout the cup. If sand is added to the cup of tea, it will not dissolve because its molecules will not interact with the water molecules, and the sand will sink to the bottom.

Molecules without positive and negative charges will often interact with substances that are very much like themselves. For instance, mixing two types of oils together will easily form a solution because the molecules of each oil are similar to each other.

Interestingly, solvents are not always liquids; it is possible for them to be solids or gases. For example, heating two kinds of metal and mixing them can form a *metal alloy*, or a "solution" that is a solid at room temperature. In addition, solutes are not always solid or liquid; a gas can be dissolved into water, such as the carbonation added to soft drinks.

5) According to Paragraph 1, how does a solution occur?
(A) A solvent dissolves a solvent.
(B) A solute is dissolved by a solvent.
(C) A solvent dissolves evenly.
(D) A solute dissolves a solvent.

6) According to Paragraph 1, the solute and solvent
(A) react to each other's charges
(B) create bonds when mixed in a liquid form
(C) are capable of dissolving most substances
(D) have molecules that harbor special properties

7) In Paragraph 2, the author states that two types of oils might create a solution because
(A) they do not have any water within their structures
(B) they are both positively charged and therefore can absorb extra charges
(C) their molecules are alike, and therefore they mix together
(D) they are made of elements that attract each other

8) According to Paragraph 3, which of the following is TRUE?
(A) Liquids cannot dissolve other liquids.
(B) Liquids, solids, and gases can act as solutes.
(C) Stirring sand into water will create a solution at first.
(D) Solvents must have positive and negative charges to dissolve solutes.

Practice #3

Read the passage. Then answer the questions that follow.

Many have argued that Antonio Meucci, a 19th-century Italian scientist, was the true inventor of the telephone. In the 1830s, Meucci developed a "voice communicator" that allowed him to converse from his ground-floor laboratory with his wife in their second-floor bedroom. Meucci said later that he was not able to obtain funding to develop his prototype.

In 1876, Alexander Graham Bell applied for a United States patent for the telephone, and it was granted. Meucci was one of several inventors who challenged the patent in court, claiming that Bell had copied his work. Meucci's case was argued for years, but in the end, he was not able to prove that his invention incorporated the use of electromagnetic transmission of sound and voice. Bell's attorneys said that Meucci's device had been based on simpler acoustic principles, and the judge agreed with the attorneys' claim.

9) According to Paragraph 1, why did Antonio Meucci claim to have invented the telephone?
   (A) He had developed hundreds of types of telephones in his laboratory.
   (B) He had used one for many years and had focused his work and publishing on it.
   (C) He had conveyed verbal messages by using his device in his residence.
   (D) He had shown Alexander Graham Bell his laboratory, including his "voice communicator."

10) According to Paragraph 1, how did Meucci explain why he had not made his invention known to the public?
   (A) He said only rich people are able to get certain types of patents.
   (B) He said a company had bought all of his prototypes.
   (C) He said that he had been planning to do so for many years.
   (D) He said that he had not had the money to move it beyond the early stage.

11) According to Paragraph 2, what did the U.S. give Bell?
   (A) Sole rights to the invention of the telephone
   (B) Legal punishment for having made a claim
   (C) Credit for acoustic principles
   (D) Materials and funding for inventing the telephone

12) Paragraph 2 states that the courts decided that
   (A) Meucci's device was electromagnetic, but he did not develop it
   (B) Meucci's invention used different technology than Bell's
   (C) Meucci invented the telephone, but he did not have the correct patent application
   (D) Bell invented the telephone, but he may have used Meucci's work

Practice #4

Read the passage. Then answer the questions that follow.

In 1701, King Charles II of Spain died without any children. At the time, Spain was the largest empire in the world, claiming the territories of present-day Spain, the Philippines, vast sections of the Americas, and parts of Italy and the Netherlands. The question of who should succeed to the throne of Charles II as King of Spain led to violence. Two European factions fought for their proposed successors in what is called the *War of Spanish Succession.*

Each faction supported a different cousin of Charles II. One was a French prince, but many in Europe objected to the fact that if he inherited the rule of France as well as Spain, he would have a huge, powerful kingdom. The other choice, supported by England, was an Austrian prince who might inherit the kingdom including what is now Germany. The selection of either prince raised the risk of the development of a European superpower.

Finally in 1713 and 1714, treaties were signed that ended the war. The French prince Philip V was declared King of Spain but was also removed from French succession so that he could not become King of France as well. Yet within a few years, Philip's grandfather, the King of France, died. Consequently, Philip claimed the vacant kingship, causing a new war.

13) What does Paragraph 1 say was the main cause of the War of Spanish Succession?
   (A) Spain claimed too much territory as part of its global empire.
   (B) Two rival groups wanted different princes to succeed to the throne of Charles II.
   (C) Charles II had too many heirs, causing civil war.
   (D) Either choice of cousins endangered Europe's balance of trade.

14) According to Paragraph 2, the major factions in the war were
   (A) Spain, Italy, the Netherlands vs. France
   (B) France, Germany, Spain vs. England, Austria
   (C) France vs. Austria, England
   (D) France, America vs. Spain, Austria, Germany

15) According to Paragraph 2, why was the succession complicated?
   (A) The French successfully took control of the Spanish kingdom.
   (B) Charles II's two potential successors belonged to different European kingdoms.
   (C) The Spanish were determined to strengthen their control over their territories.
   (D) Merging countries in Europe would cause problems for England.

16) Paragraph 3 states that the War of Spanish Succession ended because
   (A) the French agreed to limit the French prince's power
   (B) the Spanish agreed to enthrone Philip V
   (C) the Austrian prince obtained Italy and the Netherlands
   (D) the English made a treaty with Philip V

Practice #5

Read the passage. Then answer the questions that follow.

The United States does not mint* all its coins in one place. Rather, it creates metal coins at several locations. The coins intended for circulation in the regular economy come from the Philadelphia Mint or the Denver Mint. The public can tour these locations and see how coins are manufactured.

There is also a mint in San Francisco that produces "proofs." In the past, "proof" coins were samples created to ensure quality before the large-scale production of coins for actual U.S. circulation, but now they are also produced in small numbers for collectors. At West Point in New York, there is a mint that specializes in particular proofs as well as gold, silver, and platinum coins for people who want to invest in precious metals. Every coin made in the U.S. is engraved with the first letter of the mint at which it was made.

The process of creating coins begins when long strips of metal travel through a press, which punches out blank coins. A furnace then heats and softens the blanks before the washer-and-dryer stage. Next, the coins go through an "upsetting mill," which creates the rim around their edges. Finally, they are stamped with designs by a coining press. Before they are distributed, a machine counts and bags the finished coins. Afterward, they are transported to federal reserve banks and later delivered to banks across the U.S.

Mint: produce coins by shaping and stamping metal

17) Paragraph 1 states that U.S. mints
   (A) create circulating coins at all four locations
   (B) offer tours at sites where regular coins are produced
   (C) work together to produce all the money used in the U.S.
   (D) circulate coins around their production sites

18) Paragraph 2 defines coin "proofs" as
   (A) coins that can be proved to come from particular mints
   (B) coins that the U.S. government backs up in terms of purity and worth
   (C) the term used for the first coins minted in the U.S.
   (D) originally referring to a preliminary set of coins to check quality

19) What does Paragraph 2 say about U.S. mints in San Francisco and New York?
   (A) They mint many coins through large-scale production.
   (B) Coins from them are the only ones stamped with the mint's first initial.
   (C) They specialize in coins that probably will not be used as money.
   (D) U.S. Treasury-owned precious metals are stored at them.

20) According to Paragraph 3, how are coins minted?
   (A) Washed, dried, cut, engraved, then packaged
   (B) Punched, heated, washed, upset, then stamped
   (C) Punched, softened, pressed, shaped, then washed
   (D) Pressed, washed, punched, upset, then inspected

Practice #6

Read the passage. Then answer the questions that follow.

During the 1970s, disc jockeys, or DJs, in New York City began isolating the rhythmic "breakdown" sections of dance records. Taping these to play the same clip of music over and over, the DJs helped create a sidewalk phenomenon in which young street dancers competed against each other, taking turns dancing in the center of a circle of onlookers.

The activity was dubbed *breaking*, also *b-boying*, or *b-girling*, and many dancers still use those terms. Most people, however, call it *breakdancing*. The activity copied dance moves from styles of dance that were popular during the 1970s. Breakdancers then added improvised acrobatics, including sudden freezes, which are dramatic falls to the ground caught just in time; *headspins*, or spinning upside down on one's head; and various handstands.

Hip-hop music usually accompanies today's break dancers, but any type of music with a fast tempo can serve as well. Over the decades, the activity has gained worldwide popularity, and one can find "breakers" in places as distant as South Korea and Germany.

21) According to Paragraph 1, where did breakdancing first become popular?
(A) Outdoors in an urban center
(B) In recording studios with DJs
(C) Within particular circles of friends
(D) In South Korea and Germany

22) Paragraph 1 states that the dance can be traced to
(A) DJs who also liked to dance and compete
(B) acrobats who lived in New York City
(C) "breakdown" or rhythmic sections of dance records
(D) homeless youths who lived on city sidewalks

23) According to Paragraph 2, breaking requires its youthful practitioners to
(A) invert their bodies by using upper-body strength and balance
(B) know everything about hip-hop dancing
(C) always abide by the rules of competition
(D) prepare dance routines ahead of time

24) Based on Paragraph 3, what does the author believe about breakdancing?
(A) It began in the 1970s and is still associated with that decade.
(B) It started as street competitions outdoors but is now on stages.
(C) It has died out in the U.S. and now can only be seen in other countries.
(D) It has adapted to newer styles of music and different places.

Read the passage. Then answer the questions that follow.

The Statue of Liberty is an enormous green metal sculpture located on Liberty Island in the New York Harbor. The figure is a woman wearing Roman-style robes. She represents the Roman goddess of freedom, *Libertas*, who was associated with freed Roman slaves. With her right hand, she holds up a lighted torch. Her full name is *Liberty Enlightening the World*.

An artist and a politician living in France under Napoleon III's undemocratic regime came up with the idea for the statue not long after America's Civil War ended slavery in the United States. The two men organized fundraising drives in both France and the U.S. Many ordinary people contributed.

The statue's arm and torch were exhibited at the 1876 Centennial Expo in Philadelphia. Her head was exhibited at the 1878 Paris World Fair. When she was finished up to the waist, reporters were invited to lunch on a platform built within her. Finally, she was shipped to New York in 300 copper parts and then reassembled.

25) According to Paragraph 1, the statue is depicted as "enlightening" the world by
(A) reflecting greenish metallic light
(B) guarding an important harbor
(C) reminding people of the cost of slavery
(D) carrying a lighting device

26) Paragraph 1 says that the statue is modeled on a
(A) classic woman of light and learning
(B) heroine who fought for an end to Roman slavery
(C) goddess connected with liberation of slaves
(D) slave who became an icon in the ancient world

27) Paragraph 2 traces the concept for the statue to a time in history when
(A) artists could not work freely in their own countries
(B) many soldiers had died fighting Napoleon III
(C) the pursuit of freedom and democracy affected many lives
(D) French people wanted to free slaves in their own territories

28) According to Paragraph 3, the Statue of Liberty
(A) was designed for the 1878 Paris World Fair
(B) was shown to the public in segments
(C) has several platforms inside for reporters
(D) was put together and taken apart in many countries

Practice #8

Read the passage. Then answer the questions that follow.

Graceland was the home of rock-and-roll legend Elvis Presley. Located on a former farm outside of Memphis, Tennessee, Graceland got its name from Grace, a former owner's aunt. In his early 20s, Presley hoped to find quiet and privacy there and bought it in 1957 when he was at the height of his popularity. His parents, wife, daughter, and some members of his extended family lived there at different times.

Presley renovated the 23-room mansion to suit his tastes. He removed a chandelier; he added walls and gates, a racquetball court, and a TV room with three TVs; and most famously, he created a "jungle room" with an indoor waterfall. There were stereos in every room, a jukebox, and a piano. Reportedly, Presley's father had a swimming pool in his bedroom.

When Presley died in 1977, he was buried near his parents and grandmother in the home's meditation garden. The home was opened to the public in 1982 and has become one of the most-visited private homes in the United States.

29) According to Paragraph 1, what did a young Elvis Presley do?
   (A) He built a farmhouse.
   (B) He moved in with his Aunt Grace.
   (C) He purchased a residence.
   (D) He renovated his old family home.

30) Paragraph 1 suggests that Presley's home
   (A) was a place that he went to find solitude from friends and family
   (B) created a trend of having indoor jungle rooms in 1950s homes
   (C) was intended to be a quiet place where Presley could take a break from the pressures of fame
   (D) provided a place for fans to meet Presley in person

31) Paragraph 2 describes Presley's home as having
   (A) additions that gave him more privacy
   (B) several kinds of gardens
   (C) a variety of recreational facilities
   (D) special lighting and windows for tropical plants

32) According to the passage, the author says that Graceland
   (A) serves as a cemetery for the Presleys and Memphis
   (B) was purchased to provide isolation but now draws many tourists
   (C) has limited public access in contrast to its prior uses
   (D) reveals many secrets and serves as a focal point for biographers

Practice #9

Read the passage. Then answer the questions that follow.

Imprinting is the neurological process of learning a behavior quickly and permanently. In *filial imprinting*, species that depend on their parents for survival "imprint on" their mother, or what they assume is their mother, immediately after birth or hatching. Newborn animals that imprint will never forget the intense attachment formed because imprinting means that their brains have become "hard-wired" with the knowledge that their parents bring safety, food, and warmth. As a result, not only will they always recognize their parents, but they will also recognize their own kind – what is "us" and what is "them."

Imprinting is easy to identify in birds, such as geese, which leave the nest shortly after hatching. Filial imprinting is especially important to the survival of such a species. Newborns can follow their mother to search for food and safety, and they can find her again if they become lost. Imprinting also can enable young animals to recognize possible predators.

33) According to Paragraph 1, what is imprinting?
   (A) It is a lesson that mothers keep repeating until it is learned.
   (B) It is a recent development in the field of neurology.
   (C) It is a lesson that once learned, the brain never needs to learn again.
   (D) It is a kind of message that newborns communicate to caregivers.

34) Who does Paragraph 1 say is the object of filial imprinting?
   (A) The animal that gave birth
   (B) The newborn and its siblings
   (C) Whoever or whatever the newborn thinks is its parent
   (D) A part of the brain that becomes permanent

35) According to Paragraph 1, which of the following is one benefit of imprinting?
   (A) Newborns know which group they belong to and who is not like them.
   (B) All newborns can see and run right after birth; thus, they can escape predators.
   (C) Parents can temporarily leave their offspring with other "caregiver" members of the group.
   (D) Animals know survival techniques that they need to learn right away.

36) Based on Paragraph 2, animals that most obviously imprint are
   (A) those that need safety
   (B) newly hatched birds
   (C) newborns who always get lost
   (D) species that have the best parents

Practice #10

Read the passage. Then answer the questions that follow.

Noah Webster helped define American English. He labored for 22 years to produce a dictionary, learning 26 languages so that he could properly assess the origin of words. He wanted to standardize regional usage, pronunciation, and spelling within the relatively new United States. Finally in 1828, at the age of 70, he published *An American Dictionary of English Language*. The book listed 70,000 words, many more than any previous dictionary, and about 12,000 of them had American origins rather than British. For example, the word "skunk" was new, because the skunk inhabits the Americas but not Europe. He also added technological and scientific words. However, some critics said that Webster had included too many common words, calling the dictionary "vulgar."

37) According to the passage, how did Noah Webster go about defining American English?
   (A) He worked every day for 22 years and made sure that everything was proper.
   (B) He worked for decades to invent new words and trace linguistic origins.
   (C) He worked on usage standards for 26 regions to adopt.
   (D) He studied other languages and brought scientific terms into the American lexicon.

38) According to the passage, what was one of Webster's goals in producing a dictionary?
   (A) He wanted to boast about the United States.
   (B) He was interested in promoting certain fields of study.
   (C) He disliked British English and wanted to replace it.
   (D) He wanted to unify the new nation's language.

39) The author mentions *skunk* as an example of
   (A) a word that Americans use differently than British
   (B) a word that different regions of the U.S. pronounced differently
   (C) a word that did not have British origins
   (D) a word from a scientific field that would not normally have been included

40) The author says that not everyone applauded the new dictionary because
   (A) it was longer than any other dictionary
   (B) it provided American spellings for words rather than British ones
   (C) it included some words that did not seem to belong in a dictionary
   (D) it did not correctly explain the origins of words

Select the vocabulary word or phrase that has the closest meaning.

7. historical
A. fictional
B. genetic
C. counted
D. ancient

8. populated
A. inhabited
B. deserted
C. unoccupied
D. reduced

1. folklore
A. legend
B. truth
C. history
D. nonfiction

9. influential
A. invalid
B. unmoving
C. powerful
D. obscure

2. universal
A. particular
B. confined
C. irregular
D. worldwide

10. colonize
A. depart
B. settle
C. leave
D. escape

3. desperate
A. confident
B. satisfied
C. reckless
D. unworried

11. conversation
A. silence
B. dialogue
C. huddle
D. report

4. forbidden
A. outlawed
B. permitted
C. authorized
D. approved

12. studies
A. industries
B. analyses
C. outlines
D. corners

5. confirm
A. destroy
B. approve
C. oppose
D. number

13. divided
A. maintained
B. retained
C. detached
D. together

6. enjoyable
A. annoying
B. boring
C. agreeable
D. unhappy

14. boredom
A. madness
B. sadness
C. loneliness
D. dullness

15. noble
A. upper-class
B. middle-class
C. lower-class
D. senior-class

16. dissolve
A. enact
B. uphold
C. melt
D. support

17. patent
A. secret
B. habit
C. permit
D. ballot

18. grant
A. forfeit
B. award
C. refuse
D. ignore

19. transmission
A. conveyance
B. duplication
C. repetition
D. modification

20. acoustic
A. mechanic
B. electric
C. auditory
D. intellectual

21. punish
A. discipline
B. reward
C. guard
D. protect

22. successor
A. inheritor
B. winner
C. master
D. leader

23. circulate
A. distribute
B. manufacture
C. display
D. explain

24. popular
A. disliked
B. favored
C. unknown
D. loathed

25. practitioner
A. adolescent
B. amateur
C. trainee
D. expert

26. enormous
A. compact
B. gigantic
C. gleaming
D. valuable

27. recreational
A. expensive
B. entertaining
C. repairable
D. unique

28. tourist
A. native
B. fugitive
C. traveler
D. driver

29. recognize
A. distinguish
B. mislead
C. eliminate
D. entertain

30. applaud
A. disprove
B. apply
C. acclaim
D. search

I. What Is a Negative Fact Question?

Negative Fact

The negative fact question asks you to identify the answer choice that is not described in the passage or is not true according to the passage.

A. NEGATIVE FACT QUESTION MODEL

Harry Houdini was a famous magician born in Hungary in 1874. He and his family moved to the United States when Houdini was a boy. Later on, he began his career as a magician, specializing in escape acts. One of his acts was the "Milk Can Escape," in which he was put inside an enclosed, oversized milk can filled with water and had to escape in order to avoid drowning. Another of his famous escape acts was his "Straitjacket* Escape." In this stunt, Houdini was hung upside down by his ankles while wearing a straitjacket and had to free himself from the jacket.

Straitjacket: an article of clothing that resembles a jacket and restrains the arms of the person wearing it

4. According to the passage, all of the following are true about Harry Houdini EXCEPT:
   (A) He was a famous magician.
   (B) He was best known for saving himself from drowning.
   (C) He specialized in escape acts.
   (D) The "Milk Can Escape" was one of his most famous escape acts.

B. NEGATIVE FACT QUESTION FORMATS

Which of the following is NOT mentioned in the passage?

What is NOT mentioned as _____?

What is NOT given as a reason for _____?

All are examples of _____ EXCEPT _____.

All describe _____ EXCEPT _____.

All statements are true EXCEPT _____.

All are mentioned EXCEPT _____.

_____ involves all EXCEPT _____.

C. TIPS

1. When you see questions with words EXCEPT or NOT, three of the answer choices will be true.
2. Remember, you are looking for an answer that is untrue or is not included in the passage.

II. Hacking Strategy

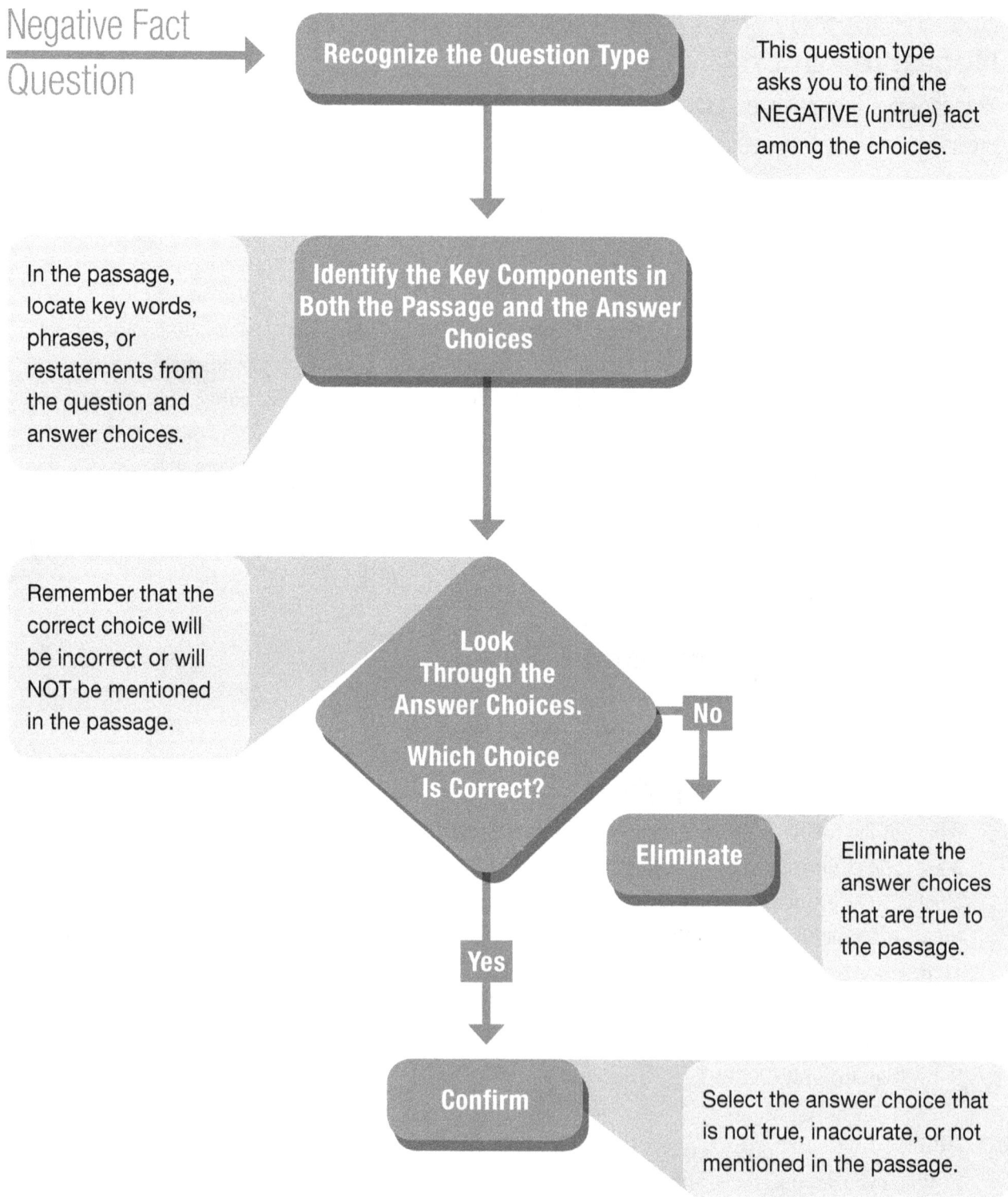

Negative Fact Question →

Recognize the Question Type

This question type asks you to find the NEGATIVE (untrue) fact among the choices.

In the passage, locate key words, phrases, or restatements from the question and answer choices.

Identify the Key Components in Both the Passage and the Answer Choices

Remember that the correct choice will be incorrect or will NOT be mentioned in the passage.

Look Through the Answer Choices.

Which Choice Is Correct?

No

Eliminate

Eliminate the answer choices that are true to the passage.

Yes

Confirm

Select the answer choice that is not true, inaccurate, or not mentioned in the passage.

Recognize the Question Type

Harry Houdini was a famous magician born in Hungary in 1874. He and his family moved to the United States when Houdini was a boy. Later on, he began his career as a magician, specializing in escape acts. One of his acts was the "Milk Can Escape," in which he was put inside an enclosed, oversized milk can filled with water and had to escape in order to avoid drowning. Another of his famous escape acts was his "Straitjacket Escape." In this stunt, Houdini was hung upside down by his ankles while wearing a straitjacket and had to free himself from the jacket.

According to the passage, all of the following are true about Harry Houdini EXCEPT:
(A) He was a famous magician.
(B) He was best known for saving himself from drowning.
(C) He specialized in escape acts.
(D) The "Milk Can Escape" was one of his most famous escape acts.

Identify the Key Components in Both the Passage and the Answer Choices

(A) He was a <u>famous magician</u>.
(B) He was best known for saving himself from drowning.
(C) He <u>specialized in escape acts</u>.
(D) The "<u>Milk Can Escape</u>" <u>was</u> <u>one of his most famous escape</u> <u>acts</u>.

Harry Houdini was a <u>famous magician</u> born in Hungary in 1874. He and his family moved to the United States when Houdini was a boy. Later on, he began his career as a magician, <u>specializing in escape acts</u>. <u>One of his acts was the "Milk Can Escape</u>," in which he was put inside an enclosed, oversized milk can filled with water and had to escape in order to avoid drowning. Another of his famous escape acts was his "Straitjacket Escape." In this stunt, Houdini was hung upside down by his ankles while wearing a straitjacket and had to free himself from the jacket.

Look Through the Answer Choices. Which Choice Is Correct?

Which choice is NOT something the passage states?

• Select **Choice B** because Houdini had to "avoid drowning," but the passage does NOT indicate that he was most famous for avoiding drowning.

Eliminate Incorrect Choices

• Eliminate **Choices A**, **C**, and **D** because they paraphrase facts about Harry Houdini that are mentioned in the passage.

Confirm

Select the correct answer — **Choice B**.

III. Quick Look

Negative Fact Questions

Look at the images below. Then select which answer choice is a negative fact.

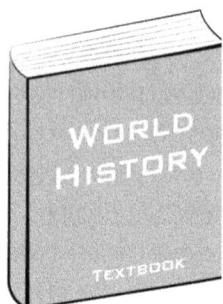

A. This is fiction.

B. This is a history book.

C. This is a textbook.

D. This is about world history.

Choice A is the negative fact because the statement that the textbook is fiction is not true (false information).

A. This is used as a scheduler.

B. This is a calendar.

C. This shows dates of the month.

D. This is used to locate other countries.

Choice D is the negative fact because a calendar is not used to locate other countries (untrue to the image).

IV. Warm Up

Choose the answer choice that does NOT belong in each group.

1. (A) turtle
   (B) snake
   (C) beetle
   (D) alligator
   (E) iguana

2. (A) oven
   (B) microwave
   (C) toaster
   (D) television
   (E) refrigerator

3. (A) reading
   (B) writing
   (C) spelling
   (D) wording
   (E) calculating

4. (A) coat
   (B) pants
   (C) sweatshirt
   (D) jacket
   (E) vest

5. (A) screwdriver
   (B) hammer
   (C) wrench
   (D) drill
   (E) broom

6. (A) tuna
   (B) halibut
   (C) trout
   (D) shrimp
   (E) salmon

7. (A) comma
   (B) period
   (C) apostrophe
   (D) semicolon
   (E) sentence

8. (A) mansion
   (B) bedroom
   (C) apartment
   (D) house
   (E) condominium

9. (A) romance
   (B) rock & roll
   (C) jazz
   (D) hip-hop
   (E) disco

10. (A) canoe
    (B) rowboat
    (C) submarine
    (D) sailboat
    (E) kayak

11. (A) clarinet
    (B) trumpet
    (C) flute
    (D) saxophone
    (E) piano

12. (A) rapid
    (B) fast
    (C) quick
    (D) continuous
    (E) speedy

13. (A) counter
    (B) argue
    (C) disagree
    (D) dispute
    (E) consent

14. (A) shampoo
    (B) soap
    (C) toothpaste
    (D) mouthwash
    (E) brush

15. (A) sundown
    (B) sunset
    (C) sunrise
    (D) twilight
    (E) nightfall

16. (A) seashell
    (B) limestone
    (C) granite
    (D) marble
    (E) sandstone

17. (A) lawyer
    (B) surgeon
    (C) pharmacist
    (D) nurse
    (E) physician

18. (A) rollerskates
    (B) skateboard
    (C) rollerblades
    (D) surfboard
    (E) bicycle

19. (A) cake
    (B) cookie
    (C) steak
    (D) ice cream
    (E) pie

20. (A) bag
    (B) purse
    (C) envelope
    (D) backpack
    (E) briefcase

V. Quick Practice

Practice #1

Read the passage. Then answer the questions that follow.

The *Council of Economic Advisers* (CEA) is an agency that offers unbiased advice to the president of the United States on domestic and international economic affairs. It also helps the president prepare economic reports for the U.S. Congress. In addition, the CEA works to increase cooperation among various governmental agencies by advising them on economic policies. The CEA is made up of a chairperson and two members, who are appointed by the president and then approved by the U.S. Senate. The CEA is supported by a staff of economic professionals, research assistants, and a statistical office.

1) Which of the following does NOT describe the CEA?
   (A) It offers unbiased advice to the U.S. President.
   (B) It only gives advice on domestic economic affairs.
   (C) It helps the president prepare an economic report.
   (D) It advises other governmental agencies.

2) Which of the following is NOT mentioned in the passage?
   (A) The U.S. Congress receives reports on domestic and international economics from the U.S. President.
   (B) The U.S. Senate selects the members of the CEA, and the president selects the chairman.
   (C) The CEA is composed of one chairperson and two members, but receives support from individuals not on the council.
   (D) The CEA gives advice to different governmental departments.

Practice #2

Read the passage. Then answer the questions that follow.

Backgammon is one of the oldest and most beloved two-player board games in the world. Researchers have found evidence that a similar game was played around 3000 BCE in Persia. Backgammon's roots also have been traced to games played in ancient Mesopotamia, Egypt, and Rome. It has been popular in Europe for centuries and is often associated with gambling. In Greece and Turkey, the game is called *tavli* and *tavla*, respectively; both are thought to be versions of the Roman backgammon known as *tabula*. Backgammon boards appear in many historic Dutch, German, and Italian paintings, and the game was first mentioned in writing in England in 1650.

3) Which of the following is NOT true about backgammon's origins?
   - (A) It has spread to many regions over about 5,000 years.
   - (B) It requires a game board and two players.
   - (C) It appears to have been played mostly by pharaohs and emperors.
   - (D) Similar games have been found in at least four ancient civilizations.

4) Which of the following is NOT true about backgammon in European history?
   - (A) It was rediscovered in the 20th century and gained popularity.
   - (B) People have often found ways to place bets on it.
   - (C) There is visual and written evidence that it has been well received.
   - (D) Linguistic evidence ties Greek and Turkish versions to ancient Rome.

Practice #3

Read the passage. Then answer the questions that follow.

Community colleges in the United States are usually funded by state governments. They offer lower-division college courses; in other words, they provide the first two years of a four-year college education. These colleges also fill many educational needs. As they are relatively inexpensive, many students find it much more affordable to attend a community college for two years and then transfer to a four-year university. Some students seek particular career training certificates granted at a community college. Most importantly, these institutions provide flexible and part-time scheduling that appeals to working and older students. Many community colleges also offer a selection of remedial classes that build basic writing or math skills before students advance to college-level courses.

5) Which of the following statements is NOT true about community colleges?
   - (A) They rely mostly on government funding.
   - (B) They usually offer college, vocational, and remedial classes many subjects.
   - (C) Their lower-division courses are easier than such courses elsewhere.
   - (D) They provide a less expensive alternative to other educational institutions.

6) What is NOT a reason given in the passage that students might choose to attend a community college?
   - (A) It provides an affordable way to attain career training certificates.
   - (B) Allowing part-time schedules means that students can work.
   - (C) Remedial classes may help students develop writing and math skills.
   - (D) The campuses offer numerous career opportunities for students.

Practice #4

Read the passage. Then answer the questions that follow.

Mahatma Gandhi is remembered worldwide for his methods of nonviolent resistance to oppression. As a young man, he trained to be a lawyer in London but found that he was too shy to speak in court. In 1893, he took a job at a law office in South Africa, which, like India, was colonized by Great Britain. During his two decades in South Africa, he became committed to social justice. He started out protesting discrimination against other Indians living there and was jailed several times. His protest movements were repressed, but the repression itself led to public outcry and thus reform. Such experiences gave him ideas that he later used in India to organize massive protests and boycotts against British rule. Great Britain finally withdrew from India in 1947, just one year before Gandhi was assassinated.

7) According to the passage, what did NOT happen in Gandhi's life?
   (A) He found he was not suited to arguing cases in court.
   (B) He grew up in South Africa and lived there for most of his life.
   (C) His first protests focused on discrimination against Indians.
   (D) He served time in jail more than once.

8) Which of the following statements is NOT true about Gandhi's career?
   (A) Early in his career, Gandhi was not committed to social causes.
   (B) Gandhi became committed to fairness in society during his time in South Africa.
   (C) Gandhi learned that nonviolence can bring about change indirectly.
   (D) The peaceful effort to evict the British from India was eventually successful.

Practice #5

Read the passage. Then answer the questions that follow.

Before they learned about oil paint around 1500 CE, artists in Europe mostly used tempera paint. *Tempera* is usually composed of powdered pigment mixed with egg yolk. It is time consuming to create tempera paintings because tempera cannot be applied thickly. It must be added in many thin layers. When European artists used tempera, they usually began by applying several coats of a chalky-white substance called *gesso* to a rigid material, usually wood, in order to create a level surface. Next, the sketching and layering of tempera could begin. The reward was that tempera dries fast and hard, has a luminous quality, and does not lose its color even after hundreds of years.

9) According to the passage, what is NOT true about European painters before 1500 CE?
   (A) They usually painted on hard surfaces such as wood.
   (B) They started by putting down a white layer to prepare the surface for painting.
   (C) They had to be patient about achieving the color they wanted on the surface.
   (D) They knew that mixing oil with pigment produced a better paint.

10) According to the passage, which of the following is NOT true about tempera?
   (A) The egg yolk makes it soft and flexible on canvas surfaces.
   (B) It is not able to be thickened or applied thickly.
   (C) It resists deteriorating for centuries once it has dried.
   (D) The gesso makes it go on smoothly.

Practice #6

Read the passage. Then answer the questions that follow.

The *pop* in *pop music* is short for *popular*. However, the term *pop music* refers to an identifiable genre, not just any music that is well liked. Pop began developing in the 1950s, alongside rock and roll, with the advent of inexpensive record singles and transistor radios. The genre borrows from many other genres of music, including rhythm and blues, gospel, country, rap, Latin music, and reggae. Despite this variety, pop music typically aims to have broad appeal. A pop song is usually fairly short, includes a catchy melody, and has a few verses interspersed with a repeating chorus. It often features soaring vocals, electric guitar, bass, and a dance rhythm. Lyrics generally focus on love and romance.

11) According to the passage, what is NOT TRUE about the pop music genre?
   (A) The name refers to whatever type of music that is popular.
   (B) It developed as recorded music became more easily accessible.
   (C) Many other sounds and styles besides rock show up in pop songs.
   (D) It tends to stick to familiar formats and messages.

12) The author describes pop songs as having the following characteristics EXCEPT:
   (A) Their creators want them to be the kinds of songs that most people enjoy.
   (B) The rhythms and lyrics often are complex and irregular.
   (C) The singing often is emotional and focused on romantic relationships.
   (D) The chorus is memorable and repeated.

Practice #7

Read the passage. Then answer the questions that follow.

In 1833, an experiment in printed media was launched in New York City: it was a newspaper called *The Sun*, featuring the motto *It shines for all*. Its founder, Benjamin Henry Day, was desperate for work during an economic downturn. His idea to fight the tough economic times was to produce an inexpensive, simple, and vividly written newspaper to sell in the city. Hence, the story of the *Sun* began.

The paper focused on news that affected common people and provided "human interest" stories. Instead of requiring subscriptions, Day sent newsboys out into the streets to sell copies. Moreover, while most daily newspapers of the day cost 6 cents, the *Sun* only charged 1 cent. Thus, it became one of the "penny papers" of the time. The *Sun* was an instant success and was published until 1950.

13) According to Paragraph 1, what is NOT true about Benjamin Henry Day?
   (A) He was unemployed during a period of tough economic times.
   (B) He wanted to start a charitable institution that would "shine for all."
   (C) He started a trend in news publishing that made good business sense.
   (D) He became the publisher of a highly successful New York daily newspaper.

14) According to Paragraph 2, the author does NOT say that the New York *Sun*
   (A) reported news that people could relate to
   (B) used simple, but lively language
   (C) printed only "human interest" stories until 1950
   (D) allowed people to buy an issue cheaply and easily

Read the passage. Then answer the questions that follow.

Brook Farm was an experimental utopia established in 1841 by George and Sophia Ripley in West Roxbury, Massachusetts. They believed that if work was shared among the community, it would allow members to engage in more leisure activities and intellectual pursuits. All residents received the same wages, worked the same hours, and paid the same for room and board, regardless of their age, gender, or social class. This was a revolutionary idea. Many of the residents had academic or religious backgrounds rather than farming experience. Although well-known literary figures, such as Nathaniel Hawthorne, were associated with Brook Farm, it was never financially stable, so in 1847 the community closed.

15) All of the following are examples of Brook Farm goals EXCEPT
   (A) reserving time for academic pursuits
   (B) creating an equal relationship among members
   (C) altering the structure of West Roxbury farms
   (D) sharing work among all members

16) According to the passage, which of the following is NOT true?
   (A) The atmosphere at Brook Farm was based on religious philosophy.
   (B) Brook Farm shut down in 1847 because it was financially unstable.
   (C) A farming background was not needed to work at Brook Farm.
   (D) All residents lived at Brook Farm and worked the same hours.

Read the passage. Then answer the questions that follow.

In 1625, a chief named Shyaam aMbul aNgoong unified several communities in part of what is now the Democratic Republic of Congo and created the powerful Kuba kingdom. Over the course of more than two centuries, Kuba power and wealth grew, largely because European traders had already begun introducing New World crops, such as squash, corn, and peanuts, to the continent. Kuba farmers were able to grow these successfully in their fertile soil and trade them widely via the area's three major rivers. The kingdom's wealth allowed it to develop a highly skilled and famed artisan class. Along with the entire Congo region, the Kuba kingdom was colonized by Belgians starting in 1885, but the kingdom has been revived and exists today.

17) The passage states that the Kuba kingdom developed for all of the following reasons EXCEPT:
   (A) A strong leader emerged and united surrounding territories.
   (B) Europeans, especially Belgians, assisted in forming the kingdom.
   (C) Good growing conditions aided in establishing popular new food sources.
   (D) Several rivers in the area made it possible to buy and sell over a wide area.

18) Which fact about Kuba does the author NOT mention in the passage?
   (A) The kingdom started when small settlements were combined in the 17th century.
   (B) Kuba was renowned for its affluence and crafters.
   (C) A European country took over the kingdom and controlled it for some time.
   (D) The kingdom rose and declined and is now only a part of history.

Practice #10

Read the passage. Then answer the questions that follow.

The Vikings were northern Germanic people who were expert sea travelers. During the Viking Age from the 8th to the 11th century, Vikings explored, attacked, traded with, and settled in territories including North Atlantic Islands, the British Isles, and Europe. The main mode of transportation that they developed was the *longship*, which was a long, narrow vessel equipped with a rectangular sail and lined with oars for rowing. It had a shallow hull, which allowed it to stay afloat in shallow waters and thus navigate up even minor rivers and land on beaches. Longships also had symmetrical front and back sections so that they could reverse direction without turning the boat around. The descendants of Vikings live in modern-day Sweden, Norway, Denmark, and Northern Germany.

19) According to the passage, which statement does NOT reflect Viking history?
   (A) Besides attacking others, Vikings also explored and traded for goods from far-away places.
   (B) Vikings spread their influence from the 700s to the 1000s.
   (C) Viking travelers always went back to their ancestral homes in the north.
   (D) Using specially designed ships, Vikings were able to settle much of Northern Europe.

20) Which of the following is NOT true about Viking seamanship abilities?
   (A) Vikings were the only people in Europe during the Viking Age who knew how to master the waves.
   (B) Vikings had a special way to make a quick retreat.
   (C) Vikings primarily powered their boats with their strength and sometimes with wind in their sails.
   (D) Vikings were able to maneuver up shallow rivers with their unique boats.

Select the vocabulary word or phrase that has the closest meaning.

7. **respectively**
   A. correspondingly
   B. certainly
   C. responsibly
   D. detrimentally

8. **require**
   A. cure
   B. fix
   C. improve
   D. need

1. **notable**
   A. famous
   B. noble
   C. royal
   D. reasonable

9. **remedial**
   A. boring
   B. corrective
   C. destructive
   D. interesting

2. **speedy**
   A. strong
   B. automatic
   C. arduous
   D. swift

10. **vocational**
    A. occupational
    B. enjoyable
    C. satisfactory
    D. playable

3. **unbiased**
   A. prejudiced
   B. impartial
   C. solid
   D. hurt

11. **oppression**
    A. objection
    B. repression
    C. nervousness
    D. replacement

4. **domestic**
   A. worldwide
   B. dated
   C. internal
   D. enduring

12. **committed**
    A. caused
    B. prepared
    C. dedicated
    D. damaged

5. **various**
   A. diverse
   B. awful
   C. dull
   D. famous

13. **discrimination**
    A. destination
    B. discovery
    C. unfairness
    D. wrongdoing

6. **associated**
   A. outgoing
   B. connected
   C. prudent
   D. charmed

14. **outcry**
    A. exclamation
    B. noise
    C. organization
    D. origin

15. **applied**
    A. favored
    B. careful
    C. supportable
    D. used

16. **luminous**
    A. brilliant
    B. relaxing
    C. occasional
    D. overwhelmed

17. **characteristic**
    A. remedy
    B. figure
    C. trait
    D. isolation

18. **focus**
    A. prefer
    B. concentrate
    C. cultivate
    D. evaluate

19. **affect**
    A. influence
    B. protest
    C. compensate
    D. recommend

20. **viewpoint**
    A. outlook
    B. explanation
    C. landscape
    D. telescope

21. **allow**
    A. amaze
    B. prohibit
    C. enable
    D. differentiate

22. **establish**
    A. found
    B. awake
    C. emphasize
    D. elect

23. **figure**
    A. character
    B. painting
    C. aspiration
    D. gesture

24. **alter**
    A. gather
    B. show
    C. change
    D. destroy

25. **fertile**
    A. frugal
    B. generous
    C. rich
    D. stingy

26. **revive**
    A. revitalize
    B. appreciate
    C. revise
    D. simulate

27. **surrounding**
    A. limited
    B. conditional
    C. suspended
    D. circumferential

28. **renowned**
    A. built
    B. hated
    C. envied
    D. famous

29. **symmetrical**
    A. institutional
    B. systematic
    C. balanced
    D. disturbed

30. **reverse**
    A. ideal
    B. contrary
    C. equal
    D. joyful

1A 2D 3B 4C 5A 6B 7A 8D 9B 10A 11B 12C 13C 14A 15D 16A 17C 18B 19A 20A 21C 22A 23A 24C 25C 26A 27D 28D 29C 30B

Exercises

Exercise #1 Read the passage. Then answer the questions that follow.

Dopamine is a hormone in the body that acts as a *neurotransmitter*; certain brain nerve cells release it to send chemical signals to other brain nerve cells. One of several distinct brain-dopamine systems plays a role in reward-motivated behavior. Dopamine can create a feeling of pleasure and helps the brain retain memories of rewarding experiences, motivating a person to repeat behaviors that resulted in a sense of pleasure. Dopamine may have developed to reinforce healthy behaviors that help maintain a body and increase its chances for survival, such as eating nourishing food.

However, most abused drugs distort the process because they also trigger the release of dopamine. For example, as a person feels pleasure from drug use, the brain may store a powerful memory of the drug and desire to repeat the experience. One aspect in overcoming addiction is that it takes time for these memories to fade.

1) According to Paragraph 1, dopamine can be described as all of the following EXCEPT
   (A) a chemical brain messenger and hormone
   (B) a feeling of motivation
   (C) a trigger for creating certain memories and desires
   (D) a brain chemical that contributes to survival

2) According to Paragraph 1, what is the function of dopamine in the brain?
   (A) Nerve cells release it as a way of creating other nerve cells.
   (B) It causes the brain to store memories of positive experiences.
   (C) It causes some people with more dopamine to find food more easily than others.
   (D) It is a neurotransmitter that triggers the brain for a "fight or flight" response.

3) Paragraph 1 says that it is likely that dopamine evolved because
   (A) it helped people find food
   (B) it creates the motivation to survive
   (C) it creates a reward-based learning system
   (D) it is a hormone and a neurotransmitter

4) According to Paragraph 2, what is NOT true about drug addiction?
   (A) The types of drugs that some people tend to abuse act on the dopamine process.
   (B) The brain remembers and craves the feeling brought on by substance abuse.
   (C) Changing drug addiction involves changing the brain at the cellular level.
   (D) People can recover from addiction and substance abuse fairly quickly.

Exercise #2 Read the passage. Then answer the questions that follow.

Wells and springs get their water from *groundwater*, a combination of rainwater and melted snow that has been filtered through the soil as it has penetrated the surface and spread out deep underground. Groundwater is not like an underground river or lake; rather, the water is stored in millions of tiny spaces between particles of rock and sand. In the United States, groundwater pumped using wells provides 20 percent of all fresh water used.

Normally, tree roots and wetlands help water permeate the Earth's deep layers to replenish groundwater. However, urbanization creates more roads and concrete-covered land and discourages rainwater from sinking into the earth. Also, people in some regions are finding that they have overdrawn and depleted the groundwater by taking out more than nature replaces. This can create disastrous shortages for farms and cities. In coastal areas, groundwater depletion can lead to permanent soil damage if salt water seeps into the tiny spaces normally filled with groundwater. Some regions channel in fresh water from elsewhere and directing it to *recharging basins*, or ponds where the water can permeate the soil.

5) According to Paragraph 1, what is groundwater?
(A) It is precipitation that has been brought up again via wells.
(B) It is the water that can be found in the spaces between underground rocks.
(C) It is subterranean water that has spread out in vast lakes.
(D) It is rain and melted snow that has collected on the surface of the land, or ground.

6) According to Paragraph 2, what are major causes of groundwater depletion?
(A) Individuals wasting too much water, and drought
(B) Saltwater in underground aquifers, and dry ponds
(C) Asphalt and concrete causing run-off, and over-pumping
(D) Channeling water from other areas, and urbanization

7) According to Paragraph 2, which of the following is NOT a consequence of groundwater depletion?
(A) Water shortages for agricultural and urban areas
(B) Soil destruction from salty water replacing pockets of groundwater
(C) Creation of basins that are filled with water from other regions
(D) Disasters such as earthquakes and flooding

8) What does the author NOT say about groundwater from Paragraphs 1 and 2?
(A) About one-fifth of America's freshwater supply is from groundwater.
(B) It is more unpolluted, fresh, and pure than above-ground water.
(C) It can reach lower levels more easily if there are roots and mud to help it.
(D) It is dispersed into tiny pockets in deep layers underground.

Exercise #3 Read the passage. Then answer the questions that follow.

Much of the American West was shaped by gold rushes. A *gold rush* is a period of time when thousands of people flock to areas where gold has been discovered, hoping to find their own nuggets or veins of gold and get rich instantly. California's gold rush started in 1848, just as the United States was taking over the territory from Mexico. A worker found a nugget in a stream next to a lumber mill that he was helping build. Within a few months, the secret was out, and by 1849, immigrants were pouring in from around the world. Many settled down and formed communities.

The changes were immense. Within just one year, California had become a state rather than a territory. While few miners or would-be miners became rich from finding gold, many people became rich by providing miners with supplies and transportation. Ranches, farms, and cities sprang up to meet the needs of the new population. The growth also had tragic results. The new settlements were generally hostile to California's native tribes, resulting in tens of thousands of natives' deaths.

Colorado also can trace its statehood to a gold rush, which started with a discovery in the Rocky Mountains 10 years after the discovery in California. Gold rushes also stimulated migration to Alaska, Arizona, Idaho, Nevada, South Dakota, Utah, and Wyoming.

9) How does Paragraph 1 define gold rushes?
(A) They are time periods when everyone becomes filled with get-rich-quick fantasies.
(B) They happen when people build fortunes on gold they have mined or found.
(C) They are episodes in history when people hurry to find gold at particular spots.
(D) They are a series of events that have many consequences for the future.

10) According to Paragraph 1, which of the following sequence of events describes the beginning of California's gold rush?
(A) The U.S. and Mexico were at war; settlers started building lumber mills; gold was mined.
(B) California was becoming part of Mexico; a man discovered gold in a stream; towns grew up.
(C) A worker found some gold next to a stream; he announced it; he and a few others became very wealthy.
(D) A worker found some gold in a stream; the land was becoming U.S. territory; people heard about the gold.

11) In Paragraph 2, the author does NOT mention that the California gold rush
(A) lasted for many years and contributed to the territory's long push for statehood
(B) caused tens of thousands of deaths of people native to the area
(C) created wealth among those who sold items to miners
(D) resulted in the permanent settling of immigrants from many places

12) According to the passage, which of the following was NOT an effect of gold rushes on the American frontier?
(A) They provided the stimulation for American settlement in much of the West.
(B) They affected the landscape because towns, farms, and roads were needed to meet miners' needs.
(C) They influenced the territorial outcome of the Mexican-American War.
(D) They sparked hostilities between immigrants and indigenous peoples.

Exercise #4 Read the passage. Then answer the questions that follow.

A Raisin in the Sun is a play written by the American playwright and author Lorraine Hansberry. It premiered in 1959 in a Broadway theater in New York City. It was the first time a play by an African-American woman had ever opened on Broadway. Moreover, it was directed by Lloyd Richards, the first African-American ever to direct a play on Broadway. It was awarded the Best Play of 1959 by the New York Drama Critics' Circle – the first time the award went to an African-American writer.

The play's title refers to a poem by African-American poet Langston Hughes, which begins, "What happens to a dream deferred? / Does it dry up / like a raisin in the sun?" The play concerns dreams that are *deferred*, or put off. It follows a poor African-American family in Chicago whose members dream of improving their lives. They receive a significant amount of money from a life-insurance policy and spend a portion as a down payment on a home. The home is in an all-white neighborhood, but it is a bargain because the housing market is weak. Their major dilemma comes when some of the white neighbors try to pay them to back out of the deal. The family must decide whether to take the money or fight for their rights. The play is based on playwright Hansberry's own experiences as a child.

13) According to Paragraph 1, *A Raisin in the Sun* marked the first time
   (A) a play written by Lorraine Hansberry was put into major production
   (B) an award-winning Broadway play featured an African American woman
   (C) a play about an African-American childhood experience was performed on Broadway
   (D) a play written by an African-American woman was produced on Broadway

14) According to Paragraph 2, why did Hansberry use the quote "a raisin in the sun" as a title?
   (A) To honor poet Langston Hughes
   (B) To set a tone of doom and the motif of sad, dry lives
   (C) To refer to a metaphor about not being able to achieve dreams
   (D) To contrast a poor agricultural setting with a comfortable suburban life

15) According to Paragraph 2, which of the following statements does NOT describe part of the plot of *A Raisin in the Sun*?
   (A) Members of a poor family living in Chicago want a better life.
   (B) Members of the family do not realize that they are buying a house in an all-white neighborhood.
   (C) People in the new neighborhood try to discourage the African-American family from moving in.
   (D) The family faces a choice about how to respond to the offer of money.

16) According to Paragraph 2, what is NOT true about the plot of *A Raisin in the Sun*?
   (A) The protagonist's family experiences racism and hostility in their poor neighborhood.
   (B) The protagonist's family receives a great deal of money because of good fortune.
   (C) The times are bad economically, so housing prices are low.
   (D) The white neighborhood is determined to remain racially exclusive.

I. What Is a Coherence Question?

Coherence

The coherence question asks you to create a more logical or coherent passage by adding a new sentence that will improve the overall information.

A. COHERENCE QUESTION MODEL

A A *ghostwriter* is a person who creates material that is credited to another person. **B** The amount of work ghostwriters contribute to the product may vary. **C** Ghostwriting is common in many fields, such as politics, music, and publishing. **D** In the music industry, a ghostwriter will often write a song that is credited to a popular singer.

5. Look at the four squares [■] that indicate where the following sentence could be added to the passage.

    Some of them may edit the credited author's work, or some may do most of the writing based on an outline given to them.

    Where would the sentence best fit?
    Circle the square [■] to add the sentence.

B. COHERENCE QUESTION FORMATS

Look at the four squares [■] that indicate where the following sentence could be added to the passage.

(A bold-faced sentence)

Where would the sentence best fit?
Circle the square [■] to add the sentence.

C. TIPS

1. When taking the official, Internet-based TOEFL test, you will be asked to *click on* the correct answer choice rather than *circle* it.
2. Understanding the purpose of the passage will help you identify the correct placement of the new sentence.
3. Look for transitions to indicate what kind of information should come next if the given information seems unrelated.
4. Check that all of the pronouns have referents. If a referent is missing, that omission can give you a clue as to where the new sentence should be placed.
5. An incorrect answer may:
    - stop the logical continuation of ideas between sentences
    - conflict with the function of the transitions
    - disrupt the relationship between a pronoun and its referent

II. Hacking Strategy

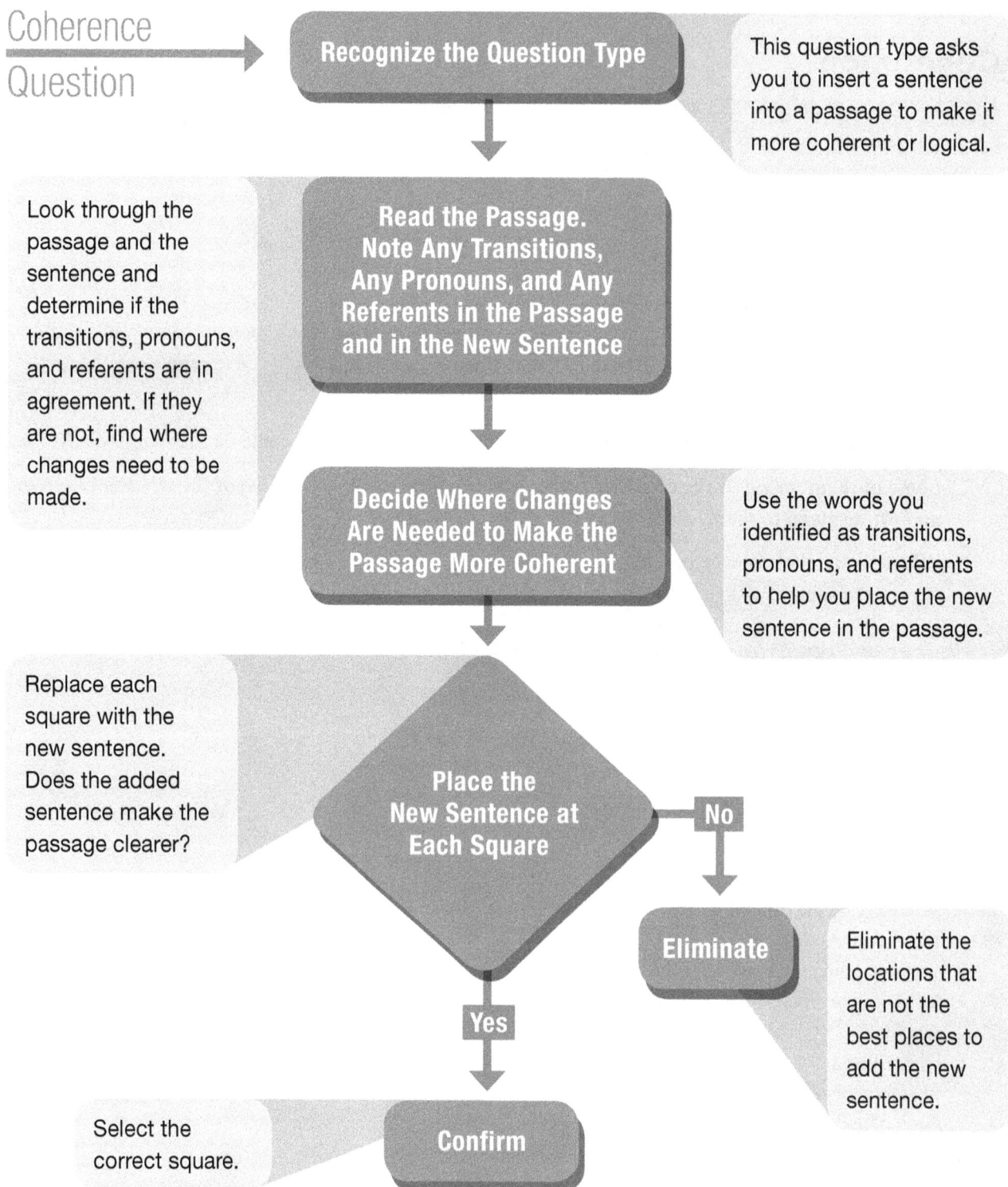

Coherence Question →

Recognize the Question Type

This question type asks you to insert a sentence into a passage to make it more coherent or logical.

Read the Passage. Note Any Transitions, Any Pronouns, and Any Referents in the Passage and in the New Sentence

Look through the passage and the sentence and determine if the transitions, pronouns, and referents are in agreement. If they are not, find where changes need to be made.

Decide Where Changes Are Needed to Make the Passage More Coherent

Use the words you identified as transitions, pronouns, and referents to help you place the new sentence in the passage.

Place the New Sentence at Each Square

Replace each square with the new sentence. Does the added sentence make the passage clearer?

No

Eliminate

Eliminate the locations that are not the best places to add the new sentence.

Yes

Confirm

Select the correct square.

(EXAMPLE

Recognize the Question Type

A A *ghostwriter* is a person who creates material that is credited to another person. **B** The amount of work ghostwriters contribute to the product may vary. **C** Ghostwriting is common in many fields, such as politics, music, and publishing. **D** In the music industry, a ghostwriter will often write a song that is credited to a popular singer.

Look at the four squares [■] that indicate where the following sentence could be added to the passage.

Some of them may edit the credited author's work, or some may do most of the writing based on an outline given to them.

Where would the sentence best fit?

Circle the square [■] to add the sentence.

Note Any Transitions, Pronouns, and Referents in the Passage and in the New Sentence

A A ***ghostwriter*** is a person who creates material that is credited to another person. **B** The amount of work <u>ghostwriters</u> contribute to the product may vary. **C** Ghostwriting is common in many fields, **such as** politics, music, and publishing. **D** **In the music industry, a ghostwriter** will often write a song that is credited to a popular singer.

Look at the new sentence that needs to be added:

Some of <u>them</u> may edit the credited author's work, or some may do most of the writing based on an outline given to them.

We can see that the underlined pronoun, "them," is plural; therefore, its referent must be plural as well. This is a big clue because the pronoun tells us that the preceding sentence will most likely have a plural referent. The sentence is saying that *some of them may edit...or some may do most of the writing....* We can infer that "them" is referring to ghostwriters because of the nature of their work (editing or writing). So let's look for a place in the passage where the word "ghostwriters" is mentioned.

Decide Where Changes Are Needed to Make Passage More Coherent

The new sentence adds more information about a ghostwriter's job, and because the pronoun "them" is used in the new sentence, the referent has to appear in the previous sentence and has to be plural.

Check the Answer Choice

Place the new sentence in each square, and eliminate incorrect squares.

As we discovered in the third step, "ghostwriters" in plural form appears in the second sentence, so let's try placing the new sentence after the second sentence.

[■] The amount of work ghostwriters contribute to the product may vary. **Some of them may edit the credited author's work, or some may do most of the writing based on an outline given to them.**

This makes sense and is the right choice. Place the new sentence at the location of the other squares to be sure that the sentence does not fit anywhere else.

Confirm

Select the correct square — **C** — by circling it.

III. Quick Look

Transitions Used in Coherence Questions

1. Addition Signals that more information similar to the previous sentence will be introduced.

Also *Another* *Other* *First, Second, etc.* *And so on*

Topic: Bookcase

Choices

2. Contrast Signals that more information contrasting to the previous sentence will follow.

Although *However* *In contrast* *While* *But*

Topic: Contrast

Choices

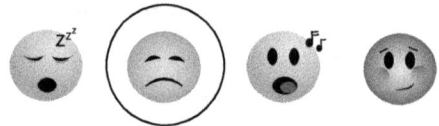

3. Cause / Result Signals that a description of the results or causes of the information in the previous sentence will follow.

Because / Since *Consequently* *Therefore* *Thus* *To conclude*

Topic: Actions

Choices

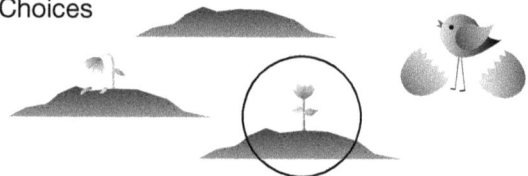

4. Example Signals that a supporting example will follow.

For example *For instance* *Including* *Such as* *First, Second, etc.*

Topic: Animals

Choices

IV. Warm Up

Read each sentence below. Then put the sentences in the correct sequence by labeling each choice as 1, 2, or 3.

1. ____ It also can be found as an ingredient in industrial products such as paint and dyes.

   ____ Seaweed is an ingredient used in many everyday products.

   ____ It is used as a thickener in products such as toothpaste and ice cream.

2. ____ However, kimonos were slowly worn less and less as Western fashions, such as suits and dresses, were introduced to Japan.

   ____ Kimonos are traditional Japanese garments that Japanese citizens wore as everyday clothing until the middle of the 20th century.

   ____ Today, kimonos are worn on special occasions such as weddings, funerals, and tea ceremonies.

3. ____ It can now be found on many different objects such as U.S. seals and on the backs of many U.S. coins.

   ____ The bald eagle has been the official emblem of the United States since June 20, 1782.

   ____ It was selected for its beauty, strength, long life, and its nativeness to the North American continent.

4. ____ A moat acts somewhat like a fortress by protecting beavers from predators such as wolves, bears, and coyotes.

   ____ Beavers are known for building dams for their colonies.

   ____ By building dams, beavers cause the water levels in streams and rivers to rise, creating moats around the dams.

5. ____ Yoga is one of the six schools of Hindu philosophy and is believed to have originated in ancient India as a physical, mental, and spiritual discipline.

   ____ The purpose of yoga is to unify the body, mind, and spirit in an experience of harmony.

   ____ In recent decades, yoga has been widely practiced in the U.S. for health benefits that may be a result of this unification.

6. _____ There is no strong evidence that proves this association.

_____ Throughout history, the full moon has been associated with erratic behavior and unexplainable events.

_____ However, it is still commonly believed that the full moon causes changes in behavior such as sleeplessness, insanity, and aggression.

7. _____ The Amazon Basin in South America is home to the most developed rainforest in the world.

_____ The Amazon Rainforest, considered one of the world's oldest tropical forests, covers the majority of the Amazon Basin.

_____ This rainforest produces 20 percent of the world's oxygen and holds two-thirds of the world's fresh water supply.

8. _____ The Day of the Dead, or *El Día de los Muertos* in Spanish, is a Mexican holiday that is celebrated on November 1 and 2.

_____ This holiday was first practiced by the Aztecs before the Spanish Conquistadors invaded the region in the 16th century.

_____ Those who now participate in the holiday gather with family and friends in cemeteries to honor the deceased with flowers, offerings, parades, and music.

9. _____ It was discovered in the Southeast Asian country of Burma in the 1950s by British mineralogist and gemologist Arthur Charles Davy Pain.

_____ *Painite* is a gemstone that is believed to be the rarest gem in the world.

_____ The color of painite varies from red to brownish to orange-red.

10. _____ In Chinese, *feng* means "wind" and *shui* means "water," which, in Chinese culture, are elements that are connected to good health.

_____ The purpose of the system is to achieve harmony and balance with nature, one's surroundings, and life.

_____ Feng shui is a Chinese system which teaches that the flow of energy, or *chi*, can be used to improve life.

V. Quick Practice

Practice #1

Read the passage. Then answer the question that follows.

Many of the western etiquette rules that are still used today originated in the 1600s royal court of Louis XIV of France. **A** The word *etiquette* comes from the Old French word for a card or label. **B** These rules dictated the social behavior and expectations of a particular class of people. **C** The upper classes used the etiquette rules as a way to separate themselves from the lower classes. **D**

1) Look at the squares [■] that indicate where the sentence below could be added in the paragraph.

In fact, when the etiquette rules were first established, they were written on a card or label for all the people who visited the royal court to see and obey.

Where would the sentence best fit?
Circle the square [■] to add the sentence to the passage.

Practice #2

Read the passage. Then answer the question that follows.

A These stories have been told by storytellers since ancient times. **B** Some scholars believe that the "golden age" of ghost stories was between the 1830s and the beginning of World War I. **C** One of the leading ghost story writers of that time was the 19th-century Irish writer Sheridan Le Fanu. He helped refine the genre during the Victorian Era (1837-1901). **D** Fanu's plots often included vampires, crimes, or suspenseful situations, aiming to create chills of fear even without ghosts.

2) Look at the squares [■] that indicate where the sentence below could be added in the paragraph.

Ghost stories **are supernatural tales in which the spirit of a dead person haunts the living.**

Where would the sentence best fit?
Circle the square [■] to add the sentence to the passage.

Practice #3

Read the passage. Then answer the question that follows.

Scientists use family studies as one way to explore the effects of environment and heredity* on human beings. **A** For example, scientists believe that shyness is often influenced by heredity. **B** They have observed that children of shy parents are more likely to be shy compared with children of parents who are not shy. **C** For instance, a child may have developed shy behavior by observing and imitating the behaviors of his or her shy parents. **D**

Heredity: the genetic passing of traits from one generation (parent) to the next (offspring)

3) Look at the squares [■] that indicate where the sentence below could be added in the paragraph.

However, other explanations cannot be excluded.

Where would the sentence best fit?
Circle the square [■] to add the sentence to the passage.

Practice #4

Read the passage. Then answer the question that follows.

Diptera is a combination of two Greek words: *di*, which means "two," and *ptera*, which means "wings." **A** According to the scientific classification in biology, Diptera is an *order* in which insects are categorized. **B** Unlike other flying insects such as dragonflies, Dipterans, also known as "true flies," have a single pair of wings. **C** Although there are more than 240,000 species of flies, only about half of them are considered "true flies." **D**

4) Look at the squares [■] that indicate where the sentence below could be added in the paragraph.

These Dipteran insects have a special characteristic that separates them from other orders of insects.

Where would the sentence best fit?
Circle the square [■] to add the sentence to the passage.

Practice #5

Read the passage. Then answer the question that follows.

Since a name is a lifelong label, many cultures have unique, socially-influenced naming systems. **A** For Romans of the Republican era, a specific system was used to name male citizens of the aristocratic class. **B** The name *Gaius Julius Caesar* provides an excellent example. First, the *praenomen* indicated the a Roman male aristocrat's *given name*, or the name that his parents chose for him. **C** Then, the *nomen gentile*, or *nomen* for short, signified the person's clan. **D** Lastly, the *cognomen*, or the last name, designated the person's family branch within the clan.

5) Look at the squares [■] that indicate where the sentence below could be added in the paragraph.

The method divided people's names into three sections.

Where would the sentence best fit?
Circle the square [■] to add the sentence to the passage.

Practice #6

Read the passage. Then answer the question that follows.

Mescaline is a powerful drug that distorts what a person sees, hears, and feels. **A** Mescaline is obtained from different types of cacti such as the peyote cactus. **B** These types of cacti grow in areas of South America and the southwestern region of North America. **C** The Native American Church, which has members from a number of tribes, is allowed to use peyote as a sacrament in religious ceremonies. **D**

6) Look at the squares [■] that indicate where the sentence below could be added in the paragraph.

Federal law prohibits the possession and use of mescaline in the United States, except for very specific purposes.

Where would the sentence best fit?
Circle the square [■] to add the sentence to the passage.

Practice #7

Read the passage. Then answer the question that follows.

A *metaphor* is a figure of speech that compares two things that would normally not be comparable. **A** For example, when people say "A heart of stone," they are using a metaphor. **B** Unlike a simile, a metaphor does not use the words *like* or *as* to suggest a comparison. **C** The statements "He is *like* a sly fox" and "He is sly *as* a fox" are similes, while the statement "He *is* a sly fox" is a metaphor. **D**

7) Look at the squares [■] that indicate where the sentence below could be added in the paragraph.

That is, characteristics of one object are used to describe another object.

Where would the sentence best fit?
Circle the square [■] to add the sentence to the passage.

Practice #8

Read the passage. Then answer the question that follows.

Many economic factors influence how much workers earn. **A** Worker salaries depend partly on the number of unemployed workers. **B** During times of economic growth, most people have jobs and are not seeking new ones, so companies will have a difficult time hiring. **C** For example, if a school district cannot find enough qualified teachers, it may raise salaries to recruit teachers from other districts. **D** On the other hand, during an economic recession, all districts may have to reduce teaching jobs, so there may be many out-of-work teachers competing for few jobs. In this case, districts can offer teachers lower salaries.

8) Look at the squares [■] that indicate where the sentence below could be added in the paragraph.

In this situation, companies are likely to pay more for employees' labor.

Where would the sentence best fit?
Circle the square [■] to add the sentence to the passage.

Read the passage. Then answer the question that follows.

Historians believe that Leucippus, a Greek philosopher in the 5th century BCE, developed one of the earliest theories about matter. **A** He theorized that all matter is made up of various indestructible pieces known as *atoms*. **B** In fact, some historians believe that Democritus overshadowed his master's work and was the one who described it extensively and then expanded it. **C** It is difficult to separate the ideas of Leucippus from those of Democritus, as their writing often appears in the same text. **D**

9) Look at the squares [■] that indicate where the sentence below could be added in the paragraph.

However, Leucippus had a student and successor named Democritus who may deserve some of the credit for the theory.

Where would the sentence best fit?
Circle the square [■] to add the sentence to the passage.

Read the passage. Then answer the question that follows.

The region that is now Louisiana has been home to many cultures. People have inhabited the area for 12,000 years. Residents built huge earthen mounds there around 3400 BCE. **A** Many settled tribes lived in the region when Spaniards first explored it in the 16th century. **B** However, France claimed the area in 1682. **C** French colonists began bringing in Africans as slaves in 1718, and Africans eventually outnumbered Europeans. **D** The negotiations of the Third Treaty of San Ildefonso, conducted between France and Spain, gave Louisiana back to France in 1800. In 1803, France sold Louisiana to the United States.

10) Look at the squares [■] that indicate where the sentence below could be added in the paragraph.

Spain ruled the territory from 1763 until 1800, a time when Spanish- and French-speaking immigrants arrived from Cuba, Haiti, and Canada.

Where would the sentence best fit?
Circle the square [■] to add the sentence to the passage.

Select the vocabulary word or phrase that has the closest meaning.

7. **official**
   A. formal
   B. novel
   C. urban
   D. specific

8. **emblem**
   A. treasure
   B. trademark
   C. appreciation
   D. remainder

1. **contribute**
   A. dedicate
   B. donate
   C. denote
   D. elicit

9. **erratic**
   A. problematic
   B. understanding
   C. erroneous
   D. unpredictable

2. **vary**
   A. excite
   B. cease
   C. activate
   D. differ

10. **invade**
    A. occupy
    B. invest
    C. modify
    D. monitor

3. **purpose**
   A. failure
   B. goal
   C. part
   D. figure

11. **gather**
    A. correct
    B. congregate
    C. abandon
    D. govern

4. **clue**
   A. color
   B. indication
   C. remedy
   D. representation

12. **deceased**
    A. dead
    B. changed
    C. alive
    D. hidden

5. **ingredient**
   A. itinerary
   B. composition
   C. element
   D. reasoning

13. **etiquette**
    A. courtesy
    B. ignorance
    C. intelligence
    D. attraction

6. **everyday**
   A. hard
   B. daily
   C. easy
   D. simple

14. **suspenseful**
    A. zealous
    B. breathtaking
    C. special
    D. hasty

15. **explore**
    A. forfeit
    B. pause
    C. probe
    D. reveal

16. **exclude**
    A. concede
    B. omit
    C. exhaust
    D. conserve

17. **consider**
    A. deem
    B. surrender
    C. force
    D. evoke

18. **separate**
    A. isolate
    B. join
    C. defeat
    D. sustain

19. **aristocrat**
    A. commoner
    B. noble
    C. authority
    D. philosophy

20. **designate**
    A. show
    B. launch
    C. compel
    D. nominate

21. **prohibit**
    A. forbid
    B. drench
    C. diversify
    D. shake

22. **distort**
    A. deny
    B. account
    C. demand
    D. alter

23. **suggest**
    A. annoy
    B. propose
    C. yield
    D. extract

24. **particular**
    A. original
    B. dormant
    C. peculiar
    D. ample

25. **theory**
    A. measurement
    B. denial
    C. hypothesis
    D. confusion

26. **indestructible**
    A. fixed
    B. immortal
    C. damaged
    D. economical

27. **extensively**
    A. broadly
    B. valuably
    C. occasionally
    D. entirely

28. **inhabit**
    A. ruin
    B. absorb
    C. strive
    D. occupy

29. **eventually**
    A. impulsively
    B. frequently
    C. ultimately
    D. virtually

30. **outnumber**
    A. surpass
    B. count
    C. adhere
    D. detect

1B 2D 3B 4B 5C 6B 7A 8B 9D 10A 11B 12A 13A 14B 15C 16B
17A 18A 19B 20D 21A 22D 23B 24C 25C 26B 27A 28D 29C 30A

I. What Is an Inference Question?

Inference

The inference question asks you to assume, or *infer*, an idea about a passage based on the information presented. In an inference question, you must be aware that an author does not directly state an idea but rather implies it. The author will state specific facts and details that will lead you to the unstated idea.

A. INFERENCE QUESTION MODEL

Ancient Egyptians believed that there was life after death. They believed that after a person has died, the person's soul visits its former body to obtain food and drink. For this reason, ancient Egyptians developed a way of preserving the body after death using special fluids and wraps. The body was placed in a tomb with its internal organs stored in jars, along with clothing, jewelry, furniture, and other objects from the deceased person's daily life.

6. What can be inferred about the ancient Egyptians burying the deceased with belongings?
   (A) They believed that such a process symbolized their love for the deceased.
   (B) They believed that such a procedure was a sacrifice that would please the gods.
   (C) They believed that the afterlife was better than life on Earth.
   (D) They believed that the deceased person's soul would appreciate having the items.

B. INFERENCE QUESTION FORMATS

What can be inferred about _____?

Which statement is MOST LIKELY true about _____?

What PROBABLY occurred after/before/during _____?

Which MOST ACCURATELY reflects the author's opinion?

It can be inferred from _____ that _____.

What can be inferred from Paragraph _____?

What is a probable belief of the author?

C. TIPS

1. An inference can be made from just one sentence or from the entire passage.
2. Often the answer choices paraphrase the ideas of the passage, so it is important to understand the passage well.
3. An incorrect answer may:
   - be too broad or unclear
   - be off-topic or unrelated to the passage
   - be false or not be supported by the stated information in the passage
   - restate the information directly given in the passage

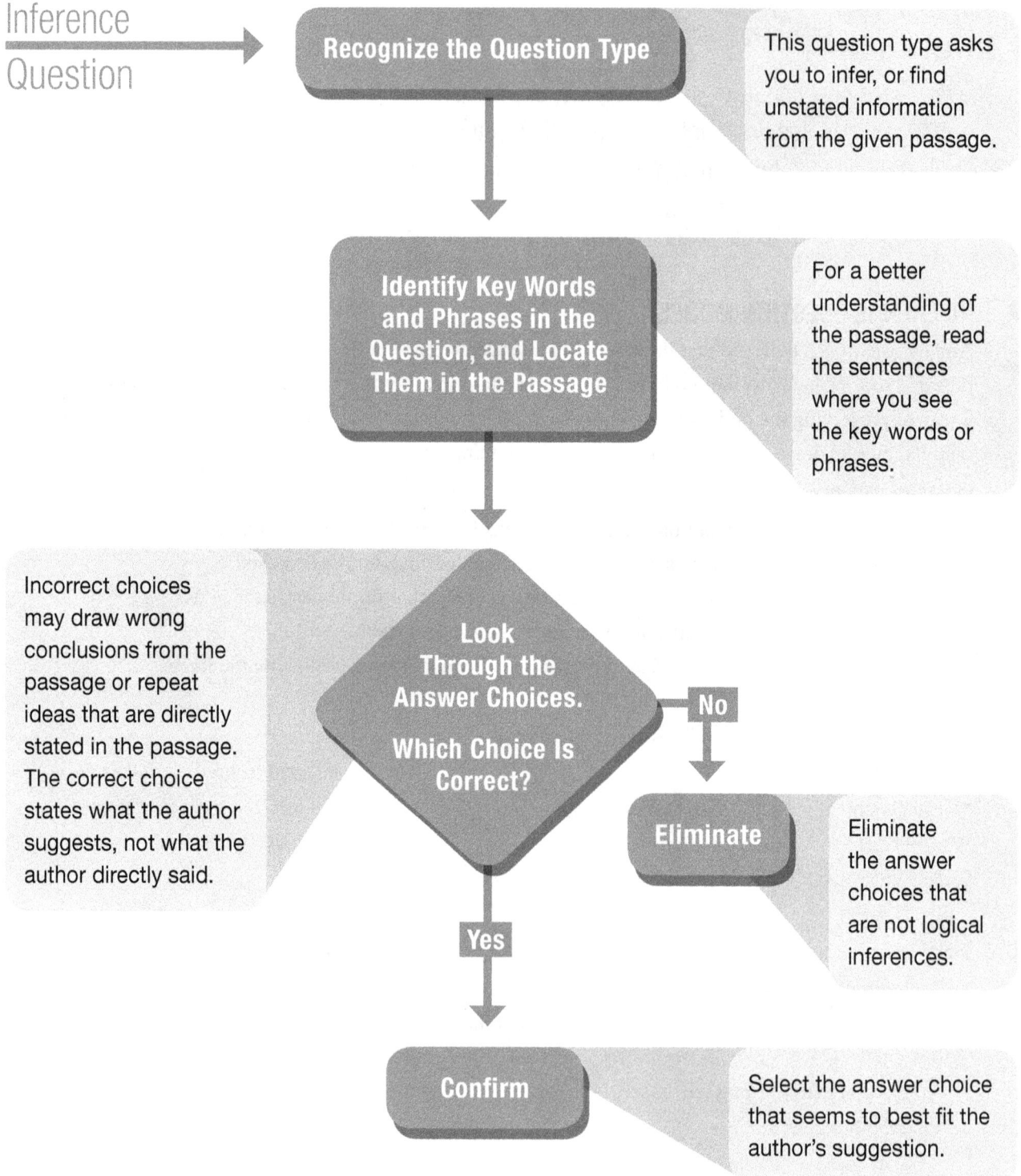

II. Hacking Strategy

Inference
Question

Recognize the Question Type

This question type asks you to infer, or find unstated information from the given passage.

Identify Key Words and Phrases in the Question, and Locate Them in the Passage

For a better understanding of the passage, read the sentences where you see the key words or phrases.

Incorrect choices may draw wrong conclusions from the passage or repeat ideas that are directly stated in the passage. The correct choice states what the author suggests, not what the author directly said.

Look Through the Answer Choices. Which Choice Is Correct?

No

Eliminate

Eliminate the answer choices that are not logical inferences.

Yes

Confirm

Select the answer choice that seems to best fit the author's suggestion.

Ancient Egyptians believed that there was life after death. They believed that after a person has died, the person's soul visits its former body to obtain food and drink. For this reason, ancient Egyptians developed a way of preserving the body after death using special fluids and wraps. The body was placed in a tomb with its internal organs stored in jars, along with clothing, jewelry, furniture, and other objects from the deceased person's daily life.

What can be inferred about the ancient Egyptians burying the deceased with belongings?

(A) They believed that such a process symbolized their love for the deceased.

(B) They believed that such a procedure was a sacrifice that would please the gods.

(C) They believed that the afterlife was better than life on Earth.

(D) They believed that the deceased person's soul would appreciate having the items.

What can be inferred about the ancient Egyptians burying the deceased with belongings?

(A)   They believed that such a process symbolized their love for the deceased.

(B)   They believed that such a procedure was a sacrifice that would please the gods.

(C)   They believed that the afterlife was better than life on Earth.

(D)   They believed that the deceased person's soul would appreciate having the items.

Ancient Egyptians believed that there was life after death. They believed that after a person has died, the person's soul visits its former body to obtain food and drink. For this reason, ancient Egyptians developed a way of preserving the body after death using special fluids and wraps. The body was placed in a tomb with its internal organs stored in jars, along with clothing, jewelry, furniture, and other objects from the deceased person's daily life.

Which choice is **NOT STATED** in the passage but is **SUGGESTED?**

• Select **Choice D** because ancient Egyptians burying their deceased with many things that the deceased used in life indicates a belief that the soul would want the items when it visited its former body, and therefore we can infer that the deceased person *appreciates having the items*.

• Eliminate **Choice A** because the passage does not mention anything about symbolizing emotions.

• Eliminate **Choice B** because burial rituals do not include a sacrifice.

• Eliminate **Choice C** because the passage does not describe the afterlife.

Select the correct answer — **Choice D**.

III. Quick Look

Making Inferences

Inference: An *inference* is an idea that you create on your own BASED ON the information that is directly stated in the passage.

1.

Choices

2.

Choices

3.

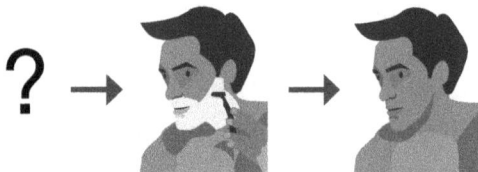

Choices

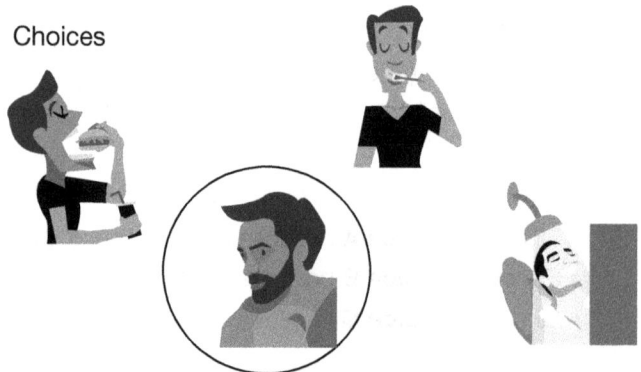

IV. Warm Up

Choose the MORE LIKELY inference from each of the following sentences.

1. The avocado, informally called the alligator pear, is an oval-shaped fruit that has leather-like skin.
   Ⓐ The avocado's skin is similar to an alligator's.
   Ⓑ The avocado's shape is similar to an alligator's.

2. On April 14, 1865, John Wilkes Booth assassinated President Abraham Lincoln.
   Ⓐ Booth disapproved of President Lincoln.
   Ⓑ President Lincoln was unethical.

3. The minimum legal age to drink alcohol in Canada is 19, but in Mexico, the minimum legal age is 18.
   Ⓐ Mexico has less young people than Canada.
   Ⓑ Canada is stricter about young adults drinking than Mexico.

4. In Japan, *slurping*, or making a loud sipping noise, while drinking soup is a sign that one enjoys the food, but in the United States, this is considered rude.
   Ⓐ Because of Japan's cultural influence, people in the U.S. slurp the soup.
   Ⓑ In the U.S. and Japan, there are different ways to express one's appreciation for food.

5. The English language originated in England and is now the official language of several nations, including the United States, one of many former British colonies.
   Ⓐ British colonization spread the English language throughout the world.
   Ⓑ The formation of the United States led to the spreading of the English language.

6. Deciduous trees and shrubs lose their leaves as the seasons change.
   Ⓐ Deciduous trees and shrubs look different each new season.
   Ⓑ Deciduous trees and shrubs become different trees each season.

7. The image of a human skull with two long bones crossed underneath it is a common symbol seen on objects such as poisonous substances.
   Ⓐ The symbol can be commonly seen on many objects.
   Ⓑ The symbol is used to warn people of something dangerous.

8. Although more modern calculating systems have developed, many Asian merchants still use the abacus, an ancient calculation tool, to keep track of inventories.
   Ⓐ The abacus makes accurate calculations despite its antiquity.
   Ⓑ People still use the abacus because of its antiquity.

9. Superhero comic books first appeared during the Great Depression of the early 20th century, and they almost immediately achieved commercial success.
   Ⓐ People enjoy reading about heroic figures during times of hardship.
   Ⓑ After the Great Depression, superhero comic books quickly lost popularity.

10. Western cultures value bread so much that the term *breadwinner* refers to the member of a family who provides financial support.
    Ⓐ Bread is a rare but desirable commodity in Western countries.
    Ⓑ Bread represents sustenance in Western cultures.

V. Quick Practice

Practice #1

Read the passage. Then answer the questions that follow.

Howard Cosell is perhaps the best-known sports broadcaster in United States radio and television history. He gained national prominence by providing play-by-play descriptions and commentary during the heavyweight boxing matches of Muhammad Ali, with whom he had a good relationship for many years. Starting in 1970, he was also a broadcaster for ABC's *Monday Night Football* for years. However, not all viewers liked Cosell because when he interviewed athletes, his questions were blunt and analytical rather than admiring. He often said, "I'm just telling it like it is."

1) Based on the passage, what is PROBABLY true about Howard Cosell?
   (A) He was a former boxer and football player.
   (B) He was not embarrassed to ask athletes about mistakes.
   (C) He was liked by the whole nation.
   (D) He only interviewed athletes who he knew personally.

2) What can be inferred from the passage about a reason for Cosell's success?
   (A) Cosell had a pleasant personality.
   (B) Cosell was not very opinionated.
   (C) Many viewers liked Cosell's honesty.
   (D) Cosell was easy to work with.

Practice #2

Read the passage. Then answer the questions that follow.

Alchemy is an ancient science that was studied for more than four millennia across three different continents. The goals of alchemy varied in time and place, but two goals remained the same: creating a philosopher's stone and creating an elixir of life. The former was thought to transform any metal into gold or silver; the latter was thought to provide eternal youth.

3) What can be inferred from the passage about alchemy?
   (A) Alchemy survived the Industrial Revolution and is still studied today.
   (B) Alchemy was associated with "black magic," or evil.
   (C) Over time, gold became less valuable, decreasing alchemy's influence.
   (D) Many people studied alchemy even though they met with only frustration.

4) What does the author PROBABLY believe about alchemists?
   (A) They were trying to fulfill the human desire for immortality and riches.
   (B) They were unintelligent and naïve and probably never realized it.
   (C) They were healers who had only good intentions.
   (D) They were forced to continue their studies by other powerful leaders.

Practice #3

Read the passage. Then answer the questions that follow.

The ancient Gaelic people of Ireland and Scotland, a branch of the Celtic people, celebrated an autumn festival they called *Samhain*, pronounced "sah-win." Samhain, which was celebrated on October 31 and November 1 to mark the end of summer, strongly influenced today's secular celebrations of Halloween. Toward summer's end, cattle were brought down from pastures and slaughtered, a practice accompanied by rituals and feasts. Gaelic people believed that the barrier between the living and the dead became thin on the night of Samhain, so they built sacred bonfires and set a place at the feast table for recently deceased loved ones. People also donned animal costumes in order to fool any spirits that they believed might harm them.

5) What can be inferred from the passage about Samhain?
 (A) It is the oldest Gaelic festival.
 (B) It coincided with a time of plentiful meat.
 (C) It may have been a way to entertain children once a year.
 (D) It was a celebration of rebirth and growth.

6) According to the passage, what was PROBABLY a Gaelic belief?
 (A) Slaughtering cattle caused the cattle spirits to be angry.
 (B) People's souls stayed around their families for a while after death.
 (C) The god of fire wanted them to celebrate one night a year.
 (D) Dressing up as animals would scare away any harmful spirits.

Practice #4

Read the passage. Then answer the questions that follow.

In the 1930s and 1940s, American folk music singer-songwriters, who drew musical inspiration from the British Isles, did not sell huge numbers of records. They were thought of as unsophisticated "hillbillies*" and associated with socialism. Folk musicians such as Woody Guthrie, who wrote "This Land is Your Land," were indeed overtly political. However, in the 1950s, the clean-cut, non-political Kingston Trio achieved commercial success by recording catchy acoustic folk songs. Ironically, their success helped pave the way for folk-based protest songs in the 1960s.

Hillbilly: a person from a remote area, especially from the mountains of the Southern U.S.

7) What can be inferred about folk music during the 1930s and 1940s?
 (A) It was more successful in live performances than on radio.
 (B) It provided music that was mostly already known because the songs were traditional.
 (C) It was praised for its socialistic messages.
 (D) It did not appeal to wealthier conservative listeners.

8) What can be inferred about the public's attitude toward buying folk and traditional music?
 (A) It improved when performers started wearing matching outfits.
 (B) Many customers who had been dismissive changed their minds in the 1950s.
 (C) People generally went from being nostalgic to being apathetic.
 (D) It was strongly affected by the protests in 1960s.

Practice #5

Read the passage. Then answer the questions that follow.

Education theorists often urge teachers to recognize "multiple intelligences" in their students. That is, each student has a preferred style of focusing on, processing, and retaining information. For example, theorist Howard Gardner says that one particular student might learn most effectively through seeing the information in writing. Another might learn best by seeing the material illustrated or by hearing it. Other students may learn best through music, collaboration, or movement.

9) What does the author PROBABLY think about learning?
   (A) Traditional schools were more effective at providing practice activities for learning.
   (B) Some children may seem less intelligent than others if information is presented in only one way.
   (C) Some students have multiple intelligences, while others may have a few.
   (D) Without music classes, a school's overall test scores are bound to decline.

10) According to Gardner, what can be inferred about how a teacher should present information?
   (A) Write new information on the board, say it, have children chant it, and then discuss it in small groups.
   (B) Alter students' learning styles so that the whole class can focus on one method of learning.
   (C) Never rely on tests to measure knowledge and intelligence.
   (D) Never interfere and have students teach themselves new material.

Practice #6

Read the passage. Then answer the questions that follow.

Throughout history, female writers have sometimes disguised their gender for publication. Some have called themselves "Anonymous"; others have used a male name or initials. George Eliot, a successful 19th-century writer, was actually a woman named Mary Anne Evans. She admitted her identity publicly only after her first novel had achieved critical acclaim. A more contemporary example is Joanne Rowling, the author of the Harry Potter series. Her publisher asked her to use the name "J.K. Rowling" so that boys would be more likely to read the books.

11) According to the passage, why did Mary Anne Evans PROBABLY use the name George Eliot on her books?
   (A) All women writers of her era used men's names.
   (B) She always pretended to be a man.
   (C) She cared more about money than women's rights.
   (D) She did not want readers and critics to be biased against her.

12) What can be inferred about J.K. Rowling's publisher from the passage?
   (A) It wanted to keep the identity of the author a well-guarded secret.
   (B) It knew that book critics would not objectively review a children's book by a female author.
   (C) It believed that boys think of books written by women as "girls' books."
   (D) It thought that parents buy more books for boys than for girls.

Practice #7

Read the passage. Then answer the questions that follow.

The insects in the flying-beetle family *Lampyridae* are often called fireflies or lightning bugs. Like animals that live in the ocean's depths, most fireflies create light within their bodies using a process called *bioluminescence*. The firefly takes in oxygen, which enters abdominal cavities where certain compounds are stored. The oxygen activates the compounds and creates cold light, which shines through the lower exoskeleton of the insect. Many firefly species are active at twilight, when they send signals to potential mates by emitting a flashing light.

13) What can be inferred from the passage about bioluminescence?
(A) It illuminates the entire surface of the insect's body.
(B) It is very common in the animal kingdom when chemical compounds interact.
(C) It potentially attracts predators.
(D) It does not generate heat, which would probably harm the insect.

14) What is MOST LIKELY true about most firefly species?
(A) They are similar in many ways to the animals of the deepest seas.
(B) They developed bioluminescence as an adaptation to allow communication.
(C) Their vision allows them to be most active in the evening.
(D) They might easily be confused if they saw a flashlight.

Practice #8

Read the passage. Then answer the questions that follow.

In ancient Egypt, most people took a break from the desert heat and bathed daily in the Nile River or used a large bowl of water at home. Wealthier people could afford to bathe in a separate room in their homes and had servants assist them during their baths. Egyptians used pasty soap made from chalk and animal fat, as well as cleansing creams made from mineral lime, oil, and perfume. Both men and women shaved their entire bodies, often including their heads. Afterward, they applied perfumes and oils to their skin.

15) What can be inferred from the passage about conditions and attitudes in ancient Egypt?
(A) Wealthy Egyptians were shy about nakedness, but others were not.
(B) Hot weather and available water contributed to a cultural value of cleanliness.
(C) Shaving and using oil and perfume had much religious significance.
(D) Egyptians were unusual in the ancient world for their knowledge about healthy habits.

16) From the passage, what can be inferred about daily bathing in ancient Egypt?
(A) They spent a fair amount of time and resources on it.
(B) They had secret recipes for making cleansers and perfume oils.
(C) Most people bathed in the evening after a long day of work.
(D) They had the first metal razors to shave off hair.

Practice #9

Read the passage. Then answer the questions that follow.

Chewing gum is inexplicably pleasant for humans. Thousands of years ago, people in various parts of the world figured out that if they boiled the liquid, or *sap*, that they found under the bark of certain trees, they could make gum. Archaeological evidence of gum from about 3000 BCE has been found in Finland. The ancient Greeks also made chewing gum. They used the sap of the "mastic" tree; as a result, *masticate* now means "to chew" in English. In the Americas, the ancient Aztec and Mayan people made gum from a tree called the *chicle*. In fact, many people in Latin America still call gum *chicle*.

17) Based on the passage, what is PROBABLY true about archaeological evidence in Finland?
 (A) It shows that ancient Greeks traded gum with people in Finland.
 (B) It included written records detailing the use of mastic trees for gum in Finland.
 (C) Some conditions in Finland preserved historic traces of chewed gum.
 (D) It proves that there were trees that produced an unusually chewy sap.

18) What can be inferred about language and gum from the passage?
 (A) The invention of gum has been a topic of conversation throughout history.
 (B) Merchants have spread the use of gum over wide cultural areas.
 (C) People have always named gum based on its tree of origin.
 (D) The origins of gum have had lasting linguistic influences.

Practice #10

Read the passage. Then answer the questions that follow.

Each year, many tourists visit General Sherman, a giant sequoia tree in California's Sierra Nevada Mountains. General Sherman has stood for more than 2,000 years in a grove of other giant sequoias and has been found to be slightly larger than its neighbor, General Grant. In fact, at 1,487 cubic meters, General Sherman may be the largest single-stem tree by volume on Earth. However, there is a taller tree, a redwood tree called "Hyperion," along the California coast. There also are wider trees, including a super-thick Montezuma cypress tree in a churchyard near Oaxaca, Mexico. Tourists like to see it because, according to legend, this particular cypress tree was planted by a priest of the Aztec wind god.

19) What can be inferred about people's attitude toward trees from the passage?
 (A) People are fascinated by trees of extreme size and age.
 (B) The government supports redwood trees because everyone loves them.
 (C) Californians take more pride in their trees than Mexicans do.
 (D) People have long considered the largest trees sacred.

20) From the passage, what is MOST LIKELY true about General Sherman?
 (A) It is larger than General Grant because it was planted earlier.
 (B) It belongs to a species that is highly resistant to stressors in the environment.
 (C) It was discovered by and named for a military leader named Sherman.
 (D) It has not changed much for at least two millennia.

Select the vocabulary word or phrase that has the closest meaning.

1. **assassinate**
   A. create
   B. finish
   C. murder
   D. protect

2. **commentary**
   A. explanation
   B. abundance
   C. similarity
   D. communication

3. **analytical**
   A. examining
   B. absurd
   C. respectful
   D. dismissive

4. **prompt**
   A. quick
   B. patient
   C. formal
   D. improved

5. **elixir**
   A. equation
   B. destiny
   C. potion
   D. duty

6. **address**
   A. neglect
   B. consider
   C. abandon
   D. discuss

7. **naïve**
   A. cautious
   B. sensible
   C. trusting
   D. impossible

8. **influence**
   A. power
   B. weakness
   C. obstacle
   D. vehicle

9. **feast**
   A. beast
   B. luxury
   C. rest
   D. banquet

10. **rebirth**
    A. pollution
    B. switch
    C. renewal
    D. triumph

11. **slaughter**
    A. bake
    B. kill
    C. trap
    D. lose

12. **commercial**
    A. financial
    B. conversational
    C. surprising
    D. confident

13. **catchy**
    A. regular
    B. memorable
    C. boring
    D. truthful

14. **pave the way**
    A. prepare
    B. finish
    C. incite
    D. scout

15. **attitude**
    A. manner
    B. altitude
    C. reason
    D. statue

16. **dismissive**
    A. humble
    B. modest
    C. simulated
    D. disdainful

17. **illustrated**
    A. spoken
    B. confirmed
    C. depicted
    D. narrated

18. **chant**
    A. chart
    B. shout
    C. return
    D. groan

19. **anonymous**
    A. named
    B. stated
    C. public
    D. unknown

20. **publicly**
    A. secretly
    B. openly
    C. visually
    D. shyly

21. **acclaim**
    A. approval
    B. disgrace
    C. belittle
    D. humble

22. **biased**
    A. genuine
    B. tolerant
    C. partial
    D. curious

23. **compound**
    A. mixture
    B. network
    C. comment
    D. event

24. **potential**
    A. helpless
    B. possible
    C. shrinking
    D. dormant

25. **confuse**
    A. bewilder
    B. explain
    C. soothe
    D. restore

26. **interact**
    A. avoid
    B. engage
    C. cancel
    D. switch

27. **pasty**
    A. smooth
    B. bright
    C. rough
    D. sticky

28. **inexplicably**
    A. fondly
    B. strangely
    C. lovingly
    D. honestly

29. **figure**
    A. determine
    B. subtract
    C. entertain
    D. surprise

30. **spread**
    A. narrow
    B. increase
    C. restrict
    D. space

Exercises

Exercise #1 Read the passage. Then answer the questions that follow.

Like most inventions, the now-iconic American blue jeans were first developed for practical reasons. In the mid-1800s, a tailor in Reno, Nevada, named Jacob Davis came up with an idea to strengthen work trousers. **A** He decided to apply for a United States patent that would give him rights to the idea. **B** He wrote to Levi Strauss, the owner of a dry-goods store he knew, asking him to help pay the patent fees. **C** The two of them obtained the patent and set up a garment factory. **D**

In their earliest days, jeans were baggy, comfortable work clothes associated with farm and factory work or with outdoor Western "cowboy" life. These characteristics began to change in the post-World War II era. The emphasis in the early 1950s on societal conformity and maintaining security led to a rising counterculture, which was popularized in films with rebellious protagonists. Marlon Brando in 1954's *The Wild One*, James Dean in 1955's *Rebel Without a Cause*, and Elvis Presley in 1957's *Jailhouse Rock*, made jeans synonymous with youthful nonconformity. As a result, many schools banned the wearing of jeans, which in turn made jeans even more popular.

1) Look at the squares [■] that indicate where the sentence below could be added to Paragraph 1.

His idea was to sew copper rivets, or fasteners, at the corners of pockets to keep them from tearing.

Where would the sentence best fit?
Circle the square [■] to add the sentence.

2) In Paragraph 2, which of the following can be inferred about jeans in American culture?
(A) The popularity of jeans dwindled as many public locations discouraged them.
(B) Young people have always demanded the right to wear jeans.
(C) The fluctuating popularity of jeans has often caused cultural confusion.
(D) Jeans appealed to people who wanted to appear daring.

Exercise #2 Read the passage. Then answer the questions that follow.

The modernist Australian literary magazine *Angry Penguins* became the center of a strange controversy in 1944. **A** Two young Australian poets, James McAuley and Harold Stewart, despised the modern style of poetry that was featured in *Angry Penguins*. **B** They hurriedly wrote 17 "modernist poems," using disjointed bits of their own poetry and lines taken from random books. **C** They signed the meaningless scribbles with a fictional name and submitted them to the magazine under the title *The Darkening Ecliptic.* **D**

Max Harris was fooled, thinking that he had discovered a poetic genius. He published and promoted the poems. Not long after, newspapers uncovered the trick and reported that the poems were fake. Harris was humiliated, and for a time the Australian public became convinced that all modernist poetry was silly and phony. However, Harris much later stated that he thought the tricksters had tricked themselves. He said that their free-association method had produced some good poems. Indeed, several recent critics and writers have agreed with him.

3) Look at the squares [■] that indicate where the sentence below could be added to Paragraph 1.

Hence, they decided to play a trick on the magazine's young, brash editor, Max Harris.

Where would the sentence best fit?

Circle the square [■] to add the sentence.

4) According to Paragraph 2, which of the following is PROBABLY the view of recent literary critics?
   (A) Harris rushed to judgment about the poems.
   (B) Harris may have been better at recognizing good poetry than people realized.
   (C) Harris was so desperate for success that he was easy to trick.
   (D) Harris must have been lacking in self-confidence and self-esteem.

Exercise #3 Read the passage. Then answer the questions that follow.

There are many uses in language and mathematics for *if-then* statements. **A** For example, "*If* he makes this goal, *then* the team will win the game" makes it clear that the condition is making the goal. **B** If the speaker added "*or else* it will lose," the speaker is giving the consequence *if* the condition is *not* met. **C** In geometry, if-then statements can be used to prove theorems: *if* two angles of a triangle are each 45 degrees, *then* the third angle will be 90 degrees. **D**

Computer programming often makes extensive use of logic and if-then commands. The commands direct a computer to make appropriate responses. A programmer can stipulate that *if* a condition is met – such as a password being correct – *then* the computer should act in a particular way. *If not* – or *else* – the computer should act in a different way. Programmers can stipulate two or more conditions by adding *else-if* commands. For instance, else-if commands can be used in the following way: "*If* the player makes the goal, or *else* if he or she makes a penalty kick, *then* the team will win."

5) Look at the squares [■] that indicate where the sentence below could be added to Paragraph 1.

These are called conditional statements because they are only true if a certain condition is met.

Where would the sentence best fit?
Circle the square [■] to add the sentence.

6) According to the passage, what can be inferred about computer programmers?
(A) They must have a strong background in geometry in order to succeed.
(B) They are able to manipulate computers in any way they want.
(C) The more conditions that they can think of, the more precise the program will be.
(D) If they write an illogical program, then it can still be partially effective.

Exercise #4 Read the passage. Then answer the questions that follow.

A At the ages of three and four, children learn through play. **B** For example, when children scoop and pour water, they are developing concepts about quantity and volume that will later help them envision math concepts. **C** When they play with dress-up clothes or puppets, they are practicing speech patterns and social skills. **D** When they draw, they are imagining scenes, a crucial aspect of later reading comprehension and writing.

Preschool teachers study early childhood education theory to learn how to set up preschool environments that maximize learning through play. Usually, teachers organize the classroom into areas, such as an area to play with blocks, an area for books, an area for painting, and so on. Children are encouraged to talk while they carry out these activities. In fact, research shows that children learn the most when they talk with other children or adults about what they are doing. The teacher must constantly assess each child's development and vocabulary by observing him or her play and talk.

7) Look at the squares [■] that indicate where the sentence below could be added to Paragraph 1.

Their games and chatting may not seem to be connected to academic learning, but they actually are.

Where would the sentence best fit?
Circle the square [■] to add the sentence.

8) What can be inferred from Paragraph 2 about early childhood education theory?
   (A) It promotes just having fun at preschool, as there are no quizzes or tests.
   (B) Building conversational skills is crucial to childhood development.
   (C) It advocates teaching language arts skills rather than science or math skills.
   (D) It is not based on academic research, but rather on common sense about child-rearing.

Exercise #5 Read the passage. Then answer the questions that follow.

Rude or unfriendly behavior is seldom tolerated for long in any culture. However, different cultures have different rules about what is "rude" and what is "polite." For example, a child in a Native American tribe may be taught to look down and speak softly when addressing an adult. If the child attends a school with a non-Native American teacher, this respectful habit might be misinterpreted as a sign of inattention or disrespect.

Anthropologist Conrad Kottak defines *enculturation* as a social process by which culture is learned and transmitted across generations. **A** The process can be direct; for example, an adult may tell a child how to hold his or her chopsticks or when to say "please." **B** However, the process is largely indirect, as people watch how others behave and also observe or experience the consequences of certain actions. **C** Thus, teachers can become enculturated by their students, for example, by recognizing that looking down and speaking softly are signs of respect in some cultures. **D**

9) What can be inferred from Paragraph 1?
   (A) Being aware of others' cultural expectations may help prevent conflict.
   (B) Some cultures have stronger moral values and higher expectations than others.
   (C) Children are often considered impolite in all cultures.
   (D) Good manners are the most important part of any culture.

10) Look at the squares [■] that indicate where the sentence below could be added to Paragraph 2.

It is also important to remember that enculturation is not only a process that affects children – it is lifelong.

Where would the sentence best fit?
Circle the square [■] to add the sentence.

Exercise #6 Read the passage. Then answer the questions that follow.

Historians consider Philip Astley, an 18th-century horse-riding instructor, to be the founder of the modern circus. Astley joined the British military in 1742 at the age of 17. Serving in the Seven Years' War allowed him to sharpen his horsemanship skills. After the war, Astley opened a riding school to profit from the then-current craze for performing tricks while riding a horse. Lessons were during the day; at night he and other riders exhibited their own trick riding.

   The audience attending Astley's exhibitions continued to grow. **A** One reason for this increasing popularity was that, unlike any other trick rider before him, Astley and his riders rode in a circle. **B** This "ring" allowed the audience to see the rider at all times and gave the rider more control over his or her balance. **C** Astley later added ropedancers, acrobats, clowns, and jugglers to keep the audience engaged between riders. **D** Thus, the concept of the performance-oriented circus for a paying audience was born.

11) According to Paragraph 1, which of the following statements is MOST LIKELY true?
   (A) Astley did not know anything about horses when he joined the military.
   (B) Astley started the evening exhibits to promote his riding classes.
   (C) Astley performed daring stunts on horseback on city streets.
   (D) Astley invented trick riding on horses after serving in the military.

12) Look at the squares [■] that indicate where the sentence below could be added to Paragraph 2.

   Then, at the age of 31, he opened the Astley's Amphitheatre in London to showcase his exhibit.

   Where would the sentence best fit?
   Circle the square [■] to add the sentence.

Exercise #7 Read the passage. Then answer the questions that follow.

A Since the beginning of agriculture, farmers worldwide have had to deal with hungry birds. **B** Birds can eat farmers' crops, leaving smaller harvests for farmers to feed their families or to sell. **C** A *scarecrow* usually refers to a human decoy dressed in old clothes and planted in a field to "scare" away birds such as "crows." **D**

   The scarecrow has appeared in different forms and shapes in different cultures. Japanese farmers at one time put rags and old fish on poles in their fields and set them on fire, and the resulting horrible smell kept birds away. Some cultures hung cloth or bones to wave and click in the wind. In many cultures, people have used *bird scarers*, or individuals who sit among the crops. When a bird comes near the crops, the bird scarer claps pieces of wood together to make loud noises, howls and shouts, or throws stones at the bird to scare it away. Updated versions of bird scarers include loud recorded noises or metallic ribbons that shimmer.

13) Look at the squares [■] that indicate where the sentence below could be added to Paragraph 1.

To prevent this, farmers in many places have used scarecrows to protect their fields.

Where would the sentence best fit?
Circle the square [■] to add the sentence.

14) According to Paragraph 2, what can be inferred about scaring birds away?
(A) Farmers in every culture respected bird scarers.
(B) Humans are more effective than devices at bird-scaring activities.
(C) Crop damage or loss from birds is no longer a problem.
(D) Most birds notice when conditions in an environment are unusual.

Exercise #8 Read the passage. Then answer the questions that follow.

During the 1890s, Austrian psychologist Sigmund Freud created *psychoanalysis*, a method of treating mental disorders. Freud wanted to help patients discover unconscious causes for their *neuroses*, or distress and anxiety. This basic idea was revolutionary and influential. Despite the significance of this idea, Freud experienced criticism from academic and clinical "neo-Freudians." They disagreed with Freud's theory that people experienced neuroses mostly because they had been forced to repress sexual impulses during childhood.

Like other Freud critics, Karen Horney, a prominent German neo-Freudian psychoanalyst, thought that neuroses had various social and cultural causes. **A** She focused on emotionally distant parents, theorizing that their children tend to be insecure. **B** Horney said that the insecurity from unmet emotional needs leads those children to try to become perfect. **C** When they cannot become perfect, they may suffer from neuroses. **D**

15) From Paragraph 1, what can be inferred about the field of psychoanalysis?
(A) Freud retired in disfavor and disgrace from the field.
(B) Many Freud critics still agreed with the importance of unconscious thought.
(C) Most psychoanalysts of the early 20th century agreed with Freud.
(D) Before Freud, psychology was more academic than clinical.

16) Look at the squares [■] that indicate where the sentence below could be added to Paragraph 2.

People who do *not* suffer neuroses, she said, may strive for ideals but are also interested in life as it really is.

Where would the sentence best fit?
Circle the square [■] to add the sentence.

I. What Is a Purpose Question?

Purpose

The purpose question asks you to identify how certain pieces of information help you understand either a detail or the main idea of the passage. A *purpose* is a reason why the author included particular information in a passage. For example, the purpose of a passage can be to inform you about a topic or to persuade the reader.

A. PURPOSE QUESTION MODEL

In ancient Greece, warriors from the city-state of Sparta inspired fear in the region for hundreds of years. Sparta focused its resources on victory in battle. For instance, all Spartan boys lived at harsh military training schools **from the age of seven**. One of the strategies that they learned was how to walk into battle in a *phalanx*, or a line of soldiers forming a wall with their shields. Spartan men continued to live in military groups rather than with wives or families even between the ages of 20 and 30.

7. Why does the author mention "**from the age of seven**" in the passage?

   (A) To describe how boys were disciplined in Sparta

   (B) To give an example of Sparta's focus on fighting

   (C) To provide details about Sparta's reputation in the region

   (D) To explain how Spartans learned to make a *phalanx*

B. PURPOSE QUESTION FORMATS

The author discusses _____ in order to _____.

The author mentions _____ in order to _____.

Why does the author discuss _____?

Why does the author compare _____ to _____?

Why does the author mention _____?

Why does the author order the information by _____?

Why does the author use the word/the punctuation mark when discussing _____?

C. TIPS

1. Generally, purpose questions ask you to create logical connections between sentences or paragraphs.

2. The overall purpose sometimes can be found in the topic sentence, which is normally the first sentence.

3. Incorrect answers are too vague, are false according to the passage, or are unrelated to the passage.

II. Hacking Strategy

Purpose
Question

→ **Recognize the Question Type**

This question type asks you to find the author's purpose for mentioning certain things.

↓

Identify Key Words and Phrases in the Question and Locate Them in the Passage to Infer the Purpose

Read the sentences where the key words and phrases appear. Read the surrounding sentences as well. Then make an inference about what the purpose is.

↓

Wrong choices will state purposes that do not make sense or are on a different topic; or they will state purposes that are too general or too specific. The correct choice will match the author's focus.

Look Through the Answer Choices. Which Choice Is Correct?

→ **No**

↓

Eliminate

Eliminate incorrect answer choices.

Yes

↓

Confirm

Select the answer choice that seems to best fit the author's purpose.

Recognize the Question Type

In ancient Greece, warriors from the city-state of Sparta inspired fear in the region for hundreds of years. Sparta focused its resources on victory in battle. For instance, all Spartan boys lived at harsh military training schools **from the age of seven**. One of the strategies that they learned was how to walk into battle in a *phalanx*, or a line of soldiers forming a wall with their shields. Spartan men continued to live in military groups rather than with wives or families even between the ages of 20 and 30.

Why does the author mention "from the age of seven" in the passage?

(A) To describe how boys were disciplined in Sparta

(B) To give an example of Sparta's focus on fighting

(C) To provide details about Sparta's reputation in the region

(D) To explain how Spartans learned to make a *phalanx*

Identify Key Words and Phrases in the Question, and Locate Them in the Passage to Infer the Purpose

Why does the author mention "**from the age of seven**" in the passage?

*Sparta focused its resources on victory in battle. For instance, all Spartan boys lived at harsh military training schools **from the age of seven**.*

Make an inference about the author's purpose. Directly before the sentence, the passage states that Sparta focused its resources on victory in battle. The reader can infer that the sentence's purpose is to add support to this general idea.

Look Through the Answer Choices. Which Choice Is Correct?

(A) To describe how boys were disciplined in Sparta

(B) To give an example of Sparta's focus on fighting

(C) To provide details about Sparta's reputation in the region

(D) To explain how Spartans learned to make a *phalanx*

Check the choices for grammatical fit and logical meaning.

• Select **Choice B** because the passage mentions *from the age of seven* to indicate how early Spartan boys started training in military schools, thus letting the readers know how much Spartans focused on fighting.

Eliminate Incorrect Choices

• Eliminate **Choice A** because the passage discusses harsh *military training schools*, but it does not talk about *how boys were disciplined*.

• Eliminate **Choice C** because the passage does not include more information about how outsiders viewed Sparta based on the age that Spartans started training.

• Eliminate **Choice D** because the passage mentions Spartan boys learning about the phalanx, but it is not the reason the author included *from the age of seven*.

Confirm

Select the correct answer — **Choice B**.

III. Quick Look

Words Used in Purpose Answer Choices	
Word	**Definition**
Argue	to try to prove a point
Caution	to warn against
Classify	to put in a category
Compare	to examine two or more things in relation to each other
Contrast	to show that one thing is different from the other
Criticize	to show something's faults
Define	to tell what something is
Describe	to give further information
Emphasize	to highlight important information
Explain	to tell why something is
Give Examples	to provide instances in order to further explain something
Identify	to tell what something is (similar to **Define**)
Illustrate	to give further information (similar to **Describe**)
Introduce	to bring forward a new idea or information
Persuade	to try to convince the reader to agree
Point Out	to bring something to attention
Praise	to admire or compliment something
Predict	to foretell something
Prove	to show that something is true
Show	to state something
Summarize	to state something in a shorter way, giving only the main ideas
Support	to show that something is true; to provide evidence for it
Trace	to follow the course of something's development
Warn	to give caution about something

IV. Warm Up

Read each topic and each detail below. Then choose whether the purpose of each detail is to:

*Persuade = PER	*Describe = DES	*Criticize = CR

1. **Topic:** European history term _____
   Detail: Scholars refer to the cultural and artistic movement that began in Italy in the 14th century as the *Renaissance*, or rebirth.

2. **Topic:** European history term _____
   Detail: To call the years between the 5th and 15th centuries the "Dark Ages" is inaccurate and misleading, as it ignores the many developments during the era.

3. **Topic:** Astrology
   Detail: Although astrology is a _____ *pseudoscience*, or not a rational field of study, in its ideal form it can give believers assurance and a sense of control and optimism.

4. **Topic:** Astrology
   Detail: Astrologers believe that there _____ are connections between human events and particular alignments of the planets, the Moon, the Sun, and the stars.

5. **Topic:** Clothing trends
   Detail: One purpose of clothing across _____ many human cultures has been to indicate social status.

6. **Topic:** Clothing trends _____
   Detail: Dressing up for Halloween has a negative impact on some children because they feel pressured to purchase a new costume each year in order to appear trendy and unique to their friends.

7. **Topic:** Dragons _____
   Detail: European dragons have been depicted for centuries as huge lizards or dinosaurs with wings; Asian dragons have tended to look more like giant serpents with legs.

8. **Topic:** Dragons _____
   Detail: Scholarly comparisons of dragons in different cultures' mythologies can provide fascinating insights.

9. **Topic:** Light bulb _____
   Detail: The most common light bulbs available today are the older incandescent bulbs and the energy-efficient compact fluorescent bulbs.

10. **Topic:** Light bulb _____
    Detail: The invention of the light bulb is hailed as a great achievement, but some researchers warn that exposure to artificial light has caused an epidemic of sleep deprivation.

II. Hacking Strategy

Practice #1

Read the passage. Then answer the question that follows.

Aquariums and zoos work to sustain animal populations whose natural habitats have been damaged. Sometimes, the institutions are able to breed nearly extinct species and reintroduce them to the wild. Reintroductions that have been successful include the California condor, a bird with a wingspan of three meters; and the *takhi*, a wild horse of Mongolia.

1) Why does the author mention "animal populations whose natural habitats have been damaged" in the passage?
   (A) To criticize aquariums and zoos for focusing only on these populations
   (B) To identify some of the species that zoos and aquariums are helping
   (C) To persuade readers that the natural environment has declined
   (D) To describe some of the species that natural environments sustain

2) Why does the author mention the "California condor" in the passage?
   (A) To interest readers in an animal that they may see in a zoo setting
   (B) To discuss the challenges of successful reintroduction of animals to each other
   (C) To describe a magnificent bird that has become extinct in the wild
   (D) To name a species that can be found in nature because of zoo programs

Practice #2

Read the passage. Then answer the question that follows.

Around the beginning of the 19th century, members of an artistic movement called *Romanticism* revolted against classicism and the rational thinking of the time. Classicists believed that **eternal**, true facts and ideals exist, and all people should strive to reach them. Romanticism, on the other hand, emphasized **originality** and feelings. Romantics valued expressing one's own imaginative thoughts and unique perspectives.

3) Why does the author mention "eternal" in the passage?
   (A) To imply the religious base of classicism
   (B) To illustrate the reasonableness of the classicists
   (C) To criticize classicism for being idealistic
   (D) To explain the classicist view of ideals

4) Why does the author mention that Romanticism valued "originality" in the passage?
   (A) To describe what Romantics aimed for in the arts
   (B) To illustrate how the Romantics read fewer books than classicists
   (C) To prove that Romantics never copied other people's ideas
   (D) To emphasize that Romantics did not tolerate facts

Practice #3

Read the passage. Then answer the questions that follow.

A long-running, popular news program in the United States called *60 Minutes* **was created in 1968** with the goal of being a news "magazine." That is, reporters investigated issues that were important to the whole country but focused on individuals who were actually experiencing those issues. The program always opens with the image and sound of a **ticking stopwatch** rather than theme music.

5) Why does the author mention "**was created in 1968**" in the passage?
   (A) To point out where the program got its name
   (B) To explain that there were important issues to investigate in 1968
   (C) To provide a detail about how long the show has been broadcast
   (D) To criticize the show as old and out-of-date at this point in time

6) Why does the author mention a "**ticking stopwatch**" in the passage?
   (A) To give an example of a type of investigative story
   (B) To describe something about the show's format
   (C) To explain the length of an episode of *60 Minutes*
   (D) To show how reporters on the show use technology

Practice #4

Read the passage. Then answer the questions that follow.

The human brain works in some ways like a **computer**. Nerve cells throughout the body and brain act like a computer's electrical wires, serving as circuits for **signals**. Like a computer processor, brain cells receive and produce signals and send them via the circuits to other parts of the body. Both the brain and the computer receive, process, and send messages. However, one basic difference is that the computer can be turned off; the brain is always receiving and sending information, even during sleep.

7) Why does the author mention a "**computer**" in the passage?
   (A) To help readers better understand how computers work
   (B) To show that a machine and a brain are completely different
   (C) To classify different areas of the brain for readers
   (D) To introduce a comparison used throughout the passage

8) Why does the author mention "**signals**" in the passage?
   (A) To provide an image of the interior of the brain
   (B) To caution that the human brain is more like a robot's than it seems
   (C) To identify something that the computer and brain have in common
   (D) To discuss how computers and brains can work so quickly

Practice #5

Read the passage. Then answer the questions that follow.

Demosthenes, who lived from 384 to 322 BCE, has long been regarded as **one of the world's greatest public speakers** and statesmen. He worked as a speechwriter and orator in the assembly in Athens, and for nearly three decades he persuaded the Athenians to stand up to the mighty Philip II of Macedon. Demosthenes' success followed an unpromising start because he initially stuttered when he spoke. Reportedly, he practiced **speaking with his mouth full of pebbles** to improve his speech.

9) Why does the author use the phrase "**one of the world's greatest public speakers**" in the passage?
    (A) To point out the importance of public speaking to a democratic world
    (B) To show the overwhelming support enjoyed by Demosthenes in Greece today
    (C) To explain the significance of a historical figure
    (D) To highlight the contribution of public speakers

10) Why does the author mention "**speaking with his mouth full of pebbles**" in the passage?
    (A) To illustrate how motivated Demosthenes was to become an orator
    (B) To point out the best way to become an effective public speaker
    (C) To criticize the Greek system for being harsh on young people
    (D) To describe the reason why Demosthenes became famous then and now

Practice #6

Read the passage. Then answer the questions that follow.

During the 1960s, United States President Lyndon B. Johnson **introduced reforms** known as the *Great Society*. These changes included laws to end racial injustice as well as to provide funding for new programs to fight poverty. Johnson's past experiences **as a teacher working with poor Latino students** motivated him to improve societal conditions. Many projects that he first proposed still continue, such as Medicare, Head Start preschools, and education funding.

11) Why does the author mention "**introduced reforms**" in the passage?
    (A) To talk about ways people were introduced to the president
    (B) To explain how changes affected President Johnson
    (C) To describe President Johnson's efforts to make changes
    (D) To criticize President Johnson for only introducing reforms

12) Why does the author mention "**as a teacher working with poor Latino students**" in the passage?
    (A) To explain one reason that President Johnson wanted the Great Society
    (B) To emphasize how much teachers benefited from the Great Society
    (C) To describe how the Head Start Preschool Program for poor children was funded
    (D) To show why President Johnson ended up as president

Practice #7

Read the passage. Then answer the questions that follow.

Eating insects is **an ancient practice of many human cultures**. Fried or roasted insects are still popular foods in parts of Latin America, Africa, Asia, and Oceania. Edible insects include types of crickets, caterpillars, and beetles. Some agriculturists now wonder if insects could become "**mini-livestock**." They suggest that raising edible insects would provide better sources of nutrition for consumers and be better for the environment than raising traditional livestock, such as cows and chickens.

13) Why does the author mention "**an ancient practice of many human cultures**" in the passage?
   (A) To contrast insect-eating with modern human cuisine and culture
   (B) To demonstrate the great variety of insects and cooking methods used
   (C) To caution readers that the practice of eating insects will be difficult to stop
   (D) To persuade readers that eating insects is not just a modern culinary trend

14) Why does the author mention "**mini-livestock**" in the passage?
   (A) To describe the size of the farms needed if insects were to be raised
   (B) To criticize people who think raising regular livestock is a good idea
   (C) To help introduce and explain the concept of farming insects
   (D) To show how minimal the environmental impact of raising insects could be

Practice #8

Practice #8 Read the passage. Then answer the questions that follow.

The Korean folktale of "Shim Chung" focuses on **the theme of *filial piety***, or respect and care for one's parents. Shim Chung is a young girl who has been raised by her poor, blind father. In order to pay her father's debt and cure his blindness, Shim Chung **volunteers to become a drowning sacrifice** to the Sea Dragon King, so she jumps in the sea. The Sea Dragon King, moved by her selflessness, saves her and allows her to return to land, where she wins the heart of a king and ultimately cures her father's blindness.

15) Why does the author mention "**the theme of *filial piety***" in the passage?
   (A) To describe the focus of all Korean folktales
   (B) To prepare the reader for upcoming plot complications
   (C) To link the Korean folktale to the field of psychology
   (D) To provide an interpretation of the story's message

16) The author mentions "**volunteers to become a drowning sacrifice**" in order to
   (A) explain Shim Chung's motivation in the story
   (B) illustrate the importance of filial piety in a folktale
   (C) inform readers about the story's conflict and resolution
   (D) explain the requirements of the powerful Sea Dragon King

Practice #9

Read the passage. Then answer the questions that follow.

In 1839, a Connecticut inventor named **Charles Goodyear** discovered how to make rubber products more resistant to extreme temperatures. Manufacturers found many ways to use the new material, including making dolls. These dolls became popular during the 1850s and 1860s. They **represented both genders and various ages**. When a rubber doll was new, it was soft and unbreakable, but it often cracked as it aged.

17) Why does the author mention "**Charles Goodyear**" in the passage?
(A) To explain why doll makers were able to start using a new material
(B) To indicate the rubber process he invented was best for tires, not dolls
(C) To add commercial appeal to the story of dolls
(D) To identify the person who invented rubber dolls

18) Why does the author mention that dolls "**represented both genders and various ages**" in the passage?
(A) To illustrate new developments in society that affected the doll industry
(B) To show how children collected dolls instead of playing with them
(C) To provide an interesting fact about dolls during the mid-19th century
(D) To indicate that children of all ages played with dolls at the time

Practice #10

Read the passage. Then answer the questions that follow.

In medieval European legends, the Holy Grail was usually a highly sought-after, special cup. French poets recorded the first Holy Grail stories at **the end of the 12th century**, and afterward, many other authors began featuring the Holy Grail in their own plots. In many of these stories, a hero must go on a *quest*, or journey, to find the grail. In legends about King Arthur, knights searched for the grail for spiritual reasons. In some stories, the grail could heal people. Grail stories may have been based on **the Celtic people's** earlier tales of a magical cooking pot.

19) Why does the author mention "**the end of the 12th century**" in the passage?
(A) To trace how European legends were written down
(B) To inform readers about the written origins of Holy Grail stories
(C) To describe when knights and other heroes looked for the Holy Grail
(D) To define medieval European legends

20) Why does the author mention "**the Celtic people's**" in the passage?
(A) To illustrate why the Holy Grail worked well in King Arthur legends
(B) To persuade readers that the Holy Grail stories were historical
(C) To identify a possible root of the Holy Grail theme
(D) To criticize medieval authors for copying other legends

POP QUIZ

Select the vocabulary word or phrase that has the closest meaning.

7. **hailed**
   A. acclaimed
   B. halted
   C. recalled
   D. interpreted

8. **artificial**
   A. fake
   B. genuine
   C. natural
   D. authentic

1. **inspire**
   A. encourage
   B. dissuade
   C. strike
   D. repress

2. **harsh**
   A. mellow
   B. smooth
   C. rough
   D. bitter

3. **energetic**
   A. lifeless
   B. active
   C. brittle
   D. clumsy

4. **alignments**
   A. altitudes
   B. ailments
   C. arrangements
   D. attributes

5. **scholarly**
   A. academic
   B. scary
   C. ignorant
   D. suggestive

6. **efficient**
   A. inept
   B. stingy
   C. effective
   D. wicked

9. **extinct**
   A. purebred
   B. exterminated
   C. extraordinary
   D. microscopic

10. **natural**
    A. unusual
    B. scarce
    C. normal
    D. elegant

11. **challenge**
    A. offense
    B. complaint
    C. difficulty
    D. product

12. **revolt**
    A. rebel
    B. crawl
    C. revive
    D. debate

13. **eternal**
    A. brief
    B. final
    C. endless
    D. regular

14. **ideal**
    A. flawed
    B. wrong
    C. perfect
    D. problematic

15. **strive**
    A. forget
    B. hassle
    C. retreat
    D. attempt

16. **romantic**
    A. loving
    B. frigid
    C. bland
    D. usual

17. **tolerate**
    A. allow
    B. check
    C. halt
    D. torment

18. **investigate**
    A. refuse
    B. examine
    C. ignore
    D. interpret

19. **orator**
    A. listener
    B. weaver
    C. framer
    D. speaker

20. **injustice**
    A. equation
    B. wrong doing
    C. praise
    D. favor

21. **roast**
    A. freeze
    B. blast
    C. pepper
    D. broil

22. **agriculturist**
    A. laborer
    B. baker
    C. farmer
    D. messenger

23. **livestock**
    A. bonds
    B. media
    C. cattle
    D. storages

24. **caution**
    A. tell
    B. warn
    C. inform
    D. teach

25. **difficult**
    A. simple
    B. pleasing
    C. fancy
    D. hard

26. **resistant**
    A. immune
    B. fragile
    C. loose
    D. feeble

27. **adapt**
    A. disturb
    B. adjust
    C. object
    D. protest

28. **search**
    A. grant
    B. demand
    C. harvest
    D. pursue

29. **heal**
    A. kill
    B. cure
    C. heighten
    D. vitalize

30. **magical**
    A. hidden
    B. enchanted
    C. obvious
    D. natural

1A 2C 3B 4C 5A 6C 7A 8A 9B 10C 11C 12A 13C 14C 15D 16A
17A 18B 19D 20B 21D 22C 23C 24B 25D 26A 27B 28D 29B 30B

I. What Is a Paraphrase Question?

Paraphrase

The paraphrase question asks you to identify the answer choice that best restates the meaning of the sentence(s) in a given passage. The restatement may summarize the main ideas in a simpler way and omit the less important details. The paraphrase may use *synonyms*, or different words that have similar meanings, to convey the same points. Furthermore, sentences may change when paraphrased: the sentence length and/or the sentence structure – the order of the words and the clauses within the sentence – may vary from the original.

A. PARAPHRASE QUESTION MODEL

Ludwig van Beethoven is one of the most famous musical composers of all time. He was born in Germany in the 1700s and began to develop his talents as a child. His father, who taught piano and violin lessons, was the first to teach Beethoven musical techniques. **Beethoven continued to compose music throughout his career, even after he became deaf later in life.**

8. Which of the following best paraphrases the highlighted sentence?

   (A) Although he lost his hearing, Beethoven continued his long composing career.

   (B) Despite his deaf condition, Beethoven wanted to become famous.

   (C) Beethoven continued to make music that could be appreciated by the deaf.

   (D) Beethoven became deaf, even though he loved making and hearing music.

B. PARAPHRASE QUESTION FORMATS

Which of the following best expresses the highlighted section?

Which of the following best expresses the highlighted section of Paragraph _____?

Which of the following best paraphrases _____?

C. TIPS

1. Look for paraphrases that contain the necessary information.
2. Incorrect answers may:
   - include unnecessary information
   - omit essential information
   - add information that is not in the passage
   - be inaccurate according to the passage
   - have a different meaning than the original passage

II. Hacking Strategy

Paraphrase Question →

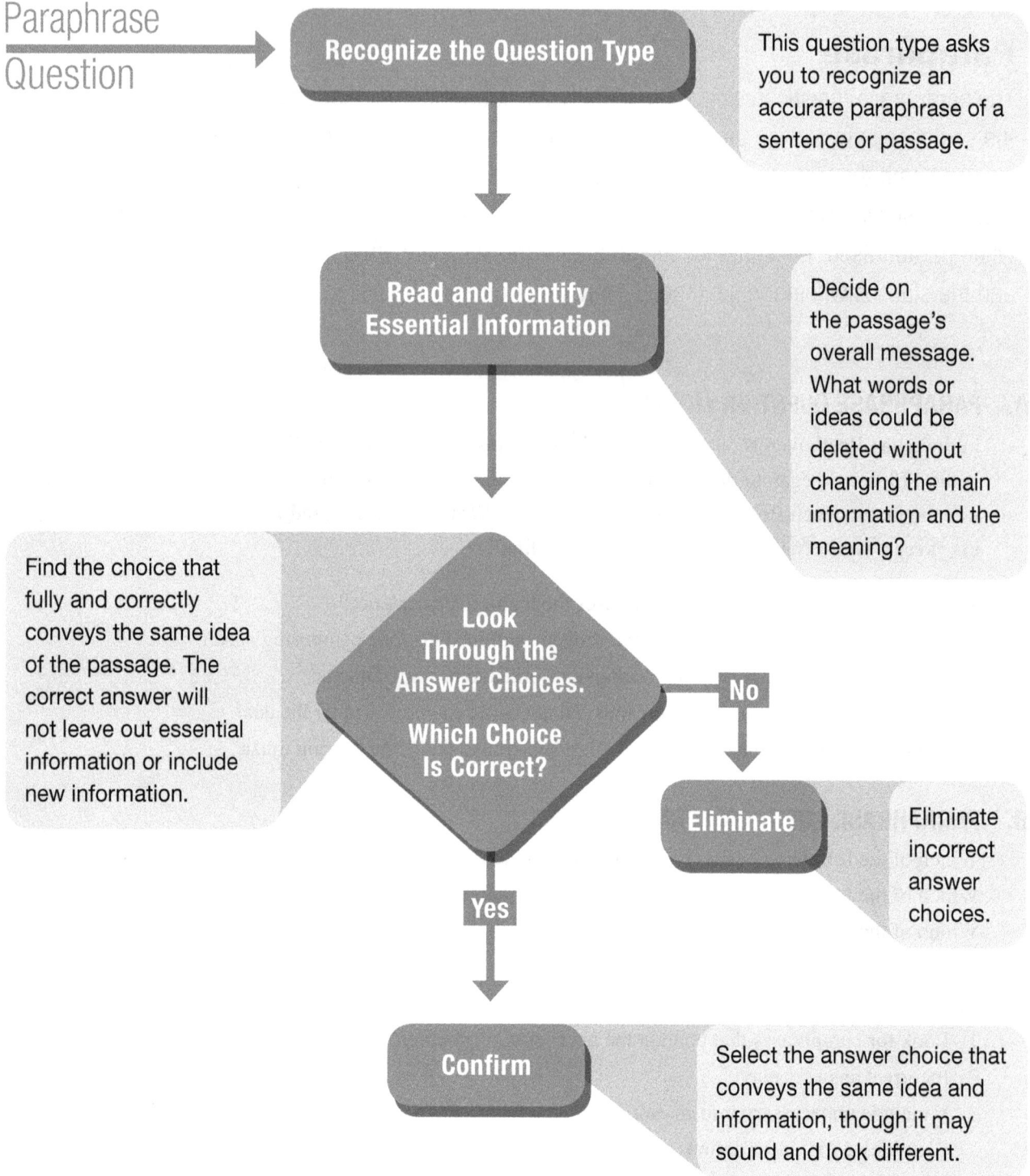

Recognize the Question Type

This question type asks you to recognize an accurate paraphrase of a sentence or passage.

↓

Read and Identify Essential Information

Decide on the passage's overall message. What words or ideas could be deleted without changing the main information and the meaning?

↓

Find the choice that fully and correctly conveys the same idea of the passage. The correct answer will not leave out essential information or include new information.

Look Through the Answer Choices.

Which Choice Is Correct?

No →

Eliminate

Eliminate incorrect answer choices.

Yes ↓

Confirm

Select the answer choice that conveys the same idea and information, though it may sound and look different.

(EXAMPLE

Recognize the Question Type

Ludwig van Beethoven is one of the most famous musical composers of all time. He was born in Germany in the 1700s and began to develop his talents as a child. His father, who taught piano and violin lessons, was the first to teach Beethoven musical techniques. **Beethoven continued to compose music throughout his career, even after he became deaf later in life.**

Which of the following best paraphrases the highlighted sentence?
(A) Although he lost his hearing, Beethoven continued his long composing career.
(B) Despite his deaf condition, Beethoven wanted to become famous.
(C) Beethoven continued to make music that could be appreciated by the deaf.
(D) Beethoven became deaf, even though he loved making and hearing music.

Read and Identify Essential Information

Beethoven continued to compose **music** throughout his career, **even after he became deaf** later in life.

The most important parts of the sentence are highlighted.

Look Through the Answer Choices. Which Choice Is Correct?

Which choice conveys the main ideas concerning *Beethoven continuing his compositions* AND *Beethoven becoming deaf*?

• Select **Choice A** because it conveys the same meaning as the highlighted sentence by using a reversed order of clauses as well as different wording.

Eliminate Incorrect Choices

• Eliminate **Choice B** because it conveys a completely different meaning than the highlighted sentence.
• Eliminate **Choice C** because neither the passage nor the highlighted sentence suggest this idea.
• Eliminate **Choice D** because it leaves out the information that Beethoven kept composing after losing his hearing.

Confirm

Select the correct answer — **Choice A**.

III. Quick Look

Paraphrase Structure Types

Type 1	Type 2	Type 3
Type 1 changes the wording and uses different sentence structure or different ordered clauses.	Type 2 uses synonyms and other expressions to convey the same idea.	Type 3 uses the referent instead of the pronoun to convey the same idea.
Original Sentence	**Original Sentence**	**Original Sentence**
Because of the increase in world 1 pollution levels, **effects of global** 1 2 **warming are more prevalent.** 2 Clause 2 Clause 1 destination (resulting sentence)	People nowadays are **more aware** of what is **going on around the world** than **they were before.** aware know	**Technology** has improved life but **it** also has created problems. Technology it referent pronoun
Paraphrase	**Paraphrase**	**Paraphrase**
The effects of global warming are 2 seen more often because world 2 1 pollution levels have increased. 1 Clause 1 Clause 2 destination (resulting sentence)	People nowadays **know more about** what is **happening in the world** than **they did in the past.** know aware	**Technology** has both improved life and created problems. Technology referent

IV. Warm Up

Read each sentence below. Then choose the answer that provides the more accurate paraphrase.

1. The gemstone jade has been appreciated throughout history. The ancient Chinese philosopher Confucius said that jade represents 11 virtues, a few of which are intelligence, justice, musical ability, and truth.

    (A) Confucius linked the gemstone jade, which has been valued throughout history, to a wide range of desirable traits.

    (B) Confucius, a respected man in ancient China, recommended jade to people in China for its traits.

2. Weight-loss supplements containing ephedra, a plant native to Central Asia, were banned in the United States in 2004 due to adverse reactions and deaths related to its consumption.

    (A) Although taking drugs containing ephedra is dangerous, some Americans still take it to lose weight.

    (B) In 2004, supplements with ephedra became illegal in the United States because of their harmful effects.

3. Benito Mussolini led the National Fascist* Party in Italy, starting in the early 1920s. He was a power-hungry, forceful leader and is often compared to Adolf Hitler. However, Mussolini did not share the same racist views as Hitler.

    (A) Although Mussolini has been compared to Hitler as a dangerously powerful leader, he believed that some races deserved to be treated as equals.

    (B) Although Mussolini and Hitler have been compared because of their powerful, dictatorial qualities, Mussolini had different views on race.

    Fascist: a follower of fascism, which is a system of government led by a ruler who suppresses opposing views by force and maintains complete power

4. William Shakespeare has been widely acclaimed as one of the greatest poets and playwrights of all time. He profoundly influenced literature and poetry. Before *Romeo and Juliet*, romance was generally not associated with tragedy.

    (A) William Shakespeare's famous works have had a significant influence on literary works, including the fusion of previously unassociated genres.

    (B) William Shakespeare's play *Romeo and Juliet* set the standard for all romantic tragedies written thereafter* and made him the most famous romantic writer of all time.

    Thereafter: afterward

5. Sigmund Freud was famous for his various theories on human behavior and experience. He believed that dreams reveal past conflicts that the dreamer experienced. His critics say that the dreams Freud used as examples do not support his theories.

   (A) Freud set forth famous theories on dreamers' experiences that many have criticized because the theories dealt with the vulnerable pasts of the dreamers.

   (B) Some of Freud's theories on dreams have been criticized for not providing adequate evidence to prove that his beliefs were correct.

6. Contrary to what the human eye sees, a polar bear's fur is not white. Its hairs are actually hollow, transparent tubes that only appear to be white because of how they reflect light.

   (A) Although a polar bear's fur is not white, many people still assume that polar bears have white fur.

   (B) Humans think that polar bears have white fur, but it is not so; their fur is actually colorless and reflects light.

7. Recent studies have suggested that the contagious quality of yawning is related to empathy. One reason for this theory is that contagious yawning occurs most often between family members.

   (A) Research has attempted to explain the contagious nature of yawning by showing that it happens most often with people that we know well and can relate to.

   (B) Research shows that people are influenced to yawn most often by their family members, thus suggesting a link between yawning and genes.

8. Dolphins have a sophisticated ability to hear underwater by a process called *echolocation*. Dolphins make sounds in the water that bounce off of other objects. The echoes then travel back to the dolphins and enable them to determine the distance, texture, size, and shape of the object.

   (A) Dolphins use echolocation to help identify and locate objects in the ocean in a sophisticated way.

   (B) Dolphins are one of the few animals that use echolocation to listen to the sounds that objects make.

9. Seahorses undergo a role reversal when it comes to pregnancy. The female seahorse deposits her eggs into the male seahorse's pouch, and he carries the eggs until the baby seahorses hatch.

   (A) Seahorses are unique in that they are the only species of fish in which the male carries the eggs and becomes pregnant instead of the female.

   (B) During the reproductive process, male seahorses bear and give birth to offspring instead of female seahorses.

10. Red ginseng has been said to have numerous health benefits, such as improving immune system function and lowering blood sugar and cholesterol levels. In addition, studies performed on mice have shown that consumption of red ginseng has inhibited the growth of cancerous tumors.

    (A) Research shows that red ginseng has stopped cancer growth completely in mice and in humans, and it also helps the latter to lose weight.

    (B) It is believed that red ginseng encourages good health in a variety of ways and also can have anti-cancer effects in mice.

V. Quick Practice

Practice #1

Read the passage. Then answer the questions that follow.

Alexander Hamilton, one of the founding fathers of the United States, helped shape the current U.S. economy. Although widely opposed at the time, Hamilton established the foundation for the national bank, called the U.S. Federal Reserve Bank, by forming the First Bank of the United States in 1791. **Hamilton believed that a national bank was necessary to improve and maintain national economic stability.**

1) Which of the following best paraphrases the first highlighted sentence in the passage?
   (A) Hamilton formed the U.S. economy during a difficult time.
   (B) Hamilton met with the founding fathers to shape the U.S. economy.
   (C) Hamilton helped create the foundation for the U.S. economy.
   (D) Hamilton shaped the U.S. economic system to found the nation.

2) Which of the following best expresses the essential information in the second highlighted sentence in the passage?
   (A) Hamilton believed that the U.S. should control and maintain its economy.
   (B) Hamilton believed that the economy would naturally fix itself.
   (C) Hamilton wanted to secure the already stabilized economy.
   (D) Hamilton wanted to create an institution to stabilize the U.S. economy.

Practice #2

Read the passage. Then answer the questions that follow.

Instinct is a term used to categorize natural behavior that is not learned from experience. **Instinctive behaviors are determined by the genetic makeup* of the organism. Learned behaviors, on the other hand, gradually develop as a result of experiences. Although behaviors can be categorized as either instinctive or learned, behaviors are mostly a combination of the two.**

*Genetic makeup: the genes that shape an organism's appearance and behavior

3) Which of the following best expresses the essential information in the first highlighted part of the passage?
   (A) Instinctive behaviors are determined by both the genetics and the experiences of a living thing.
   (B) Organisms develop behaviors instinctively due to genetics, but it is more common for them to form a behavior from their experiences.
   (C) Organisms form behaviors because of genetics they have learned gradually from experiences.
   (D) A learned behavior is slowly developed from experiences; in contrast, an instinctive behavior is inherited through genes.

4) Which of the followinge best expresses the second highlighted part of the passage?
   (A) Although scientists have different ways of categorizing behaviors, few use that system.
   (B) All types of behavior can be organized as either instinctive or learned.
   (C) Many behaviors are not based only on instinct or learning.
   (D) It is easier to discuss issues related to instinct and learning by exploring one issue at a time.

Practice #3

Read the passage. Then answer the questions that follow.

Solar heating requires an efficient absorber to collect sunlight and convert it to heat. **The absorber may be made of heat-absorbing ceramic, metal, plastic, or other materials and is usually painted black. A good absorber collects 95 percent or more of the solar radiation at its surface and converts it into heat energy. At the same time, the absorber retains 80 percent more heat than an ordinary surface would.**

5) Which of the following best paraphrases the first highlighted sentence in the passage?
   (A) Different black-painted substances, such as metal or ceramic, can be used as solar absorbers.
   (B) Absorbers should be painted black and have textured surfaces no matter what material they are made of.
   (C) Solar absorbers may look like copper, steel, or ceramic plates, but they are actually coated in black paint.
   (D) Textured absorbers such as ceramic are more complicated than black-painted absorbers.

6) Which of the following best expresses the essential information in the second highlighted part in the passage?

(A) Only about 5 percent of the sun's energy is used by an absorber, but a good one can convert that into 80 percent more energy than an ordinary power plant.

(B) An efficient solar absorber gathers almost 100 percent of the sun's energy and wastes only a small amount of that energy.

(C) Although ordinary surfaces can be used as absorbers, they produce 20 percent less heat and waste 95 percent of the radiation they absorb.

(D) 95 percent of solar radiation can be gathered by a good absorber, but only 20 percent can be gathered by an ordinary surface.

Practice #4

Read the passage. Then answer the questions that follow.

A *spoils system* is the practice of granting government positions as a reward for political party loyalty. The system is used in many countries. **Many people consider the practice reasonable when a party appoints capable individuals to high offices where policy is to be made. However, many feel that the practice is unjustifiable when leaders dismiss able employees from government jobs to make room for others who have only demonstrated strong support for the party.**

7) Which of the following best paraphrases the first highlighted sentence in the passage?

(A) According to many, the reason for the spoils system is to place qualified people in positions to make important policies.

(B) Some feel that the spoils system is acceptable if qualified individuals are chosen to make policy.

(C) If suitable policy makers held high positions, many people would regard the spoils system as moral.

(D) When policy is made in high offices, many feel that the system is reasonable.

8) Which of the following best expresses the essential information in the second highlighted sentence of the passage?

(A) People who give their support to political parties and are not concerned with public policy like the spoils system the most.

(B) The spoils system is unforgivably wrong when it is only used to make policies that support a particular political party.

(C) Many people do not like the spoils system if it is used to reward a candidate's supporters while firing qualified workers from government jobs.

(D) According to many people, a person should not work for the government if there is no strong support from the person's political party.

Practice #5

Read the passage. Then answer the questions that follow.

Plautus was an important Roman playwright of comedy. His plays borrow much of their material from Greek New Comedy, which centered on fictional situations and "everyday" citizens such as young men in love with slave girls, cunning* servants, and deceived masters. **Plautus added earthy Italian comic elements and his own boisterous* wit. He was more concerned with making people laugh than subtle techniques of plot construction and characterization.**

Cunning: tricky or deceptive

Boisterous: loud, noisy, and lacking in restraint or discipline

9) Which of the following best paraphrases the first highlighted section in the passage?
   (A) Roman and Greek New Comedy have the same Italian comic element.
   (B) Italian comic elements influenced Greek New Comedy with its boisterous wit.
   (C) Plautus was greatly influenced by Italian comic elements that emphasized average citizens.
   (D) Plautus added his own twist to Greek New Comedy by including new elements and unrestrained humor.

10) Which of the following best expresses the essential information in the second highlighted section?
   (A) Giving his audience a good time was more important to Plautus than the intricate aspects of playwriting.
   (B) Plautus' humor was simple, not complex, and that is why audiences laughed so much when seeing his plays.
   (C) Because Plautus did not care about his plot or characters, this often produced very funny results on stage.
   (D) To create a story with good characters and humor, Plautus did not put any pressure on himself.

Practice #6

Read the passage. Then answer the questions that follow.

Vapor is the gaseous state of heated solids or liquids. **In a technical sense, vapor includes both oxygen and steam. However, it is also possible to make a distinction between the two. Oxygen, which can be categorized as gas, remains gaseous when compressed at ordinary temperatures. On the other hand, steam, which can be categorized as vapor, resumes* its liquid or solid state at ordinary temperatures.**

Resume: to begin again after interruption

11) Which of the following best expresses the first highlighted part in the passage?
   (A) Oxygen and steam are types of vapor that are indistinguishable from each other.
   (B) The distinction between oxygen and gas is technical, but they are both considered steam.
   (C) Although oxygen and steam are technically both vapors, they can also be differentiated.
   (D) Technically speaking, steam is a gas, and oxygen is a vapor.

12) Which of the following best expresses the second highlighted part in the passage?

(A) While steam changes back into its natural state when exposed to normal temperatures, gases do not.

(B) Both oxygen and steam can become gases and vapors when they are exposed to naturally temperate environment.

(C) While vapors become steam under the right pressure and temperature, all gases change into oxygen in such situations.

(D) Steam vapors change from liquid to solid when put under a high single-temperature container, but oxygen gases do not do this.

Practice #7

Read the passage. Then answer the questions that follow.

Infants begin to be delighted by "peek-a-boo" games at around five months of age. **In peek-a-boo games, a person "hides" behind his or her hands or some other type of screen, and then gently pops into the baby's view again.** Developmental psychologist Jean Piaget theorized that **babies enjoy this game because they do not yet realize that objects or people continue to exist even when the babies cannot see them**. The game helps babies learn that objects or people are permanent.

13) Which of the following best paraphrases the information in the first highlighted sentence in the passage?

(A) Many people enjoy some form of a game that entertains babies by hiding and reappearing.

(B) Playing peek-a-boo means surprising a baby by moving out of and coming into the baby's sight.

(C) Babies enjoy peek-a-boo, but adults must be sure to "pop" out gently.

(D) Staying hidden behind hands, screens, blankets, or furniture is essential when playing peek-a-boo with a baby.

14) Which of the following best expresses the information in the second highlighted part of the passage?

(A) Before they know who people are, babies love to look at them in the game of peek-a-boo.

(B) Babies do not have completely developed sight yet, and therefore they are amused by seeing people.

(C) Babies are pleasantly surprised by peek-a-boo before they learn of object permanence.

(D) Babies need to know that parents will always come back.

Practice #8

Read the passage. Then answer the questions that follow.

The Great Depression of the 1930s was a period of intense economic hardship that affected countries worldwide. It originated in the United States when the stock market prices suddenly plunged. **This event was called the Stock Market Crash of 1929. Following the crisis, 25 percent of Americans became unemployed. More than 40 percent of America's banks were forced to shut down. Banks had no money to operate, as their customers began withdrawing all of the money that they had previously deposited into their bank accounts.**

15) Which of the following best expresses the first highlighted part in the passage?
   (A) One fourth of Americans were out of work and almost half of the country's banks ceased to exist after the massive crash.
   (B) As a result of the devastating crash, more than 40 percent of the banks in America suffered.
   (C) In 1929, the American economy was hurt because some banks were forced to close and Americans lost their jobs.
   (D) America experienced all of the symptoms of a crisis with its high unemployment rate and massive reduction of banks.

16) Which of following best expresses the second highlighted section in the passage?
   (A) Many banks could no longer be in business because their former customers, who once deposited money, began stealing all of banks' reserves.
   (B) At the same time that customers began to withdraw money from their accounts, the government banks were forced to close down.
   (C) Even though banks had made deposits into their own accounts, customers began taking out this money, so the banks had to close down.
   (D) Because their customers were depleting their own bank accounts, banks no longer had enough money to function.

Practice #9

Read the passage. Then answer the questions that follow.

Karl Jaspers was a German existentialist. Originally a psychiatrist during World War I, he had turned to philosophy by the time the Nazis banned his works in World War II. **Perhaps because of these experiences, Jaspers highly valued independent thinking.** He even titled one of his books *Philosophy Is for Everyman*. **He wanted all people to engage in philosophy because he believed that everyone has access to it at any time.**

17) Which of the following best paraphrases the first highlighted sentence in the passage?
   (A) Jaspers always thought for himself, and therefore had many experiences.
   (B) Jaspers praised the value of individuals thinking about their experiences.
   (C) Jaspers engaged in war experiences, and knew how important it was for individuals to take part in history.
   (D) Jaspers' past experiences may be the reason he wanted people to think for themselves.

18) Which of the following best paraphrases the information in the second highlighted sentence of the passage?
   (A) Jaspers felt that philosophical thinking was available to all people.
   (B) Jaspers likened rationality to keeping secrets, and wanted people to know the answers.
   (C) All people at all times should study philosophy in school, according to Jaspers.
   (D) The reason for people to live, in Jaspers' writing, is to uncover the open secrets of life.

Practice #10

Read the passage. Then answer the questions that follow.

According to popular myth, Benjamin Franklin "invented" electricity. In 1752, Franklin supposedly flew a kite with an iron key attached to its silk string during a storm. **Franklin predicted that if lightning were electrical and if electricity could be transferred, then the wet kite string and metal key would conduct negative charges from a storm cloud. This dangerous experiment may or may not have taken place, but it is certain that Franklin did invent the lightning rod.** The rod conducted lightning's electricity harmlessly away from rooftops.

19) Which of the following best expresses the information in the first highlighted sentence?
   (A) Franklin planned to manipulate electrical currents from lightning by flying a kite high enough.
   (B) Franklin hypothesized that he could find a use for the electricity from lightning, such as lights.
   (C) Franklin thought that a storm's negative electrical charges could probably flow through wet material and metal.
   (D) Franklin transferred electricity through paper, wood, silk, and iron metal.

20) Which of the following best expresses the information in the second highlighted sentence?
   (A) Franklin was able to put his knowledge to good use and was able predict dangerous settings.
   (B) Franklin developed the lightning rod even though it is not clear if the kite experiment actually took place.
   (C) Franklin used lightning rods to prove that lightning was electrical and that it was not as dangerous as people thought.
   (D) Some people argue that the lightning rod would not exist if Franklin had not done the experiment.

Select the vocabulary word or phrase that has the closest meaning.

7. empathy
A. discord
B. understanding
C. disdain
D. contempt

8. texture
A. balance
B. original
C. element
D. structure

1. compose
A. destroy
B. scatter
C. excite
D. construct

9. reversal
A. validity
B. switch
C. recovery
D. enactment

2. banned
A. permitted
B. outlawed
C. approved
D. sanctioned

10. immune
A. resistant
B. vulnerable
C. exposed
D. sensitive

3. adverse
A. negative
B. enormous
C. helpful
D. notable

11. stabilized
A. developed
B. successful
C. flexible
D. balanced

4. vulnerable
A. closed
B. secured
C. exposed
D. guarded

12. genetic
A. ancestral
B. external
C. original
D. internal

5. contrary
A. similar
B. opposite
C. proper
D. native

13. gradually
A. unevenly
B. constantly
C. suddenly
D. abruptly

6. contagious
A. healthy
B. sanitary
C. annoyed
D. infectious

14. convert
A. remain
B. sustain
C. change
D. continue

15. ceramic
A. clay
B. steel
C. fiber
D. wood

16. reasonable
A. expensive
B. incredible
C. doubtful
D. tolerable

17. demonstrate
A. assure
B. cause
C. clear
D. show

18. deceive
A. disprove
B. receive
C. fool
D. impose

19. earthy
A. native
B. complex
C. refined
D. crude

20. boisterous
A. unrestrained
B. creative
C. attractive
D. thoughtful

21. subtle
A. decent
B. delicate
C. amazing
D. perfect

22. intricate
A. elaborate
B. obvious
C. distinct
D. evident

23. technical
A. scientific
B. demanding
C. approximate
D. unrealistic

24. temperate
A. violent
B. stormy
C. furious
D. moderate

25. delighted
A. pleasured
B. tricked
C. educated
D. trained

26. permanence
A. fluctuation
B. stability
C. change
D. irregularity

27. withdraw
A. remain
B. pursue
C. defend
D. remove

28. praise
A. criticize
B. berate
C. scorn
D. acclaim

29. uncover
A. conceal
B. reveal
C. suppress
D. withhold

30. certain
A. evident
B. doubtful
C. surprising
D. wonderful

1D 2B 3A 4C 5B 6D 7B 8D 9B 10A 11D 12A 13B 14C 15A 16D
17D 18C 19D 20A 21B 22A 23A 24D 25A 26B 27D 28D 29B 30A

Exercises

Exercise #1 Read the passage. Then answer the questions that follow.

On August 2, 1923, Warren G. Harding, the 29th president of the United States, died unexpectedly while in office. Consequently, his vice president, Calvin Coolidge, was sworn into office as the new president in the **early morning of August 3, 1923**. Coolidge was called "Silent Cal" because he was not very talkative. However, his stance on civil rights and the rapid economic growth during his administration **brought back public confidence** in the White House after **Harding's scandal-driven administration**. Coolidge was a popular president who won a second term and **remained in office until 1929**.

1) Why does the author MOST LIKELY mention "**early morning of August 3, 1923**" in the passage?
   (A) To show the process of the U.S. presidential transfer of power
   (B) To emphasize how urgent it was to transfer presidential power immediately
   (C) To indicate that President Harding urgently wanted to transfer power
   (D) To describe how U.S. vice presidents usually became president during this period

2) Why does the author mention that Coolidge "**brought back public confidence**" in the passage?
   (A) To state that Coolidge earned the trust of the Americans
   (B) To de-emphasize the president's role in confidence in the White House
   (C) To list Coolidge's accomplishments during his presidency
   (D) To argue that Coolidge had no confidence until the public gave it to him

3) Why does the author mention "**Harding's scandal-driven administration**" in the passage?
   (A) To show that the public liked Harding more
   (B) To explain the extent of Harding's corruption and dishonesty
   (C) To contrast Harding's and Coolidge's administrations
   (D) To describe the challenges that Harding's administrative staff faced

4) Why does the author mention that Coolidge "**remained in office until 1929**" in the passage?
   (A) To argue that Coolidge honored his commitments
   (B) To define the length of a presidential term in the U.S.
   (C) To provide evidence that Coolidge was popular
   (D) To compare the time period of his presidency with others

Exercise #2 Read the passage. Then answer the questions that follow.

Classical music that was called *Impressionist* developed in the late 19th and early 20th centuries in France. **Like Impressionist art, this music sought to create a mood or feeling. Sometimes it attempted to evoke a place or a natural phenomenon.** For example, one of the pieces by Impressionist composer Maurice Ravel is *Jeux d'eau*, or "Water Games," which he said was inspired by "the noise of water." **Composer Claude Debussy's orchestral piece *Nocturnes*, or "Nights," tried to convey nighttime clouds, brightly lit festivals, and the mythical Sirens luring people into the sea.**

5) Which of the following best expresses the information in the first highlighted sentence of the passage?

   (A) When musical Impressionists write, they aim to make people become very emotional, just as Impressionist artists do.

   (B) Impressionism in art and music is similar in that the intent is to intrigue and mystify.

   (C) Audiences may not understand Impressionist music or art, as there may not be a narrative.

   (D) Impressionists try to evoke a sensation, an atmosphere, a setting, or an image for people.

6) Which of the following best expresses the information in the second highlighted sentence of the passage?

   (A) Claude Debussy's musical concept of "night" exemplifies Impressionist musical composition goals.

   (B) Claude Debussy was famous for attempting to create sounds for festivals and nightlife.

   (C) Claude Debussy tried very hard to capture the sounds of the sea and sky at night in *Nocturnes*.

   (D) Expressions of the natural, social, and mystical aspects of night are all parts of Debussy's *Nocturnes*.

Exercise #3 Read the passage. Then answer the questions that follow.

Euhemerus, a Greek scholar of the 4th century BCE, developed the earliest known theory about the origins of myths. He suggested that myths are stories with some basis in historical truth. For example, Euhemerus said that stories about **Zeus**, the Greek's most powerful father-god, could have grown out of exaggerations of an actual early king of Crete, for whom people felt great awe. The problem with this approach is that **modern scholars** usually have no evidence to determine if there is such a factual basis for any particular myth.

Max Müller, a 19th-century scholar who focused on Indian culture, proposed that myths created gods by accident. He noticed that in the ***Vedas***, or Hindu scriptures, the gods seemed like forces of nature. He theorized that people first used the names and stories of gods as a means of talking about nature. Over time, people forgot that the myths were simply metaphors and began to think of them as real. For example, Müller said that the name *Zeus* comes from an ancient word meaning **"shining" or "radiance"**; thus, Zeus was metaphor for the all-powerful Sun.

7) Why does the author mention "**Zeus**" in Paragraph 1?
 (A) To give details about what Greece's gods were like
 (B) To describe Euhemerus' religion when he started theorizing
 (C) To criticize the way people exaggerate legends of human beings
 (D) To compare a god to a real ancient ruler

8) Why does the author mention "**modern scholars**" in Paragraph 1?
 (A) To persuade readers to accept Euhemerus' theory of myths as modern
 (B) To introduce a newer theory about myths into the passage
 (C) To point out a weakness in using Euhemerus' theory to study myths
 (D) To show that Euhemerus' theory has been persistent

9) Why does the author mention the "***Vedas***" in Paragraph 2?
 (A) To contrast Müller's theory of myths with that of Euhemerus
 (B) To imply that Müller's theory made sense in only one culture
 (C) To describe how Müller spent his career reading books about Hindu deities
 (D) To identify a source from which Müller developed a theory of myths

10) Why does the author put quotation marks around "**shining**" and "**radiance**" in Paragraph 2?
 (A) To explain that Müller was interested in Greek and Hindu gods' appearances
 (B) To show how a natural force may have been personified as a god
 (C) To illustrate the Greek image of beautiful gods and goddesses
 (D) To prove that Müller's theory focuses on translating languages

Exercise #4 Read the passage. Then answer the questions that follow.

Aristotle, the Greek writer who lived in the 300s BCE, is usually remembered as a great philosopher. However, he was also a natural historian and wrote extensively about *zoology*, or the study of animals. **As a natural historian, he observed many animals in their habitats. He also looked in fishermen's nets and dissected some animals to learn more.** He described the parts of many animals, such as species of fish and octopuses. Aristotle realized the difference between sea mammals and fish, and he accurately classified sharks and rays in one group. He also studied the development of chickens inside their eggs by breaking open and studying fertilized eggs at intervals.

  From his observations, Aristotle developed and introduced the idea of arranging animals on a scale from simple to complex based on their anatomy and behavior. His classification of animals represented a huge leap forward for his time and was used for about 2,000 years.

11) Which of the following best expresses the information in the highlighted section of Paragraph 1?
 (A) Aristotle made a habit of quietly thinking about natural areas and fishing ports.
 (B) Aristotle studied by watching creatures' ordinary lives and cutting some open.
 (C) Aristotle was the first person to value examining the habitats of animals.
 (D) Aristotle studied zoology by himself, as there was no one to teach him about it.

12) Which of the following best expresses the information in the highlighted part of Paragraph 2?
 (A) Aristotle organized life forms along a scale based on how smart they were and how capable they were.
 (B) Aristotle came to conclusions by thinking about complicated animals and how they act.
 (C) Aristotle arranged life forms from least to most complex by behavior and structure.
 (D) Aristotle's arrangement of animals is based on how their bodies developed over time.

Exercise #5 Read the passage. Then answer the questions that follow.

The West African country of Liberia suffered through **14 years of brutal civil war** that ended in 2003. The decrease in violence was credited to a women's peace movement led by Leymah Gbowee. She had organized volunteers to reach out to women at churches, mosques, and marketplaces, urging them to come to interfaith prayer meetings and **nonviolent demonstrations**. At great personal risk, thousands of women gathered daily and eventually pressured the warring sides to negotiate for peace.

When the **negotiators could not come to an agreement**, hundreds of women sat down in the lobby of the hotel where the negotiations were taking place. The women threatened that if the leaders tried to leave without making a peace treaty, the women would take off their own clothes. In Liberian culture, seeing an older or married woman naked is a curse. Finally, the negotiators came to an agreement, and the fighting ended. Gbowee was awarded the **Nobel Peace Prize** in 2011 for what she accomplished.

13) The author PROBABLY mentions "**14 years of brutal civil war**" in Paragraph 1 to
(A) emphasize how terrible war always is, especially if it lasts as long as 14 years
(B) give a reason why Liberian women risked their safety for peace
(C) criticize militant groups of the Liberian civil war as being unnecessarily brutal
(D) describe what happened in Liberia in the 1990s

14) Why does the author mention "**nonviolent demonstrations**" in Paragraph 1?
(A) To illustrate an important characteristic of the Liberian peace protests
(B) To demonstrate how much violence the Liberian civil wars caused
(C) To describe situations in which activists demonstrated how to be peaceful
(D) To persuade the reader that the Liberian women were serious

15) Why does the author mention "**negotiators could not come to an agreement**" in Paragraph 2?
(A) To indicate where the peace talks were taking place
(B) To give an example of why the women were startled
(C) To provide a possible reason that the civil wars took place
(D) To describe the warring parties' unwillingness to compromise

16) The author most likely mentions the "**Nobel Peace Prize**" in Paragraph 2 in order to
(A) tell how much influence the peace movement gained starting in 2011
(B) show that the global community admired the Liberian peace movement
(C) discuss the aims of the Liberian women's organizations
(D) demonstrate how long it took for the world to notice her effort

Exercise #6 Read the passage. Then answer the questions that follow.

Robinson Crusoe, a novel by Daniel Defoe, was first published in England in 1719. The tale's narrator, named Robinson Crusoe, recounts the 28 years that he spent on an island after being shipwrecked. **Soon after it was released, Robinson Crusoe caught the public's imagination and has enjoyed centuries of popularity ever since. However, the source of Defoe's ideas is still a mystery.**

Some scholars assert that the novel was based on the published experiences of Alexander Selkirk, a Scottish sailor who was actually stranded on a deserted island for four years. **Others pointed to translations of *Hayy ibn Yaqdhan*, the tale by Ibn Tufail about a boy raised by a gazelle on a deserted island.** However, it is likely that *Robinson Crusoe* was strongly influenced by the story of Henry Pitman, a surgeon who was sent to a Caribbean island as a prisoner, only to escape and get shipwrecked on another island before making his way back to London.

17) Which of the following best expresses the information in the highlighted section of Paragraph 1?
   (A) The public argues about whether Defoe's novel deserves its popularity, as it may have been copied from several sources.
   (B) The public imagined the story and enjoyed the mystery of where so many ideas could have come from.
   (C) Although Defoe's personal life is still a mystery, his novel has slowly gained popularity over many generations.
   (D) The sources that inspired the novel remain unknown, but many readers have enjoyed it for hundreds of years.

18) Which of the following best expresses the essential information in the second highlighted sentence?
   (A) Ibn Tufail wrote a story about a boy on a deserted island that may have been the inspiration for *Robinson Crusoe*.
   (B) In *Hayy ibn Yaqdhan*, Ibn Tufail wrote about his time of being stranded on a deserted island with a boy and a gazelle.
   (C) *Hayy ibn Yaqdhan*, which is a story about a boy raised by a gazelle on a deserted island, was the only inspiration for *Robinson Crusoe*.
   (D) Ibn Tufail inspired Daniel Defoe to write about a boy who was raised by a gazelle on a deserted island.

Exercise #7 Read the passage. Then answer the questions that follow.

Many gardeners in North America treasure the nasturtium, an annual flower that must be reseeded each year. Originally from the **Andes Mountains**, the beautiful and edible plant consists of long vine-like stems and has bright red, orange, or yellow flowers. Each flower has five petals, eight stamens, and a tube that **protrudes from the back** and holds nectar. The flat, rounded leaves seem as though they could be tiny green umbrellas.

All parts of the plant can be eaten and can be described as slightly peppery in taste. The flowers and leaves can be tossed into salads or pressed into a frosted cake for decoration. Insects, especially **butterfly and moth larvae**, like to eat the plant. Some gardeners actually plant the nasturtium in vegetable gardens just because it attracts helpful insects. However, in some areas, the nasturtium is considered a problem, as it has invaded natural habitats and **crowded out** native species.

19) Why does the author mention the "**Andes Mountains**" in Paragraph 1?
 (A) To add information that helps describe the appearance of nasturtiums
 (B) To suggest the conditions to which the plant is naturally most adapted
 (C) To provide an example of a place where nursery plants come from
 (D) To describe the beginning of the process of getting the plant to grow in North America

20) Why does the author mention "**protrudes from the back**" in Paragraph 1?
 (A) To point out one of the flower's identifying features
 (B) To explain how the flower holds nectar
 (C) To illustrate how the flower's name was determined
 (D) To contrast the nasturtium flower with other flowers

21) Why does the author mention "**butterfly and moth larvae**" in Paragraph 2?
 (A) To illustrate something about the roots and stems of the nasturtium
 (B) To caution readers to look for caterpillars on the leaves before eating
 (C) To describe a characteristic of nasturtiums that gardeners may or may not like
 (D) To advise those who want to grow nasturtiums not to grow them

22) Why does the author mention "**crowded out**" in Paragraph 2?
 (A) To help the reader visualize the nasturtium in its natural habitat
 (B) To inform readers what happens when people plant too many nasturtiums
 (C) To explain how the nasturtium can become invasive in a natural area
 (D) To provide details about the interactions of crowds with the plant

Exercise #8 Read the passage. Then answer the questions that follow.

The calculator is a device that is used for both fundamental math problems and more complicated operations. Throughout history, people have devised calculating devices. **The abacus, invented around 2000 BCE, was one of the first adding machines. Other methods developed to facilitate calculations since that early time have included logarithm tables in 1614, the slide rule in 1622, the mechanical calculator in 1642, and workable adding machines in the 19th century. Desktop electronic calculators became available in the 1960s, and by the 1970s, people could buy pocket-sized calculators.**

In the 1990s, a new range of calculating tools reached the market. **In order to meet the expanding needs of the consumer, engineers created the graphing calculator, which plots graphs and performs advanced calculations for electronics and engineering work.** With the explosion of the Internet, webmasters began creating online calculating tools for every possible use.

23) Which of the following best expresses the information highlighted in Paragraph 1?
(A) Humans have used tools to calculate numbers for at least four millennia.
(B) By the 1960s, consumers could purchase pocket calculators.
(C) People have developed many useful counting devices, but the abacus has been superior to all other methods.
(D) People used only the abacus until electronic calculators appeared.

24) Which of the following best expresses the highlighted sentence in Paragraph 2?
(A) The name of a calculator is decided by its function.
(B) The need for calculating aids skyrocketed as more advanced calculators such as graphing calculators were introduced.
(C) More advanced calculators were developed to respond to the needs of the public.
(D) As a result of demands by engineers, graphing calculators were developed to perform complex functions.

I. What Is a Summary Question?

Summary

The summary question asks you to select the sentences that best explain the main idea of a given passage. A summary states the most important and major ideas in a shorter form.

A. SUMMARY QUESTION MODEL

Acupuncture is based on the Taoist principle that there is a natural flow of *qi* ("chee"), or life force, through each living thing. *Qi* is made up of the opposing forces of *yin* and *yang*. Acupuncturists believe that *qi* flows inside the body along branching meridians. When these channels become blocked, the result is illness and pain. Therefore, through careful observation, listening, and pulse-taking, acupuncturists diagnose the blockages and insert slim needles into the skin at those points. They believe that this allows *qi* to flow freely again and *yin* and *yang* to balance.

9. **Directions**: An introductory sentence for a brief summary of the passage is provided below.
Complete the summary by selecting the THREE answer choices that express the most important ideas in the passage. Some sentences do not belong in the summary because they express ideas that are not presented in the passage or are minor ideas in the passage. **This question is worth 2 points.**

Acupuncture aims to restore health by unblocking the body's energy system.
-
-
-

Answer Choices
1. Principles of acupuncture are based on Taoist text that also identifies meridians in the body.
2. *Qi*, made up of *yin* and *yang*, can become stuck at points in the body, causing sickness and pain.
3. Needles can release the blocked *qi*, resulting in relief of symptoms.
4. Needles are used to locate spots where the *qi* cannot travel freely.
5. Practitioners must run extensive tests before treatment.
6. Recovery takes place with an exact balance of two opposite energies.

B. TIPS

1. Make sure that you choose an answer that includes the most important ideas in the passage.
2. You can choose a paraphrase that omits minor ideas as long as the passage's meaning remains the same.
3. Incorrect answers are inaccurate or irrelevant, or they contain minor ideas and details.
4. Because these questions ask you to select multiple correct answers, they are worth up to two points rather than one point.
5. You must select two correct answers to receive 1 point and three correct answers for 2 points.

II. Hacking Strategy

Summary
Question

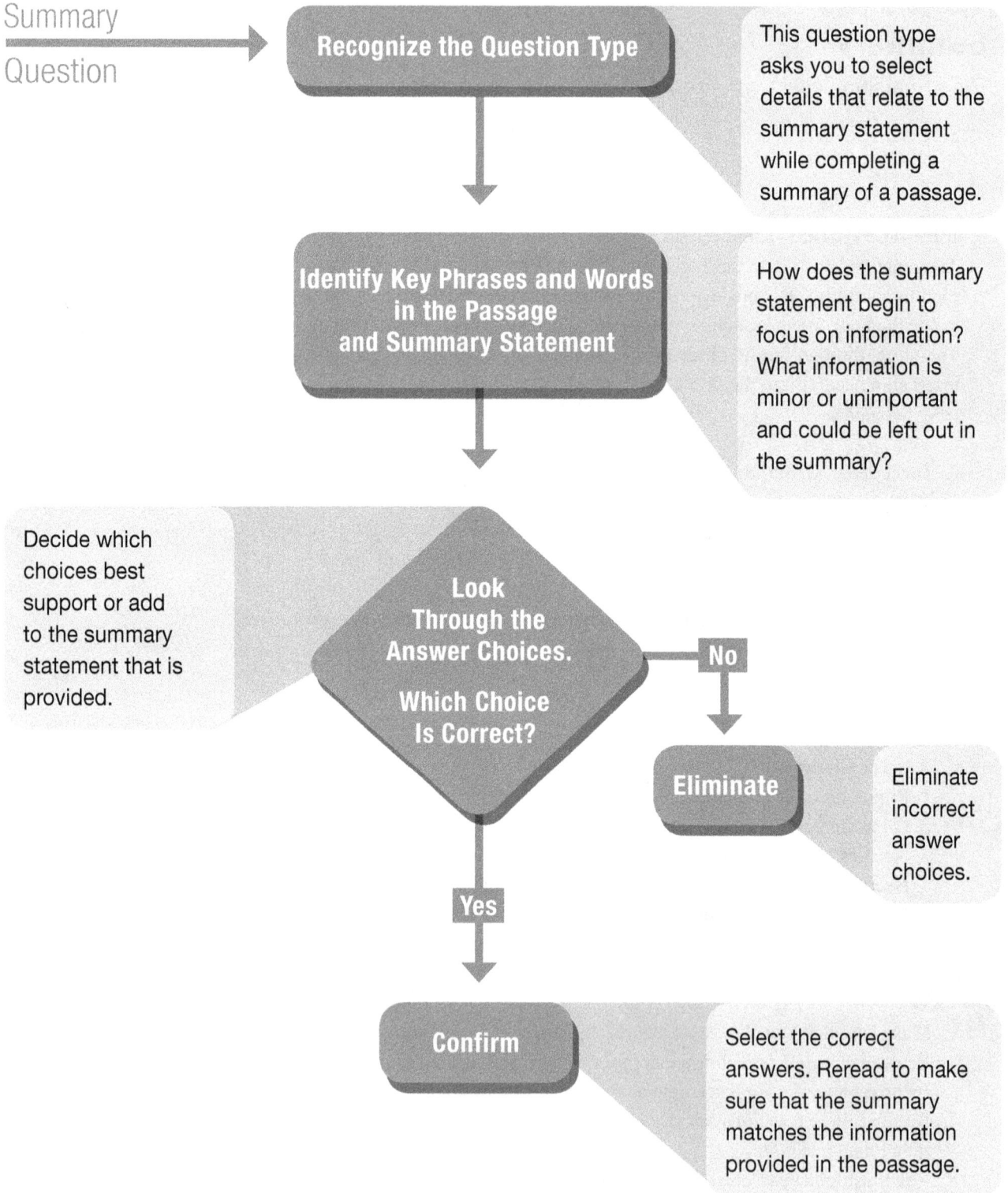

Recognize the Question Type

This question type asks you to select details that relate to the summary statement while completing a summary of a passage.

Identify Key Phrases and Words in the Passage and Summary Statement

How does the summary statement begin to focus on information? What information is minor or unimportant and could be left out in the summary?

Decide which choices best support or add to the summary statement that is provided.

Look Through the Answer Choices.

Which Choice Is Correct?

No

Eliminate

Eliminate incorrect answer choices.

Yes

Confirm

Select the correct answers. Reread to make sure that the summary matches the information provided in the passage.

Recognize the Question Type

Acupuncture is based on the Taoist principle that there is a natural flow of *qi* ("chee"), or life force, through each living thing. *Qi* is made up of the opposing forces of *yin* and *yang*. Acupuncturists believe that *qi* flows inside the body along branching meridians. When these channels become blocked, the result is illness and pain. Therefore, through careful observation, listening, and pulse-taking, acupuncturists diagnose the blockages and insert slim needles into the skin at those points. They believe that this allows *qi* to flow freely again and *yin* and *yang* to balance.

Acupuncture aims to restore health by unblocking the body's energy system.

-
-
-

Answer Choices

1. Principles of acupuncture are based on Taoist text that also identifies meridians in the body.
2. *Qi*, made up of *yin* and *yang*, can become stuck at points in the body, causing sickness and pain.
3. Needles can release the blocked *qi*, resulting in relief of symptoms.
4. Needles are used to locate spots where the *qi* cannot travel freely.
5. Practitioners must run extensive tests before treatment.
6. Recovery takes place with an exact balance of two opposite energies.

Identify Key Phrases and Words in the Passage and Summary Statement

Acupuncture aims to restore health by unblocking the body's energy system.
Acupuncture is based on the Taoist principle that there is a natural flow of *qi* ("chee"), or life force, through each living thing. *Qi* is made up of the opposing forces of *yin* and *yang*. Acupuncturists believe that *qi* flows inside the body along branching *meridians*. When these channels become blocked, the result is illness and pain. Therefore, through careful observation, listening, and pulse-taking, acupuncturists diagnose the blockages and insert slim needles into the skin at those points. They believe that this allows *qi* to flow freely again and *yin* and *yang* to balance.

Look Through the Answer Choices. Which Choice Is Correct?

Find choices that are discussed in the passage AND logically connect to the introductory sentence:
Acupuncture aims to restore health by unblocking the body's energy system.
- Select **Choice 2** because the passage states that "the result is illness" when channels become blocked, which a restatement of this choice
- Select **Choice 3** because the passage states that "slim needles" unblock channels, which is synonymous with this choice.
- Select **Choice 5** because the passage describes "careful observation" and a number of other diagnostic methods, or *extensive tests*.

Eliminate Incorrect Choices

- Eliminate **Choices 1**, **4**, and **6** because they are speculation and are not mentioned in the passage.

Confirm

Select the correct answers — **Choices 2**, **3**, and **5**.

III. Quick Look

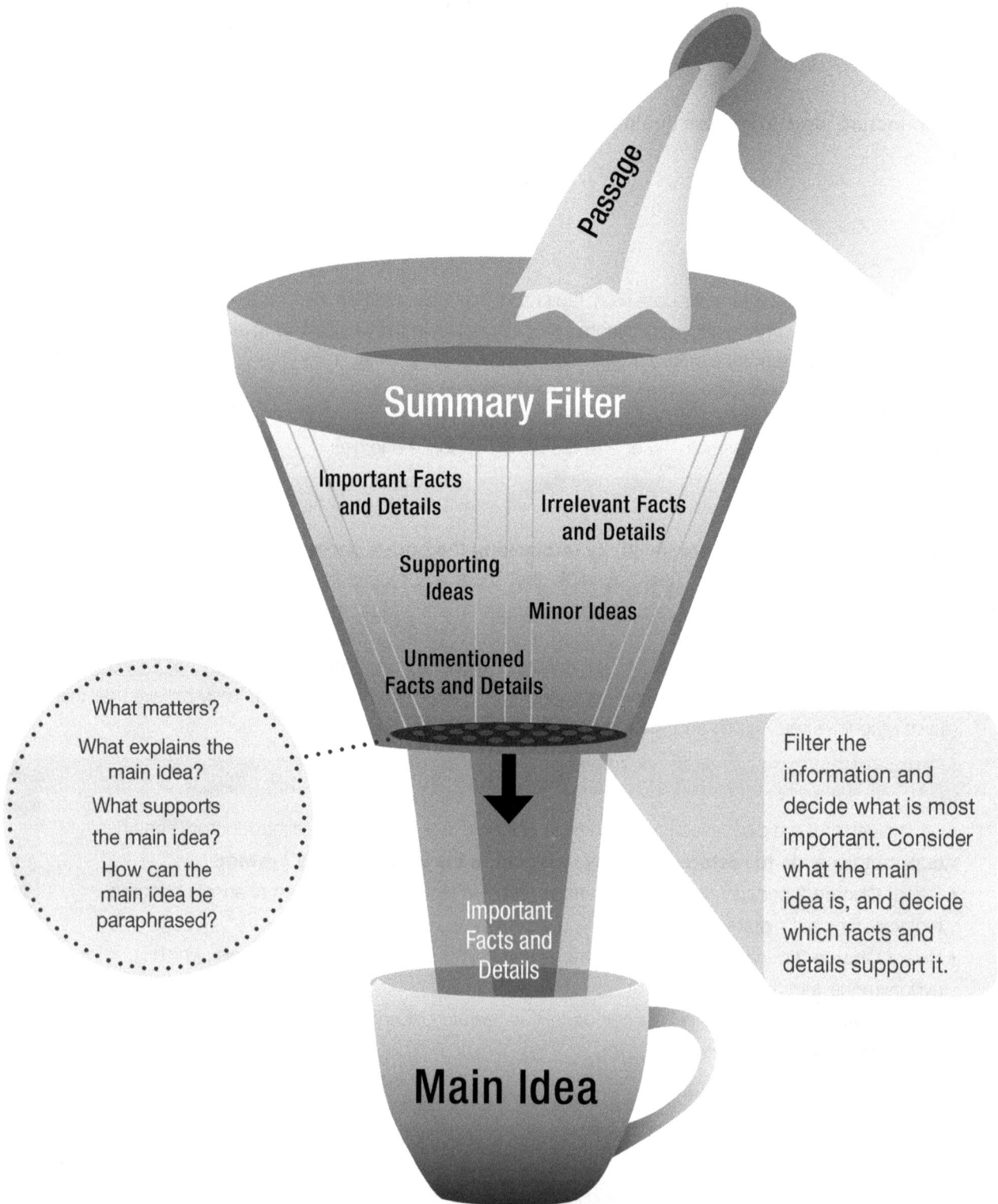

Passage

Summary Filter

Important Facts
and Details

Irrelevant Facts
and Details

Supporting
Ideas

Minor Ideas

Unmentioned
Facts and Details

What matters?

What explains the
main idea?

What supports
the main idea?

How can the
main idea be
paraphrased?

Filter the
information and
decide what is most
important. Consider
what the main
idea is, and decide
which facts and
details support it.

Important
Facts and
Details

Main Idea

IV. Warm Up

Below is a topic sentence and three supporting details. Put a check mark next to the one detail that does NOT support the main idea.

1. Topic sentence: **There are a variety of styles of artistic painting.**
   ____ Support #1: Abstract painting is a style of painting that does not depict realistic scenes, but rather it uses shapes, lines, and color.
   ____ Support #2: One of the most famous paintings in the world is the portrait *Mona Lisa* by the renowned Renaissance artist Leonardo da Vinci of Florence, Italy.
   ____ Support #3: Developed in ancient China, ink wash painting is an art style in which the artist uses only black ink to paint the image.

2. Topic sentence: **Edgar Allan Poe was an American writer and literary critic, well known for dealing with the theme of death.**
   ____ Support #1: Poe wrote a short story entitled "The Cask of Amontillado," which is about a man who seeks revenge on an old friend by leading him to his death.
   ____ Support #2: "The Masque of the Red Death" is a short story by Poe about a deadly plague that takes the lives of a prince and his guests at a masquerade ball.
   ____ Support #3: In Poe's "The Tell-Tale Heart," the narrator insists that he is not insane, but the reader can tell that he is.

3. Topic sentence: ***The Phantom of the Opera*, by French author Gaston Leroux, tells a tragic tale of love and horror involving the Paris Opera House.**
   ____ Support #1: Leroux was a successful journalist, critic, and novelist until his death in 1927.
   ____ Support #2: One of the main characters, Christine, becomes romantically involved with a much-feared and mysterious man known as the "Opera Ghost of Paris."
   ____ Support #3: In the novel, the "Opera Ghost" is a man named Erik with a hideously* disfigured* face, which brings terror and fear to anyone who sees it.

   Hideously: of a horrible, frightening, and ugly nature
   Disfigured: deformed in appearance

4. Topic sentence: **The island of Bali is famous for its dance performances, which attract many tourists.**
   ____ Support #1: The dance of *Barong* features a battle between two of Bali's mythological characters, who represent good and evil.
   ____ Support #2: Much like the dancers of India, Balinese dancers use exaggerated eye and facial expressions to enhance the performance.
   ____ Support #3: Bali is also known for other highly developed arts such as colorful paintings and sculptures depicting its culture and religion.

5. Topic sentence: **When an eclipse occurs, a celestial body obscures* either the Sun or Moon.**

_____ Support #1: A solar eclipse occurs when the Sun is partially or fully hidden by the Moon.

_____ Support #2: Looking directly at the Sun can cause permanent eye damage.

_____ Support #3: A lunar eclipse results when the Moon passes through the Earth's shadow.

Obscure: conceal, hide

6. Topic sentence: **Several types of berries contain significant amounts of antioxidants, which are praised for their potential to help prevent infection and disease.**

_____ Support #1: Like berries, spinach has a significant amount of disease-fighting antioxidants.

_____ Support #2: Cranberries, known to help maintain urinary tract health, have been shown to have high levels of antioxidants.

_____ Support #3: According to nutritionists, blueberries contain the most antioxidants among all fruits.

7. Topic sentence: **Following a gluten-free diet has become quite common in the United States in recent years for a few reasons.**

_____ Support #1: Some people have *celiac disease*, in which the intestine becomes inflamed* when gluten is consumed.

_____ Support #2: Gluten can be found in some cosmetics and hair products, in addition to foods processed from wheat.

_____ Support #3: People may have a sensitivity to gluten, which causes considerable negative side effects such as stomach pain.

Inflammation: (scientific definition) swelling that causes pain

8. Topic sentence: **The Baroque era, which started in Italy, is characterized by its style of art.**

_____ Support #1: The Baroque style of painting featured exaggerated lighting and intense impressions.

_____ Support #2: The word "baroque" may have derived from the Portuguese word *barroco*, which means an irregular pearl.

_____ Support #3: Some Baroque sculptures are characterized by human forms that exude* great movement and energy.

Exude: to give out or emit

9. Topic sentence: **The number 13 is considered unlucky in various countries, including the United States.**

_____ Support #1: The number 4 has a great deal of symbolism in various religions because it represents the four elements: air, fire, earth, and water.

_____ Support #2: Many hotels in the U.S. do not have a 13th floor simply because of a superstitious belief.

_____ Support #3: When the 13th day of the month falls on a Friday, it is traditionally considered an unlucky day.

10. Topic sentence: **In Greek mythology, Zeus was the god of the sky and the supreme god of all others.**

_____ Support #1: Zeus was known to punish gods and humans he considered wicked, or who had lied or broken oaths.

_____ Support #2: Zeus was the rain god and cloud gatherer, and his weapon was the thunderbolt, which he would throw at those who displeased him.

_____ Support #3: Zeus' brother, Poseidon, ruled the sea, and their other brother, Hades, ruled the Underworld.

IV. Quick Practice

Practice #1

Read the passage. Then answer the question that follows.

Much of William Shakespeare's fame comes from his ability to create complex characters in his plays. These individuals voice emotions that most people find hard to put into words. Although he created his characters during the late 16th and early 17th centuries, they still make audiences laugh, cry, and gasp in horror. Shakespeare's characters often try to cope with timeless themes of loyalty, ambition, leadership, parenting, fate, regret, truth, and love. Their clever or moving lines also contributed greatly to the richness of the English language, establishing many new words and phrases.

1) **Directions**: *An introductory sentence for a brief summary of the passage is provided below. Complete the summary by selecting the THREE answer choices that express the most important ideas in the passage. Some sentences do not belong in the summary because they express ideas that are not presented or are minor ideas in the passage.* **This question is worth 2 points.**

> **William Shakespeare is considered one of the greatest English dramatists of all time.**
> -
> -
> -

Answer Choices
1. Shakespeare's portrayal of characters strongly appeals to the audience's emotions.
2. Shakespeare wrote his plays because he knew that they would be timeless.
3. The characters tend to be ambitious but loyal, which moves audiences.
4. Audiences still relate to the basic problems that the characters face.
5. Actors have to memorize many clever or moving lines to play their characters.
6. Shakespearian English immensely influenced the modern English language.

Practice #2

Keeping a pet can have a number of benefits. Some pets can perform very specific tasks that are difficult for humans: certain breeds of dog can very effectively herd sheep or cattle, and cats are experts at catching small, elusive rodents. However, even pets that do not help humans accomplish daily tasks, such as hamsters and fish, can provide companionship, which potentially reduces an owner's anxiety and makes him or her feel more relaxed. Though keeping a pet has many potential rewards, caring for it requires time and responsibility. Therefore, people, especially children, may learn empathy and accountability when they are allowed to help care for a pet.

2) **Directions**: *An introductory sentence for a brief summary of the passage is provided below. Complete the summary by selecting the THREE answer choices that express the most important ideas in the passage. Some sentences do not belong in the summary because they express ideas that are not presented or are minor ideas in the passage.*
This question is worth 2 points.

> **There are many benefits to caring for animals.**
>
> ●
> ●
> ●

Answer Choices

1. Keeping pets in a household can have a soothing effect.
2. Any animal can become a pet given time and patience.
3. Playing with large pets requires people to constantly exercise.
4. Some pets can be trained to fulfill a particular function.
5. Pets are usually more important to people than are their family members.
6. Children can learn about work and compassion through animal care.

Practice #3

Read the passage. Then answer the question that follows.

The planet closest to Earth is Mars. Because it is so close, Mars can be seen with the naked eye, which has long caused people to wonder about it. In ancient times, Romans named the planet Mars after their god of war, possibly because its color reminded them of blood. Scientists now know that the red color comes from Mars' iron-rich soil. Furthermore, using telescopes, astronomers observed that the planet's surface appeared to have been carved by rivers and seas, and theorized that life might be present. Robotic rovers continue to search for signs of past or present life.

3) **Directions**: *An introductory sentence for a brief summary of the passage is provided below. Complete the summary by selecting the THREE answer choices that express the most important ideas in the passage. Some sentences do not belong in the summary because they express ideas that are not presented or are minor ideas in the passage.*
This question is worth 2 points.

People have been curious about Mars since ancient times.

-
-
-

Answer Choices

1. Myths about gods creating the planet were commonplace.
2. Some ancient people probably associated the planet with bloodshed.
3. Continued research has not yet revealed which gases or types of ice are at the planet.
4. Scientists continue to investigate the red color on the planet's surface.
5. Humans have examined Mars in many ways, including with "rovers" on its surface.
6. Due to its proximity to Earth, Mars was scrutinized long before there were telescopes.

Practice #4

Read the passage. Then answer the question that follows.

Sleep is not a waste of time. When people sleep, much more is occurring than simple muscle rest and renewal. In fact, researchers have found that during sleep, bodies are repairing cells and maintaining immune systems. Furthermore, experiments have shown that brains are also active during sleep, busy sorting, storing, and discarding information received during the day. Consequently, people remember information more efficiently when they are allowed to sleep right after learning it. An individual deprived of sleep for too long may fall into *microsleeps*, periods in which the brain is in a sleep state for a few seconds without the person realizing it.

---

4) **Directions**: *An introductory sentence for a brief summary of the passage is provided below. Complete the summary by selecting the THREE answer choices that express the most important ideas in the passage. Some sentences do not belong in the summary because they express ideas that are not presented or are minor ideas in the passage.*
This question is worth 2 points.

Sleep is important for learning and for maintaining health.

-
-
-

Answer Choices

1. Letting one's body rest is crucial for avoiding muscle injury.
2. Sleep helps the body sustain its ability to fight sickness.
3. During sleep, the brain preserves meaningful new concepts.
4. Sleep activates the body to restore itself on the cellular level.
5. The body allows a person to avoid sleep for a long time.
6. While sleeping, people develop defenses that make them unable to get sick.

Practice #5

Read the passage. Then answer the question that follows.

Beavers are the largest furry rodent in North America. They are known for their paddle-like tails and their habit of cutting down trees with their long teeth to build dams in streams. Beavers were trapped to near extinction during the 1800s, as beaver fur was made into felt for warm hats and coats, creating a huge market for the material in the United States and Europe. Europeans, Americans, and Native Americans trapped beavers so that they could trade the furs for supplies. Native Americans and early settlers also consumed beaver meat.

5) **Directions**: *An introductory sentence for a brief summary of the passage is provided below. Complete the summary by selecting the THREE answer choices that express the most important ideas in the passage. Some sentences do not belong in the summary because they express ideas that are not presented or are minor ideas in the passage.*
This question is worth 2 points.

> **At one time, people trapped beavers for many reasons.**
> ●
> ●
> ●

Answer Choices
1. Beaver fur was suited to making outerwear for chilly places.
2. People valued beaver fur because it was adapted to wet conditions.
3. Beavers were hunted because they depleted lumber supplies needed to build dams.
4. Trappers engaged in an unending quest to keep beavers from damming streams.
5. Beaver skins served as a kind of currency for bartering with others.
6. People who trapped beavers used them for culinary and mercantile purposes.

Practice #6

Read the passage. Then answer the question that follows.

Fashion modeling may bring fame and glamour, but it is hard work. Models are independent contractors, so they must apply for each modeling assignment separately. Generally, to be considered for a job, models must be very tall and thin, have clear skin, and possess the "look" that the industry is seeking at the time.

Modeling jobs may take place in studios under hot lights, on runways, or outdoors in all types of weather. Models may be asked to express a particular emotion or mood. While a few models become wealthy, most models earn very little. It has been suggested that nearly half of all professional models suffer from eating disorders, anxiety, or depression due to pressures of the job.

6) **Directions**: *An introductory sentence for a brief summary of the passage is provided below. Complete the summary by selecting the THREE answer choices that express the most important ideas in the passage. Some sentences do not belong in the summary because they express ideas that are not presented or are minor ideas in the passage.*
This question is worth 2 points.

There are many negative aspects of the fashion modeling profession.

-
-
-

Answer Choices

1. Models have little job security and must continually compete for work.

2. A model's basic appearance may be favored inconsistently by the fashion industry.

3. Working for no pay is the norm for entry-level modeling applicants.

4. It is common for models to experience mood disorders and lose too much weight.

5. Fashion models can expect to become at least moderately wealthy over time.

6. The fashion industry rarely hires the same model twice.

Practice #7

Read the passage. Then answer the question that follows.

Language is not just grouping words together; it conveys meaning within the context of a culture. The Hawaiian language is an example of one that is heavily dependent on context and inference. Most linguists agree that Hawaiian consists of only five vowels and eight consonants, but these numbers vary based on region and interpretation. Despite the limited number of letters in the Hawaiian alphabet, some Hawaiian words have multiple meanings, which are called *kaona*. The kaona of a word depends on the situation. For example, the Hawaiian word *aloha* can mean "love," "affection," "peace," "compassion," "mercy," "hello," or "goodbye." Native speakers using the language are not confused, just as native speakers of English know when the word "mouse" refers to a rodent or a computer cursor controller. Therefore, to understand the kaona of Hawaiian, it is helpful to know the historic legends, experiences, and beliefs of the people.

---

7) **Directions**: *An introductory sentence for a brief summary of the passage is provided below. Complete the summary by selecting the THREE answer choices that express the most important ideas in the passage. Some sentences do not belong in the summary because they express ideas that are not presented or are minor ideas in the passage.*
This question is worth 2 points.

Hawaiian is a language with interesting characteristics.

-
-
-

Answer Choices

1. It includes words that have a precise meaning only when used in a sentence.

2. There is no way a non-native speaker can learn the many hidden meanings of it.

3. Like the Hawaiian language, most English phrases are expressed as metaphors.

4. Its syllables are formed with a relatively small number of consonants and vowels.

5. It uses many inferences, making it a complicated language.

6. Its grammar is simpler than English, but its word order is more complicated.

Practice #8

Read the passage. Then answer the question that follows.

When children are home-schooled in the United States, they spend days working on state-approved learning activities at home with a parent. They may meet with a teacher once a week or more. Although home-schooling is still rare and controversial among those who believe that peer interactions develop crucial social skills, some parents believe that it is the ideal way to educate their children. For instance, they may feel critical of the quality of public schools, or they may want to stress religious values. Sometimes, the family may live too far away from any schools, or the child may have a time-consuming job or interest, such as acting. Finally, some parents may feel that children learn best when children themselves are allowed to make more decisions.

---

8) **Directions**: *An introductory sentence for a brief summary of the passage is provided below. Complete the summary by selecting the THREE answer choices that express the most important ideas in the passage. Some sentences do not belong in the summary because they express ideas that are not presented or are minor ideas in the passage.*
   This question is worth 2 points.

> **There are several reasons that some U.S. families home-school their children.**
> -
> -
> -

Answer Choices

1. The parents are able to teach whatever they think is important.
2. Schools may be too remote or inaccessible for the children.
3. The parents may be critical of government-funded educational methods and results.
4. Children may learn more if they are allowed to be more autonomous.
5. The parents may value spending recreational time with their children at home.
6. The parents may want their children to be in charge of all learning activities.

Practice #9

Read the passage. Then answer the question that follows.

Fluoridation is the addition of the chemical fluoride to water supplies. Many authorities believe that drinking fluoridated water slows down the loss of tooth enamel, resulting in fewer dental problems. Dentists and public health officials say that this is especially helpful for poor children. Despite the benefits, local water district officials sometimes face opposition when they attempt to fluoridate water. Opponents point to rare cases of excessive fluoride causing harm to bones and say that fluoride can discolor children's teeth and may cause other health issues. Opponents further point out that more research is needed to justify public water fluoridation and believe that individuals should have the right to decide for themselves whether or not to use fluoride.

---

9) **Directions**: *An introductory sentence for a brief summary of the passage is provided below. Complete the summary by selecting the THREE answer choices that express the most important ideas in the passage. Some sentences do not belong in the summary because they express ideas that are not presented or are minor ideas in the passage.*
   This question is worth 2 points.

There are two sides in the debate over fluoridation.

-
-
-

Answer Choices

1. Opponents say that tooth enamel is not strengthened by it.
2. Supporters say that it helps prevent tooth decay for everyone.
3. Opponents are in agreement that its harmful side effects are overstated.
4. Opponents argue that excess fluoridation has damaged health on occasion.
5. Opponents say that more research about fluoride is necessary.
6. Supporters want fluoride added to every drink served to poor children.

Practice #10

Read the passage. Then answer the question that follows.

Slang is the use of new informal words or phrases or the use of familiar words or phrases in new ways. Sometimes people begin using slang to express concepts brought about by new technology. For example, development of the Internet spurred new terms such as *cyber* (dealing with the Internet). Sometimes members of a certain group use slang in order to express a sense of shared identity. For example, jazz musicians invented terms such as *gig* (performing job) and *axe* (a person's instrument). People also borrow foreign words as slang. In English, the slang word *klutz*, or clumsy person, comes from Yiddish. In Spanish, a slang term for "lunch" is *lonche*, borrowed from English and used instead of the Spanish word for lunch, which is *almuerzo*.

---

10) **Directions**: *An introductory sentence for a brief summary of the passage is provided below. Complete the summary by selecting the THREE answer choices that express the most important ideas in the passage. Some sentences do not belong in the summary because they express ideas that are not presented or are minor ideas in the passage.*
This question is worth 2 points.

Slang words develop in a language for different reasons.

-
-
-

Answer Choices

1. All languages have slang, which comes from informality.
2. Newly invented tools often require the creation of new words.
3. People might use slang to feel more connected to each other.
4. Musicians have the biggest influence on slang words in most societies.
5. Slang can be used for awhile before a more formal expression replaces it.
6. Sometimes other languages contribute slang words to a lexicon.

Select the vocabulary word or phrase that has the closest meaning.

1. slim
A. thin
B. bulky
C. pointy
D. bent

2. treatment
A. injury
B. charity
C. policy
D. therapy

3. depict
A. confuse
B. portray
C. distort
D. engrave

4. plague
A. delight
B. torture
C. poison
D. epidemic

5. hideously
A. stupidly
B. adequately
C. horribly
D. wrongly

6. enhance
A. complicate
B. minimize
C. reinforce
D. improve

7. deformed
A. misshapen
B. improved
C. perfected
D. stacked

8. gatherer
A. detractor
B. collector
C. governor
D. commentator

9. individual
A. solitary
B. ordinary
C. womanly
D. cursory

10. horror
A. delight
B. fear
C. repose
D. calm

11. cope with
A. suffer from
B. deal with
C. apply to
D. bring up

12. regret
A. refuse
B. remorse
C. relish
D. resent

13. soothe
A. control
B. reveal
C. intensify
D. ease

14. naked
A. burned
B. bald
C. bare
D. bold

15. bloodshed

A. playing
B. ordering
C. striking
D. killing

16. research
A. estimate
B. interrogate
C. investigate
D. contemplate

17. repair
A. remember
B. replace
C. amend
D. exchange

18. immune
A. resistant
B. receptive
C. responsive
D. reactive

19. discard
A. desert
B. preserve
C. manage
D. destroy

20. micro
A. large
B. modest
C. simple
D. minute

21. extinction
A. starting out
B. dying out
C. dealing in
D. coming in

22. glamour
A. boredom
B. dullness
C. elegance
D. interest

23. assignment
A. rule

B. task
C. choice
D. time

24. suffer
A. believe
B. assist
C. agonize
D. comfort

25. anxiety
A. worry
B. peace
C. creeps
D. relief

26. relatively
A. precisely
B. exactly
C. appropriately
D. comparatively

27. district
A. characteristic
B. distinction
C. region
D. establishment

28. clumsy
A. unhappy
B. awkward
C. clever
D. graceful

29. informality
A. calmness
B. inertness
C. quietness
D. casualness

30. sometimes
A. constantly
B. occasionally
C. regularly
D. frequently

17C 18A 19A 20D 21B 22C 23B 24C 25A 26D 27C 28B 29D 30B
1A 2D 3B 4D 5C 6D 7A 8B 9A 10B 11B 12B 13D 14C 15D 16C

I. What Is an Organization Question?

Organization

The organization question asks you to identify the facts and details that best fit the two to three subtopics of the passage. A passage has one main topic. To support the main topic, a passage can have multiple subtopics. Subtopics are supported by their facts and details.

A. ORGANIZATION QUESTION MODEL

Geography and geology are both studies of the Earth. In fact, the prefix *geo-*, which is found in the words *geography* and *geology*, means "Earth." Geographers are associated with map making, as the suffix *-graph* means "written" or "drawn." Geographers may use maps to show how land is changing over a long period of time, or they may quickly draw up maps to show firefighters how a forest fire is moving. In addition, geographers may be called upon to study an area's environment, resources, and human cultures in order to assist in planning or problem solving. On the other hand, geologists focus on the actual rocks and soils of the Earth, as the suffix *-logy* means "study." Geologists may study layers of rock formations, determining their age to answer questions about the Earth's past. These scholars may assist in the search for oil or other natural underground resources. Geologists also study natural disasters, such as the forces causing earthquakes and tsunamis.

10. **Directions**: Select the sentences that most appropriately match the descriptions of each area of study. TWO of the answer choices will NOT be used.

Answer Choices	Areas of Study
1. This field may map contours of land. 2. This field may focus on the rotations and orbit of Earth. 3. This field studies the ages of rock and soil formations. 4. This field may help with mining or oil drilling. 5. This field includes the study of dinosaurs. 6. This field sometimes may overlap with *social sciences*, or the studies of human cultures.	**Geography** • • **Geology** • •

All other organization questions have either five or seven correct answer choices. Above is a simplified example.

B. TIPS

1. Note any facts in the paragraph that refer to a subtopic.
2. Correct answers should be easily found in the passage.
3. An incorrect answer will be inaccurate, unrelated, or illogical according to the passage.
4. Because these questions ask you to select multiple correct answers, they are worth either 3 or 4 points.
5. If you are asked to select five correct choices, you must answer three out of five correctly for 1 point, four out of five for 2 points, and five out of five for 3 points. If you are asked to select seven correct choices, you must answer four out of seven correctly for 1 point, five out of seven for 2 points, six out of seven for 3 points, and seven out of seven for 4 points.

II. Hacking Strategy

Organization
Question →

Recognize the Question Type

This question type asks you to organize information by sorting it into categories.

Identify the Categories and Key Components in Both the Passage and the Answer Choices

After examining the categories, identify the key words and phrases that are seen both in the answer choices and the passage.

Do the answer choices fit in a category? If so, which category? Wrong choices may be inaccurate or not mentioned in the passage. Correct choices will fit one of the two categories.

Look Through the Answer Choices.

Which Choice Is Correct?

No →

Eliminate

Eliminate the answer choices that do not fit into a category, are inaccurate, and/or are not mentioned.

Yes ↓

Confirm

Sort the correct answers into the correct categories.

(EXAMPLE

Geography and geology are both studies of the Earth. In fact, the prefix *geo-*, which is found in the words *geography* and *geology*, means "Earth." Geographers are associated with map making, as the suffix *-graph* means "written" or "drawn." Geographers may use maps to show how land is changing over a long period of time, or they may quickly draw up maps to show firefighters how a forest fire is moving. In addition, geographers may be called upon to study an area's environment, resources, and human cultures in order to assist in planning or problem solving. On the other hand, geologists focus on the actual rocks and soils of the Earth, as the suffix *-logy* means "study." Geologists may study layers of rock formations, determining their age to answer questions about the Earth's past. These scholars may assist in the search for oil or other natural underground resources. Geologists also study natural disasters, such as the forces causing earthquakes and tsunamis.

Areas of Study

Geography	Geology
•	•
•	•

Answer Choices

1. This field may map contours of land.
2. This field may focus on the rotations and orbit of Earth.
3. This field studies the ages of rock and soil formations.
4. This field may help with mining or oil drilling.
5. This field includes the study of dinosaurs.
6. This field sometimes may overlap with *social sciences*, or the studies of human cultures.

Identify the Categories and Key Components in Both the Passage and the Answer Choices

The category types are "geography" and "geology."

Geography and geology are both studies of the Earth. In fact, the prefix *geo-*, which is found in the words *geography* and *geology*, means "Earth." Geographers are associated with map making, as the suffix *-graph* means "written" or "drawn." Geographers may use maps to show how land is changing over a long period of time, or they may quickly draw up maps to show firefighters how a forest fire is moving. In addition, geographers may be called upon to study an area's environment, resources, and human cultures in order to assist in planning or problem solving. On the other hand, geologists focus on the actual rocks and soils of the Earth, as the suffix *-logy* means "study." Geologists may study layers of rock formations, determining their age to answer questions about the Earth's past. These scholars may assist in the search for oil or other natural underground resources. Geologists also study natural disasters, such as the forces causing earthquakes and tsunamis.

Look Through the Answer Choices. Which Choice Is Correct?

Compare key words in the choices to key words in the passage. Do they have the same information? Does the choice fit into one of the categories?

Geography
- Select **Choice 1** because the third sentence states that "Geographers are associated with map making."
- Select **Choice 6** because the fifth sentence states that "Geographers may be called upon to study... human cultures."

Geology
- Select **Choice 3** because the seventh sentence states that "Geologists may study layers of rock formations...to answer questions about the Earth's past."
- Select **Choice 4** because the eighth sentence states that geologists "search for oil or other natural underground resources."

Eliminate Incorrect Choices

- Eliminate **Choices 2** and **5** because they are not mentioned in the passage.

Confirm

Select the correct answers and put them into the correct category.

Geography — Choices 1 and 6 / Geology — Choices 3 and 4

III. Quick Look

Organization Diagram

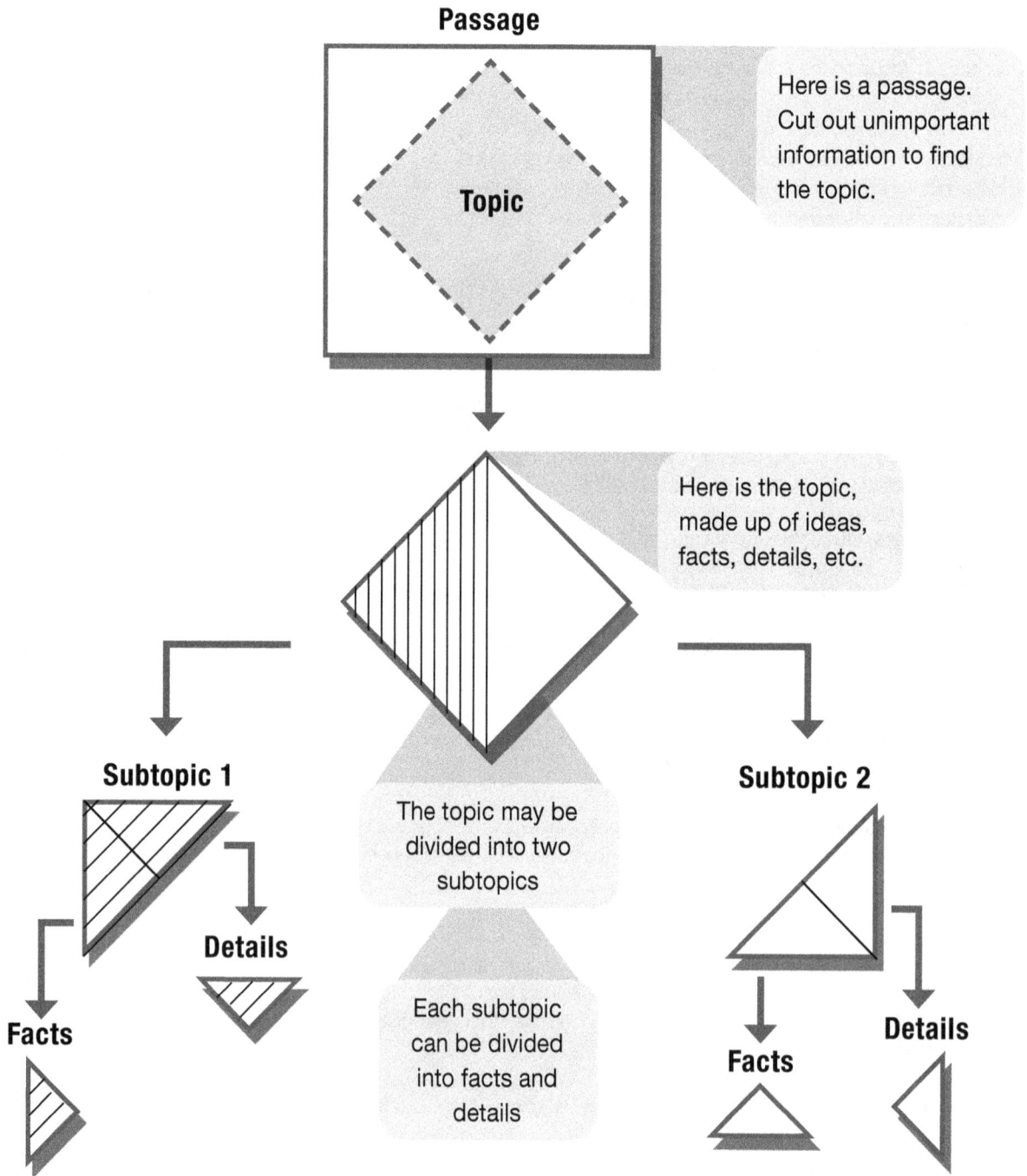

Passage

Topic

Here is a passage. Cut out unimportant information to find the topic.

Here is the topic, made up of ideas, facts, details, etc.

The topic may be divided into two subtopics

Subtopic 1

Details

Facts

Each subtopic can be divided into facts and details

Subtopic 2

Facts

Details

IV. Warm Up

Below are two categories and eight answer choices. Six of the answers belong in the categories. Two of the answers do not. Put the six appropriate answer choices into their corresponding categories.

1. **Choices**	Train	Plane
1. This uses rails to cross terrain.	____	____
2. This travels between locations at non-specific times.	____	____
3. This must regulate oxygen levels.	____	____
4. This sometimes includes bunk beds for long journeys.		
5. This generally has separate engine controls in the front and the back.		
6. Opening a door while this is operating would be disastrous.		
7. Ocean currents must be consulted before taking this mode of travel.		
8. This requires passengers to turn off their electronic devices during takeoffs and landings.		

2. **Choices**	Play	Movie
1. This is performed in front of a live audience.	____	____
2. If an actor misses a line, the error can be corrected.	____	____
3. This allows the use of a wide range of special effects.	____	____
4. Pets are welcome to attend this.		
5. This originated centuries ago in Greece.		
6. The audience can see the spotlights used to focus on actors.		
7. This is recorded, edited, and then shown to audience.		
8. A character's actions and emotions are not important.		

3. **Choices**   **Whale**   **Shark**

   1. This includes a species that is Earth's largest animal.   _____   _____

   2. This creature most likely requires a frozen habitat.   _____   _____

   3. This can smell blood in the water and is attracted to it.   _____   _____

   4. This creature can maneuver on land as well as in water.

   5. This breathes through gills, or slits, that are located on its sides.

   6. This is feared as a stealthy hunter of swimmers.

   7. This animal is not a fish; it is a mammal.

   8. This comes to the surface and blows out air.

4. **Choices**   **Brain**   **Computer**

   1. It was developed in the 1900s.   _____   _____

   2. It requires a constant flow of blood and oxygen to survive. _____   _____

   3. Electricity gives it the power to operate.   _____   _____

   4. It is most often used as a tool to transport items.

   5. People are able to think with it.

   6. It gives people the ability to have emotions.

   7. It is operated using an engine.

   8. It can be turned on and off.

5. **Choices**   **Golf**   **Tennis**

   1. The playing area for this game is called "the green."   _____   _____

   2. Players of this game must wear goggles.   _____   _____

   3. In this game, it is possible to earn the score of "love."   _____   _____

   4. Paddles are used to hit a ball in this game.

   5. This game requires people to use rackets.

   6. Players of this game "serve" the ball to their opponents.

   7. The winner of this game is the one who strikes the ball the least.

   8. Balls from this game may easily land in a pond or shrubbery.

6. **Choices**   **Italy**   **Egypt**

   1. Pharaohs once ruled this country.   _____   _____
   2. The language of this country originated from Latin.   _____   _____
   3. This country is famous for its Viking stories.   _____   _____
   4. The Roman *Coliseum* stands here to this day.
   5. This country was known as a large producer of *papyrus*.
   6. This country is mostly made up of islands.
   7. *Gladiators* were a part of this country's ancient history.
   8. The *Sphinx* is a famous statue that can be found here.

7. **Choices**   **Ocean**   **Lake**

   1. It is comprised of salt water.   _____   _____
   2. It is most often composed of fresh water.   _____   _____
   3. Official ice hockey games are now played on it.   _____   _____
   4. It supports freshwater organisms such as frogs.
   5. It creates an environment in which cacti can survive.
   6. This body of water is sometimes found on top of a mountain.
   7. The waves that it creates make it suitable for people to surf.
   8. The deepest depths can be found in this body of water.

8. **Choices**   **Comedy**   **Tragedy**

   1. This is a type of movie, play, or story that evokes sadness. _____   _____
   2. This is designed to make people laugh.   _____   _____
   3. This type of story is frightening and often leaves the reader disturbed. _____   _____
   4. Someone would most likely watch this type of movie to relieve stress.
   5. The famous story of *Romeo and Juliet* is an example of this.
   6. Emotions like misery and despair are prevalent in this.
   7. One is not supposed to take this genre very seriously.
   8. Critics usually prefer this type.

9. **Choices**

	Chemist	Psychologist
	____	____
	____	____
	____	____

1. This person studies how molecules interact with one another.
2. This person may study the relationship between wealth and happiness.
3. This person may conduct therapy sessions.
4. This person designs and oversees the construction of buildings.
5. This person uses beakers and test tubes when experimenting.
6. This person may spend time observing the behavior of others.
7. This person attempts to heal injuries or sickness in animals.
8. This person must have a strong understanding of the Periodic Table of Elements.

10. **Choices**

	Energy	Fatigue
	____	____
	____	____
	____	____

1. This feeling has little to do with quantity of sleep.
2. Caffeine provides a temporary elevation in this.
3. This can make people reluctant to socialize.
4. When this occurs, accomplishing a task is challenging.
5. The body may feel this when fighting an illness.
6. Nutritious foods contribute to building this.
7. Animals may be immune to this.
8. More of this can help a team win a game.

V. Quick Practice

Practice #1

Read the passage. Then answer the question that follows.

Adults and adolescents use their brains differently because the human brain takes around 25 years to completely develop. The brain matures from back to front, or from the more primitive areas that regulate movement and instinct toward the areas at the front that govern planning, strategizing, and organizing.

As a result, adolescents tend to react to their surroundings more on "gut-level" instincts, using more basic and impulsive parts of the brain, while adults tend to use the frontal cortex as they react, relying more on memories, experience, and reasoning.

Adolescent brains are also more sensitive than adult brains to neural hormones that are released when a reward is given. Hormonal sensitivity may be what makes adolescents more likely to take risks for rewards, especially social rewards such as approval from friends. Evolutionarily, the adolescent brain may have needed to be more risk-and-reward oriented so that young people could move away from home and into new territory with peers. The adult brain, meanwhile, may have needed to mature to make wiser decisions that supported stability.

1) **Directions**: *Select the sentences that most appropriately match the descriptions of each stage of brain development. TWO of the answer choices will NOT be used.* ***This question is worth 3 points.***

Answer Choices	Stages of Brain Development
1. It develops from back to front.	**Adolescent brain**
2. It is more active at the reasoning, strategizing level.	●
3. Social rewards especially affect it.	●
4. Memory and experience play a bigger role in decisions.	**Adult brain**
5. People in this stage feel as if time passes more quickly.	●
6. It is more impulsive and open to taking risks.	●
7. At this stage, people more often choose to be stable rather than adventurous.	●

Practice #2

Read the passage. Then answer the question that follows.

Two types of volcanos are *shield volcanos* and *stratovolcanos*.

So-called shield volcanos resemble a warrior's "shield," sloping gently down from the vent at the center. They develop this shape from repeated eruptions of fiery liquid rock, or *lava*, which cools and solidifies as it flows downward, creating a broad, low mountain. Some of the largest volcanos on Earth, such as Mauna Loa in Hawaii, are shield volcanos.

Stratovolcanos, on the other hand, explode from the vent and emit more solid debris. These solid materials then build up near the vent, forming a steep-sided mountain. Most stratovolcanos are smaller and erupt less often than shield volcanos. The name comes from the word *strata*, which refers to the layers of solid materials that make up the volcano's cone. Stratovolcanos, such as Vesuvius in Italy, are the most common type of volcano.

2) **Directions**: *Select the sentences that most appropriately match the descriptions of each type of volcano. TWO of the answer choices will NOT be used.* **This question is worth 3 points.**

Answer Choices	Types of Volcanos
1. All of these are located in Hawaii. 2. Large quantities of solid material comes out when these erupt. 3. These are the most prevalent kind of volcano. 4. These are named after something used in ancient battles. 5. These never erupt because they are so small. 6. This name comes from the materials that form the volcano. 7. Mostly liquid rock comes out when these erupt.	**Shield volcanos** ● ● **Stratovolcanos** ● ● ●

Practice #3

Read the passage. Then answer the question that follows.

Folk dances are the dances that developed among people in villages throughout the world and have been passed down from generation to generation. The step patterns as well as the hand and arm movements are usually repetitive and can be either simple or complicated. Dancers often stand in a circle and sometimes join hands or hold each other by the shoulders as they dance. It is likely that most of these dances were developed to be performed at festivals, celebrations, or religious rituals.

During Europe's Medieval period, royal and aristocratic social circles began altering European folk dances to meet their social needs. These modified dances, called *social dances*, include dancing with a partner at a social event, and they became identified with elegance and refinement. Details of etiquette, such as how to approach a partner, and of style, such as how to position one's head, became important. Soon, graceful social dancing became an indispensable skill for those in the elite classes.

3) **Directions**: *Select the sentences that most appropriately match the descriptions of each form of dance. TWO of the answer choices will NOT be used.* **This question is worth 3 points.**

Answer Choices	Forms of Dances
1. These were sometimes developed for religious purposes.	**Folk dances**
2. These required a high level of energy.	●
3. These mostly developed in small, rural communities.	●
4. Learning these was important for affluent Europeans.	**Social dances**
5. These almost always feature a special mode of dress.	●
6. These were done with a partner but still in a group setting.	●
7. These often represented one's sophistication and nobility.	●

Practice #4

Read the passage. Then answer the question that follows.

Ropes and knots were likely developed by prehistoric peoples to meet needs in fishing, hunting, lifting, pulling, clothing, and bandaging. Some of the common knots today are the square, bowline, and granny knots.

The square knot is probably the best known and most widely used. Formed by two overhand knots turned in opposite ways, the square knot can join two ropes or cords. Thus, it is useful for tying shoelaces and wrapping packages. Doctors use a form of a square knot to tie stitches that close up wounds.

The bowline knot, on the other hand, uses just the end of one rope. The knot forms a circle that will not slip if properly tied. It can hold sailboats to a dock, and it can also be used to anchor small airplanes to the ground. In addition, a bowline knot can be used as a seat to lift someone during a rescue.

4) **Directions**: *Select the sentences that most appropriately match the descriptions of each kind of knot. TWO of the answer choices will NOT be used.* ***This question is worth 3 points.***

Answer Choices	Kinds of Knots
1. This is effective when tying two ropes together.	**Square knot**
2. Prehistoric people probably invented this to meet a practical need.	●
3. This is best used to capture animals while hunting and fishing.	●
4. Only one rope is needed to make this circular knot.	**Bowline knot**
5. This has a particular role to play in medical surgeries.	●
6. This provides support for those who must be lifted.	●
7. This effectively secures a movable thing to a post, peg, or dock.	●

Practice #5

Read the passage. Then answer the question that follows.

Mapmakers create maps for many different purposes. Two of the common types are general reference maps and thematic maps.

The most common type of map is the *general reference map*, which shows the names and locations of natural and constructed features. Such features may include mountains, lakes, rivers, roads, schools, and city boundaries. The map may show the whole world or magnify a small area, such as the house lots in a neighborhood. The primary purpose of a general reference map is to help people find places.

Another variety of map is a *thematic map*, one that illustrates the distribution of population, rainfall, or a natural resource over an area. To depict the quantities or qualities of the distribution, a thematic map may use colors, thematic symbols, or variations in the sizes or shapes of the symbols. For example, a map of petroleum trade in a region may show thick arrows for large oil exports and thin arrows for small oil exports.

5) **Directions**: *Select the sentences that most appropriately match the descriptions of each type of map. TWO of the answer choices will NOT be used.* **This question is worth 3 points.**

Answer Choices	Types of Maps
1. This helps builders construct better houses.	**General reference map**
2. This shows how a specific characteristic is spread over a location.	●
3. This can show very large or very small areas.	●
4. This aims to help in planning a route ahead of time.	●
5. This has different colors and symbols to reveal information.	**Thematic map**
6. This gives the location of natural and man-made features.	●
7. This should be unchanging and permanent.	●

Practice #6

Read the passage. Then answer the question that follows.

There are several kinds of ceramic pottery, including earthenware and stoneware.

Although researchers once associated ceramics with the arrival of farming, recent archaeological evidence indicates that humans have used earthenware since the time of hunting and gathering during the late glacial period. People around the world continue to cook and serve food with earthenware, as the clay used to produce earthenware is easier to work with and less expensive compared to other clays. Earthenware is coarse, easily chipped or broken, and not watertight unless a glaze is added to its surface. Because earthenware is fired at lower temperatures than other types of pottery, potters can use more colorful glazes on it.

Stoneware was invented in China around 1400 BCE, but Europeans did not learn how to make it until the 1600s CE. This type of pottery is made from different clays that can be fired at high temperatures. Because it is nonporous, stoneware is smooth, glass-like, and able to hold liquids. The pottery is also dense and tough – even a steel point cannot scratch it. Potters usually glaze their pieces to decorate them.

6) **Directions**: *Select the sentences that most appropriately match the descriptions of each type of pottery. TWO of the answer choices will NOT be used.* **This question is worth 3 points.**

Answer Choices

1. Potters have been specializing in this type of pottery for centuries.
2. Potters can mold this easily and decorate it colorfully.
3. This resembles glass in some ways, though one cannot see through it.
4. People in China originally developed this pottery.
5. Europeans tend to prefer this, though it is easy to chip.
6. This is dense enough to hold water and is usually glazed.
7. People may find this to be affordable but fragile.

Types of Pottery

Earthenware
- ●
- ●

Stoneware
- ●
- ●
- ●

Practice #7

Read the passage. Then answer the question that follows.

When engineers consider the construction of new bridges, two of the types that they may propose are girder bridges and truss bridges.

A girder bridge resembles a sophisticated version of a log placed over a creek. Modern girder bridges, such as freeway overpasses or bridges over vast waterways, are flat beams supported underneath by massive posts that form the shapes of either rectangles or the capital letter "I." Romans built strong girder bridges of stone and mortar. Today, modern builders still favor the girder bridge design but instead use steel and concrete as building materials.

Before strong steel and concrete were developed, people often built truss bridges. These take advantage of tall vertical triangular shapes to redistribute the tension and compression on the bridge when weight is added to it. The "triangles" often stick up along the sides of the bridge, and sometimes a cover is added over the top. Truss bridges offer great strength and can be built with simple materials such as wood and iron. Truss bridges provide the advantage of not having supporting posts underneath that can interfere with streams or traffic below them.

7) **Directions**: *Select the sentences that most appropriately match the descriptions of each style of bridge. TWO of the answer choices will NOT be used.* ***This question is worth 3 points.***

Answer Choices

1. This uses circular shapes to provide special support.
2. This basically uses horizontal planks supported by vertical posts.
3. This divides force among specially designed supports.
4. This can be built for pedestrians, automobiles, or trains.
5. This can be built with relatively simple materials but can still hold up tremendous weight.
6. Today's construction of this uses concrete and durable metals.
7. This allows things to pass under it without obstruction.

Styles of Bridges

Girder bridge
- ●
- ●

Truss bridge
- ●
- ●
- ●

Practice #8

Read the passage. Then answer the question that follows.

Two of the powerful empires in the Americas in the 15th and 16th centuries were the Incas of the Andes Mountains and the Aztecs of present-day Mexico. Each empire organized its economy according to its own unique needs.

The Incas had no *currency*, or money system, and no markets. The government did not tax but rather required people to produce goods for the government or to work on farms or public projects such as irrigation systems. Government officials collected, stored, and redistributed most food, tools, and clothing; citizens did not have to buy anything. This highly controlled system helped prevent hunger in a challenging mountain environment.

On the other hand, the Aztecs, who lived on flat plains that were easier to farm, collected tributes or taxes from their subjects but did not regulate the subjects' lives as much as the Inca government did. The Aztecs allowed individuals to form marketplaces and become merchants and traders. The currency used in markets was cacao beans used for making chocolate. The merchant class was allowed to travel freely in Aztec-controlled land and in foreign or even enemy territories. Many merchants who traveled were also employed as spies for the Aztec state.

8) **Directions**: *Select the sentences that most appropriately match the descriptions of each type of economic system. TWO of the answer choices will NOT be used.* **This question is worth 3 points.**

Answer Choices	Types of Economic Systems
1. People could negotiate for goods in a central location or foreign territory.	**Incas**
2. Traveling to barter often had a hidden purpose beyond profit.	●
3. People had to provide labor to produce community goods.	●
4. Discontent with the government was an issue in this economy.	**Aztecs**
5. This empire relied on hunting and gathering to support its basic economy.	●
6. Food was challenging to grow and thus had to be shared.	●
7. For a citizen, taxation was mandatory.	●

Practice #9

Read the passage. Then answer the question that follows.

Among the most important breeds of dairy cows are the Holstein-Friesian and the Jersey.

The Holsteins probably developed in the Schleswig-Holstein region of Germany. They have a spotted black-and-white coat. This type of cow tends to be the largest of the dairy breeds, with broad hips and a long, thick body. Worldwide, dairy farmers have more Holsteins than any other breed because they usually produce the most milk. However, their milk usually contains less butterfat than the milk of other breeds.

Jersey cattle, another common breed, are opposite from the Holsteins physically. The Jersey breed is the smallest of the dairy breeds. Jerseys tend to have wide faces, short foreheads, and short horns, and range in color from gray to reddish-brown. They usually produce less milk than other dairy cows, but their milk contains the most butterfat and protein. Jersey cows came from the tiny British island of Jersey in the English Channel.

9) **Directions**: *Select the sentences that most appropriately match the descriptions of each breed of cow. TWO of the answer choices will NOT be used.* **This question is worth 3 points.**

Answer Choices	Breeds of Cows
1. This breed has the advantage of producing great quantities of milk.	**Holstein cow**
2. This breed is the strongest among the cow breeds.	●
3. This breed has the longest horns of any dairy cattle breeds.	●
4. This breed produces milk that is denser in fats per liter than milk from other breeds.	●
5. This breed is the littlest in size of the dairy cow breeds.	**Jersey cow**
6. This breed looks as if it might have been blotched with black ink.	●
7. This breed happened to develop as the largest of the dairy breeds.	●

Practice #10

Read the passage. Then answer the question that follows.

Most writers use a combination of description and imagery techniques to help readers picture stories.

Description gradually "paints" a scene piece by piece using adjectives and descriptive phrases. Henry David Thoreau uses such descriptions in *Walden*: "When I first took up my abode *in the woods*, my house was not finished for winter, but was...*without plastering or chimney*, the walls being of *rough, weather-stained* boards, with *wide chinks*, which made it *cool at night*."

Writers use imagery when they want to add an extra layer of meaning or feeling. Imagery usually employs unexpected comparisons to another object or idea. In *The Great Gatsby*, F. Scott Fitzgerald describes two women in a room with wind blowing through. He writes that they were sitting on a couch that was "like an anchored balloon," and their white dresses "were rippling and fluttering as if they had just been blown back in after a short flight around the house." This imagery leads the reader to associate the women with flight and air and paradoxically with being held down or "anchored."

10) **Directions**: *Select the sentences that most appropriately match the descriptions of each type of literary technique. TWO of the answer choices will NOT be used.* **This question is worth 3 points.**

Answer Choices	Types of Literary Techniques
1. This technique constructs a picture bit by bit with adjectives.	**Description**
2. This technique may give the reader extra associations with characters.	●
3. This technique may say that an apple is "smooth, red, and a bit shiny."	●
4. This technique is used most often by serious writers.	**Imagery**
5. This technique may describe a city bus as a "whale."	●
6. This technique is especially useful for describing female characters.	●
7. This technique often uses surprising comparisons.	●

Select the vocabulary word or phrase that has the closest meaning.

7. comprise
A. collect
B. connect
C. combine
D. contain

8. frightening
A. normal
B. amazing
C. scary
D. tasty

1. disaster
A. germ
B. property
C. occurrence
D. catastrophe

2. terrain
A. zone
B. organ
C. limit
D. land

3. device
A. apparatus
B. creation
C. molecule
D. nomination

4. habitat
A. behavior
B. custom
C. resource
D. home

5. stealthy
A. mean
B. furtive
C. vulgar
D. brutal

6. survive
A. complete
B. persevere
C. encounter
D. neglect

9. misery
A. sorrow
B. pleasure
C. trouble
D. concern

10. reluctant
A. repeated
B. unwilling
C. roaming
D. ready

11. nutritious
A. rotten
B. corrupt
C. healthy
D. sound

12. govern
A. rule
B. indicate
C. make
D. cover

13. cortex
A. trigger
B. practice
C. material
D. covering

14. neural
A. sensitive
B. sensible
C. sensory
D. senseless

15. oriented
A. cautioned
B. disordered
C. adjusted
D. operated

16. emit
A. release
B. extend
C. catch
D. absorb

17. debris
A. remains
B. illusions
C. grounds
D. packets

18. vent
A. place
B. outlet
C. fence
D. motor

19. repetitive
A. recurring
B. defective
C. sensitive
D. introductory

20. royal
A. massive
B. expensive
C. responsible
D. noble

21. graceful
A. fragile
B. elegant
C. careless
D. smooth

22. indispensable
A. imperative
B. disposable
C. independent
D. unnecessary

23. sophisticated
A. ancient
B. simple
C. refined
D. dangerous

24. stitch
A. sew
B. cook
C. glue
D. spook

25. rescue
A. ignore
B. save
C. release
D. escape

26. variation
A. uniformity
B. similarity
C. source
D. difference

27. porous
A. spongy
B. sheer
C. slender
D. steady

28. tribute
A. offering
B. blame
C. neglect
D. ransom

29. breed
A. project
B. feather
C. number
D. species

30. chink
A. object
B. crack
C. noise
D. window

17A 18B 19A 20D 21B 22A 23C 24A 25B 26D 27A 28A 29D 30B
1D 2D 3A 4D 5B 6B 7D 8C 9A 10B 11C 12A 13D 14C 15C 16A

Exercises

Exercise #1 Read the passage. Then answer the question that follows.

Currently, the average global birthrate is declining slightly. About half of the world's population lives in places where birthrates are below "replacement levels." In other words, fewer than two babies are born per two adults. Now at more than 7 billion, the planet's population could reach a high point of 9 or 10 billion in this generation and then may begin to decline. If the whole globe had an average replacement rate of 1.5 babies for every two adults, the global population could fall to half of what it is today by the year 2300.

A decline in global population will have both positive and negative consequences. A reduction in population will ease environmental problems and global shortages of food, fresh water, and energy. However, a population decline may also lead to a problematic demographic shift: huge economic burdens result when there are fewer young people supporting greater numbers of an aging population.

Directions: *An introductory sentence for a brief summary of the passage is provided below. Complete the summary by selecting the THREE answer choices that express the most important ideas in the passage. Some sentences do not belong in the summary because they express ideas that are not presented or are minor ideas in the passage.* ***This question is worth 2 points.***

> **The global population may begin to decline, with mixed results.**

-
-
-

Answer Choices

1. Average childbearing rate in many countries is fewer than two babies per couple.
2. More than half of the world's population lives in Asian countries.
3. Fresh water will likely be in shorter supply.
4. There may be more resources for everyone.
5. A decline in youthful segments of the population can create economic problems.
6. Seniors have traditionally been supported by people who are able to work.

Exercise #2 Read the passage. Then answer the question that follows.

There are two types of languages: genderless language and gendered language. Each of these most likely has developed from many different cultural aspects of language.

Genderless languages tend to have more gender-neutral words. For example, the Malay language does not have different words for "he" and "she." Also, instead of using words such as "boy" or "girl," Malay more commonly uses neutral words such as "child." When Malay speakers want to be specific about gender, they can add the words "female" or "male," but it is not the norm. Other fairly genderless languages include Finnish, Turkish, Hungarian, Mandarin, and Cantonese.

Gendered languages may divide words into feminine or masculine categories. For example, in Spanish a flower is feminine while a tree is masculine. German, Russian, Swahili, and Arabic are among those languages that are gendered.

Some psychologists study how these differences in language shape human thinking. Some researchers say that when a language is more gendered, people think in a more stereotypical way about women. Others suggest the opposite – that when a language is genderless, people tend to think of everything as masculine, and women become more "invisible."

Directions: *Select the sentences that most appropriately match the descriptions of each type of language. TWO of the answer choices will NOT be used.* **This question is worth 3 points.**

Answer Choices

1. This type of language may use "sibling" more often than "sister" or "brother."
2. More populations may speak this type of language.
3. A reference to a "teacher" could mean either a male or female one.
4. Its grammar may be more difficult to learn.
5. It may require memorizing masculine and feminine categories of words.
6. Listeners to this type of language may assume that most things are masculine.
7. A Hindi speaker knows that a "cup" is masculine, while a "plate" is feminine.

Types of Languages

Genderless languages
-
-
-

Gendered languages
-
-

Exercise #3 Read the passage. Then answer the question that follows.

Reasoning is a process in which people think about information, evaluate it, and make a judgment accordingly. Although it may not always be accurate or true, reasoning combines different pieces of information to draw conclusions that seem to "make sense." For example, in a criminal case a jury has to consider the facts and then use careful reasoning to decide whether the defendant is guilty or not guilty of the crime.

Reasoning can be deductive or inductive. *Deductive reasoning* draws a conclusion based on general statements, as in "If A is true, then B has to be true." For example, a scientist may conclude that if oxygen-dependent humans are able to exist in an environment, then oxygen must be available in that environment. *Inductive reasoning*, on the other hand, uses observations or specific examples to come to conclusions. For example, a person looking outside and seeing puddles may conclude that it has rained, even though there may be other explanations.

Directions: *An introductory sentence for a brief summary of the passage is provided below. Complete the summary by selecting the THREE answer choices that express the most important ideas in the passage. Some sentences do not belong in the summary because they express ideas that are not presented or are minor ideas in the passage.* **This question is worth 2 points.**

> **Reasoning is a process for making decisions or judgments.**

-
-
-

Answer Choices

1. It can help people realize what facts or observations may mean.
2. It is generally relied upon primarily in law and science.
3. It can use either general or specific information to help draw conclusions.
4. It is a useful way to come to a conclusion, but it is not always correct.
5. It is built upon facts proven by research.
6. It is the opposite of creative, imaginary thought processes.

Exercise #4 Read the passage. Then answer the question that follows.

A crane is a machine that lifts and transports heavy objects, usually on construction sites. There are two main types of cranes – the crawler-mounted crane and the tower crane – each with its own special use.

Crawler-mounted cranes are mobile; they can "crawl" around on their own undercarriages over all kinds of surfaces. This crane uses a long arm, or *boom*, and a system of cables, wheels, and blocks to raise and lower a load. Heavy weights on the back of the crane help prevent it from tipping over and increase the weight of the load that can be lifted.

A tower crane is shaped like a "T" and is typically fixed in one place. The vertical section is made up of segments that form a steel framework, or support tower, called a *mast*. An arm called a *jib* forms the horizontal section. One side of the jib holds the load, and the other holds a counterweight. Tower cranes are often built temporarily in elevator shafts of tall buildings under construction. They extend above the top of the building and move heavy objects, tools, and materials between the ground and construction area. As the building grows, tower cranes can also be increased in height. Some tower cranes are fixed to the ground and others are mounted on tracks so they can move.

Directions: *Select the sentences that most appropriately match the descriptions of each type of crane. TWO of the answer choices will NOT be used.* **This question is worth 3 points.**

Answer Choices

1. This can change its height to match the height of the building that it is serving.
2. This is used to build railroads and railroad tracks.
3. This moves over many different surfaces with no trouble.
4. This can be assembled inside buildings that are being constructed.
5. This has problems tipping over because it is too light.
6. This contains "T"-shaped vertical and horizontal sections.
7. This has heavy loads on the back to keep it from falling over.

Types of Cranes

Crawler-mounted crane
●
●

Tower crane
●
●
●

Exercise #5 Read the passage. Then answer the question that follows.

In 1920, the 18th Amendment to the United States Constitution banned the production, transportation, and sale of alcoholic beverages in the U.S. In other words, Americans could drink alcohol, but they were not allowed to make it or sell it. Supporters of the amendment expected that most people would stop drinking alcohol, thereby reducing crime, health problems, and poverty.

However, while alcohol consumption in the U.S. did drop, other problems erupted. Because legitimate alcoholic beverage companies were shut down, organized criminal gangs took over production and sales of alcohol. Violence increased as the gangs fought each other. *Speakeasies*, or nightclubs where people could buy alcoholic drinks illegally, flourished. Political corruption rose as officials were paid to ignore the distribution of alcohol. In 1933, voters ratified the 21st Amendment, which repealed the 18th Amendment – the only time in U.S. history that an amendment has been removed from the Constitution.

Directions: *An introductory sentence for a brief summary of the passage is provided below. Complete the summary by selecting the THREE answer choices that express the most important ideas in the passage. Some sentences do not belong in the summary because they express ideas that are not presented or are minor ideas in the passage.* **This question is worth 2 points.**

> **The 18th Amendment had unintended effects and became unpopular.**

-
-
-

Answer Choices

1. The law did not prevent crime but rather increased it.
2. More public servants became corrupted.
3. American public's alcohol consumption level skyrocketed.
4. Poverty rates decreased.
5. Some crime bosses became infamous.
6. Voters overturned a Constitutional amendment.

Exercise #6 Read the passage. Then answer the question that follows.

Diabetes is a serious disease that prevents the body from converting sugars and starches, or *glucose*, into the energy that the body needs to function. People are most commonly diagnosed with Type 1 or Type 2 diabetes.

Type 1 diabetes, formerly known as juvenile diabetes, commonly strikes a person during childhood and can quickly develop over the course of weeks. This form of diabetes is typically an *autoimmune disease*, as the body's own immune system attacks part of the body. In this case, the immune system destroys the beta cells that produce the hormone insulin. Normally, insulin causes the body to absorb and store glucose from the blood. Without insulin, glucose cannot enter the body's cells, and cells can starve. At the same time that cells can suffer glucose deprivation, glucose can be building up in the bloodstream to toxic or life-threatening levels. People with Type 1 diabetes thus require regular administration of insulin to maintain normal levels of insulin in the body.

Type 2 diabetes is much more widespread. It typically forms in people who are over the age of 30 and often takes years to fully develop. For sufferers of Type 2 diabetes, their beta cells are not destroyed, but their bodies become *insulin-resistant*; they do not respond properly to insulin. Researchers do not know exactly why Type 2 diabetes develops in some people, but risk factors include obesity and lack of exercise. Also, for unknown reasons, Type 2 diabetes is more likely to strike people whose genetic heritage is African, Hispanic, Asian, or Native American.

Directions: *Select the sentences that most appropriately match the descriptions of each type of diabetes. TWO of the answer choices will NOT be used.* **This question is worth 3 points.**

Answer Choices

1. The chances of getting this may be reduced with good habits.
2. This causes excessive production of insulin, which becomes toxic.
3. The body cannot obtain the cells that it needs.
4. People experience a rapid onset of this.
5. People develop this before they reach adulthood.
6. The body's protective system attacks the body's own cells.
7. People with certain ethnic backgrounds may be more susceptible to this.

Types of Diabetes

Type 1 diabetes
-
-
-

Type 2 diabetes
-
-

Exercise #7 Read the passage. Then answer the question that follows.

Swamps, or areas filled with stagnant water and many trees, have played vital roles in American history. For example, when the first English colonists landed in 1607 in what is now Virginia, the surrounding swamps may have been their most significant enemy. Mosquitoes from the swamps spread deadly malaria, and many colonists died of dysentery and typhoid from drinking dirty water.

Despite the risks of disease, the swamps along the east coast of the United States often served as popular hiding places. In the 1700s, the South Carolina swamps were known to shelter pirates. During the Revolutionary War, rebels such as Francis "Swamp Fox" Morton were able to surprise British troops with attacks from the swamps and then vanish back into them. And until the Civil War, escaped slaves sometimes lived in secret communities in swamplands. These days, most of the swamps have been logged and drained, but some sections are protected wilderness areas.

Directions: *An introductory sentence for a brief summary of the passage is provided below. Complete the summary by selecting the THREE answer choices that express the most important ideas in the passage. Some sentences do not belong in the summary because they express ideas that are not presented or are minor ideas in the passage.* **This question is worth 2 points.**

Swamps have affected the history of the United States in several ways.

-
-
-

Answer Choices

1. Swamps were an obstacle for the first English settlers.
2. Swamps have served as important sources of clean drinking water for settlements.
3. Swamps were home to many of the most infamous pirates in America's history.
4. Swamps were used to frustrate the British army during the Revolutionary War.
5. Swamps harbored runaway slaves who lived together in secluded settlements.
6. Swamps have disappeared ever since people discovered their dangerous nature.

Exercise #8 Read the passage. Then answer the question that follows.

Solar power comes from converting sunlight to electricity. Two types of conversion systems are thermal and photovoltaic.

Thermal systems operate by gaining and storing heat from sunlight. The heat is generated by focusing a great deal of reflected light onto a single spot. For example, the system may use a mirrored dish, a tower surrounded by mirrors, or a parabolic trough* to reflect and focus light onto a central tube filled with water, molten salt, or oil. The heated fluid can then be used to create steam to turn turbines, generating electricity.

Photovoltaic, or PV, systems generate electricity directly from light by exposing panels of materials to the Sun. These materials are particular types of silicon semiconductors that can absorb photons of light and release electrons. The electrons are captured to create an electric current. PV system panels can be large and used in a power station, or small enough to be placed in a windowsill to charge a battery. The panels can be placed on the roofs of homes or carports, in livestock pastures, or on spacecraft.

Trough: a receptacle that is long, narrow, and open on top

Directions: *Select the sentences that most appropriately match the descriptions of each system of solar power. TWO of the answer choices will NOT be used.* **This question is worth 3 points.**

Answer Choices

1. This is a system that harnesses the powers of the wind and the Sun.
2. This works by arranging mirrors to reflect light on a single point.
3. This concentrates sunlight onto a container of liquid.
4. This is highly effective because it makes use of synthetic energy.
5. Heat energy is a key component of this.
6. This relies on a type of material that gives off electrons when exposed to light.
7. Flat panels used in this system can create electricity anywhere there is sunlight.

Systems of Solar Power

Thermal
-
-
-

Photovoltaic
-
-

Actual Practice

Our **Actual Practice** section provides 12 academic passages with a variety of associated questions to give students an opportunity to apply skills acquired throughout the first ten chapters before proceeding onto a simulation of a full-length TOEFL iBT Reading Test.

01

The Gaia Hypothesis

A *The Gaia Hypothesis* describes the Earth as an **immensely** interactive system. **B** The hypothesis proposes that while physical features on Earth, such as rocks and water, affect how living things evolve, living things also affect how their physical surroundings evolve. **In fact, living things as a whole sustain the conditions that in turn sustain them.** **C** Supporters of the hypothesis point to evidence that organisms influence many conditions necessary for the continuation of life, including global temperatures and the chemical makeup of the atmosphere and ocean. **D**

Tropical rainforests demonstrate the principle. Rainforest trees absorb rainwater and release some of **it** back into the air as vapor. The process, known as *transpiration*, increases the air's humidity. The increased humidity then adds to the area's cloud cover, which both shades the trees to keep them cool and provides plenty of rain.

In the late 1960s while he was studying the possibility of detecting life on Mars, British scientist James Lovelock started developing the idea that living organisms control conditions. Lovelock proposed that researchers could determine the presence or absence of life on other planets by looking for atmospheric chemicals, such as oxygen and methane, produced by living plants or animals. American microbiologist Lynn Margulis later collaborated with **him** to further expand the theory based on proven concepts, with emphasis on microbial interactions. The theory met with **skepticism** in the science community at first. **However, as the Gaia Hypothesis has become more refined, it has been used in many academic disciplines, including biogeochemistry and climate science.**

1) The word "**immensely**" in Paragraph 1 is closest in meaning to
   (A) importantly
   (B) instantaneously
   (C) extremely
   (D) unimaginably

2) Look at the squares [■] that indicate where the following sentence could be added to Paragraph 1.

   It was named for *Gaia*, the ancient Greek Earth goddess.

   Where would the sentence best fit?
   Circle the square [■] to add the sentence.

3) In Paragraph 1, the author suggests that the Gaia concept
   (A) explains the origin of rocks and water on Earth
   (B) divides the Earth by type of phenomenon
   (C) claims that the environment is one organism with many complicated parts
   (D) states that the present world would be unsustainable without a variety of living organisms

4) Which of the following best paraphrases the highlighted sentence in Paragraph 1?
   (A) Indeed, organisms create and maintain the ecosystems that they need.
   (B) Actually, living creatures need the most interrelated conditions of life.
   (C) Naturally, inorganic matter is part of any life form's ecosystem.
   (D) In other words, habitats are more conceptual than physical.

5) In Paragraph 2, the author explains the Gaia Hypothesis by
   (A) stressing an environmental problem
   (B) describing an environmental process
   (C) arguing for more environmental knowledge
   (D) giving a history of an important environment

6) The word "**it**" in Paragraph 2 refers to
   (A) the principle
   (B) rainwater
   (C) vapor
   (D) humidity

7) Why does the author mention "*transpiration*" in Paragraph 2?
   (A) To show what transpires in the rainforest
   (B) To describe how trees become endangered
   (C) To introduce a concept that supports the hypothesis
   (D) To caution against harming rainforest trees

8) Paragraph 3 states all of the following about the Gaia Hypothesis EXCEPT:
   (A) It was popularized in the 19th century.
   (B) It has been developed mainly by two scientists.
   (C) It was first developed to identify signs of life on Mars.
   (D) It has become more accepted as it is further developed.

9) According to Paragraph 3, Lovelock proposes that the existence of life on other planets could be determined by
   (A) looking for water and rocks on their surfaces
   (B) analyzing the atmospheres for particular gases
   (C) searching for signs of rainforests
   (D) determining the presence or absence of a water cycle

10) The word "**him**" in Paragraph 3 refers to
    (A) James Lovelock
    (B) life on other planets
    (C) a researcher
    (D) Lynn Margulis

11) The word "**skepticism**" in Paragraph 3 means
    (A) belief
    (B) doubt
    (C) conviction
    (D) trust

12) What can be inferred based on the highlighted sentence in Paragraph 3?
    (A) The Gaia Hypothesis needs further proof before it can be applied in scientific communities.
    (B) Many scientists have been working to improve the Gaia Hypothesis.
    (C) Few scientists fully understand the Gaia Hypothesis.
    (D) Biogeochemistry mainly uses the Gaia Hypothesis.

13) **Directions**: An introductory sentence relating to the passage is written below. Complete the exercise by choosing THREE answers that support the sentence. Some sentences do not belong because they do not support the sentence. **This question is worth 2 points.**

The Gaia Hypothesis is that Earth's nonliving matter and living beings affect each other.

   ●
   ●
   ●

Answer Choices
1. Evolution leads to changes only in organisms.
2. Tropical rainforests help maintain their climate.
3. Things that are not living are actually alive.
4. Organisms affect the chemistry of the surrounding sea, land, and air.
5. Even tiny microbial creatures support the conditions that support them.
6. Climate change is occurring faster than predicted.

Stonehenge

Stonehenge is a prehistoric **monument** in South West England. The site includes a circular group of massive stones, many of them broken, standing in a grassy field on the Salisbury Plains. No one knows exactly how or why **it** was constructed. **Archaeological digs have revealed that the site was used as a burial ground at several points in time,** but the area also may have been employed for religious ceremonies, a tribal gathering area, a healing center, or an astrological observatory. Similar, less famous sites exist elsewhere in Great Britain and **Ireland**.

A Archaeologists believe that the Stonehenge site was utilized from around 8000 BCE, based on the remains of wooden posts. **B** Around 3100 BCE, people built a mud bank encircling the Stonehenge site; there may have been a wooden structure inside of it. **C** Then around 2600 BCE, people began erecting stones. **D** **Somehow they transported the enormous stones to the site** and arranged a ring of **4-meter** high stones, topped by horizontal stones nearly a meter thick. Within the ring, builders erected stones nearly **7 meters** high, each weighing as much as two large buses.

The stone builders probably lived in a community about 3 kilometers away. Domestic animal teeth found in the community prove that people came from as far away as the Scottish Highlands to visit the monument. Stonehenge seems to have been used for at least 1,000 years, but it was abandoned by 43 CE when Romans conquered the area and **forbade** local religious practices.

Engineers and astronomers have helped archaeologists theorize about the site's layout. **The monument seems to have been built so that certain stones marked the Sun's rising on the *summer solstice*, or the longest day of summer.** In addition, evidence of avenues to and from the nearby river, other wooden structures a few kilometers away, and huge fire pits may mean that people incorporated the site as part of ritual processions.

While some people certainly must have known about Stonehenge over the 2,000-year period following the Roman invasion, it was not until 1922 that the British government began to restore the monument and promote public attention for it. Today, Stonehenge is one of Britain's major tourist attractions, drawing more than 1 million visitors each year.

---

1) The word "**monument**" in Paragraph 1 is closest in meaning to
   (A) landmark
   (B) house
   (C) monograph
   (D) reminder

2) The word "**it**" in Paragraph 1 refers to
   (A) Stonehenge
   (B) South West England
   (C) grassy field
   (D) circular group

3) What can be inferred from the highlighted phrase in Paragraph 1?
   (A) Local ghost stories refer to graves at the monument.
   (B) The stones and mounds were built in memory of deceased leaders.
   (C) Archaeologists have found human remains in the soil at the site.
   (D) Ancient people left markings on the stones that probably refer to death.

4) Based on Paragraph 1, all of the following have been suggested as ancient uses of Stonehenge EXCEPT
   (A) a place for watching the stars, Moon, and Sun
   (B) a place for spiritual and religious observances
   (C) a place for studying the effects of certain plants
   (D) a place for the sick and injured to seek help

5) The author mentions "**Ireland**" in Paragraph 1 because
   (A) it has a similarly famous astronomy site
   (B) it contains grassy fields and massive stones, though they are less accessible
   (C) it contains sites that share features with Stonehenge
   (D) another Stonehenge is located there in the southwestern part

6) Look at the squares [■] that indicate where the following sentence could be added to Paragraph 2.

   Over the next five millennia, earthen and stone parts of the monument were added in phases.

   Where would the sentence best fit?
   Circle the square [■] to add the sentence.

7) According to Paragraph 2, people started adding big stones to the monument at Stonehenge starting around
    (A) 8000 BCE
    (B) 3100 BCE
    (C) 2600 BCE
    (D) 1922 CE

8) What can be inferred from the highlighted phrase in Paragraph 2?
    (A) People in prehistoric times were bigger and stronger than now.
    (B) The stones at Stonehenge were moved many times.
    (C) It is not known exactly how people transported the stones.
    (D) It is thought that the stones were transported all at once.

9) Paragraph 2 MOST LIKELY mentions "**4-meter**" and "**7 meters**" in order to
    (A) describe something amazing about the monument
    (B) provide details about the stones' importance
    (C) analyze the significance of the stones' different sizes
    (D) support the argument that the site was used for gatherings of many people

10) The word "**forbade**" in Paragraph 3 is closest in meaning to
    (A) obeyed
    (B) forfeited
    (C) permitted
    (D) prohibited

11) Which of the following statements is closest in meaning to the highlighted sentence in Paragraph 4?
    (A) It seems that the monument had something to do with solar eclipses.
    (B) Builders appear to have placed the stones to best emphasize a particular day.
    (C) The positioning of the stones makes the best of hot summer and freezing winter conditions.
    (D) The placement of some stones near the monument lines up with lunar eclipses.

12) According to the passage, which of the following statements is NOT true about Stonehenge?
    (A) Researchers from diverse fields have collaborated to study it.
    (B) Romans demolished the site in 43 CE.
    (C) The public largely ignored it for 2,000 years.
    (D) The British government now considers it culturally significant.

13) **Directions**: Select the sentences that most appropriately match the descriptions of each use for Stonehenge. TWO of the answer choices will NOT be used. **This question is worth 3 points.**

Uses that are certain

  -
  -

Uses that are theorized

  -
  -
  -

Answer Choices

1. Human remains were buried there in different historical periods.
2. Romans ruled the area at the beginning of the first millennium.
3. Certain stones indicate pagan worship practices.
4. Stones seem to line up with the Sun's position at daybreak on the day of the summer solstice.
5. All structures at the site are arranged in concentric circles.
6. People came to the site to heal injuries or illness.
7. The British government manages the site for tourists.

03

Aesthetics

The word *aesthetic* relates to something that is pleasing to the senses or beautiful. Not surprisingly, the branch of philosophy known as *aesthetics* has often been **regarded as** the study of what is beautiful. However, aesthetics has actually developed into a much broader study of art theories.

A Aestheticians study the arts **in general**, comparing them across cultures and times. **B** These scholars attempt to organize information systematically in order to answer the basic questions: What is art? **C** Moreover, how should art be judged and valued? **D**

One example of a debate within the discipline of aesthetics is the art-world phenomenon of Relational Aesthetics, or RA. This movement was first defined in the 1990s by French art curator and critic Nicolas Bourriaud. Writing about RA at that time, Bourriaud maintained that the trend emphasized the viewer's experience of art. Examples might include artists exhibiting works that invited visitors to create art, encounter an **odd situation**, or view human models in poses. Some works of "art" did not seem to be art, such as an exhibit that showed visitors how to illegally connect a television to a network cable or exhibits that invited **them** to taste food that the artist was cooking. **Bourriaud applauded such projects for de-emphasizing the artists and helping viewers connect to the experience. Some critics, however, said that the RA exhibits obviously did not qualify as art.**

Aestheticians often take an *interdisciplinary approach* to answer the many questions that they ask. That is, aestheticians use concepts and research from other **fields**. They may use psychology to understand why an art experience becomes meaningful. They may look to anthropology and sociology to understand how creating art relates to other human endeavors, such as religion. These approaches may shed light on how the idea of "art" varies in relation to people's **physical, social, and cultural environments**.

1) In Paragraph 1, the author introduces the philosophy of modern aesthetics by
   (A) comparing it to another philosophy
   (B) illustrating how it connects to people's lives
   (C) contrasting it with its earlier purpose
   (D) describing aesthetic architects working in the field

2) The term "**regarded as**" in Paragraph 1 means
   (A) compared with
   (B) replaced with
   (C) considered as
   (D) disguised as

3) Why does the author most likely use the term "**in general**" in Paragraph 2?
   (A) To explain that aestheticians examine all of the arts as a concept
   (B) To indicate the unfocused path that the study of aesthetics usually takes
   (C) To prove that the performing arts are as important as visual art
   (D) To argue that aestheticians should try to create art themselves

4) Look at the squares [■] that indicate where the following sentence could be added in Paragraph 2.

   What should art be like?

   Where would the sentence best fit?
   Circle the square [■] to add the sentence.

5) In Paragraph 3, what can be inferred about the Relational Aesthetics phenomenon?
   (A) Mainly art critics and aestheticians participated in it.
   (B) It emphasized viewer participation rather than completed objects.
   (C) It was popular with gallery owners and museum directors.
   (D) Children could appreciate it more than adults.

6) Based on Paragraph 3, one of Bourriaud's jobs is
   (A) to create Relational Aesthetic works of art
   (B) to provide discipline for various academic and art endeavors
   (C) to publish evaluations of art exhibits at museums and galleries
   (D) to explain French art-world movements to the rest of the world

7) What can be inferred about the term "**odd situation**" in Paragraph 3?
(A) Visitors were able to experience something that they had not encountered before.
(B) Many of the art exhibits made visitors feel uncomfortable.
(C) Artists invited visitors to have personalized experiences.
(D) Visitors were given the odd feeling that they were being observed and followed.

8) The word "**them**" in Paragraph 3 refers to
(A) artists
(B) human models
(C) works of "art"
(D) visitors

9) Which of the following best paraphrases the highlighted sentences in Paragraph 3?
(A) Bourriaud said that RA can hold viewers' attention because of the interaction between the artist and the viewers.
(B) According to Bourriaud, the unconventional art projects, such as cooking, attracted viewers because of their distinguishing features.
(C) Some art critics loved the phenomenon of RA, while others said that it was crazy because it was too innovative.
(D) While Bourriaud praised RA for its unique characteristics, some critics said that it should not be viewed as art at all.

10) The word "**fields**" in Paragraph 4 probably means
(A) movements
(B) disciplines
(C) faculties
(D) resources

11) According to Paragraph 4, aestheticians may carry out all of the following EXCEPT
(A) discuss how religious themes are reflected in art
(B) write about art trends and their impact on viewers
(C) set prices for works of art that are for sale
(D) consult with an anthropologist

12) Why is the phrase "**physical, social, and cultural environments**" mentioned in Paragraph 4?
(A) To illustrate methods for pursuing art studies
(B) To describe the past environment for art criticism
(C) To explain why people may have different concepts of what "art" is
(D) To discuss how modern aestheticians plan art exhibits

13) **Directions**: An introductory sentence relating to the passage is written below. Complete the exercise by choosing THREE answers that support the sentence. Some sentences do not belong because they do not support the sentence. **This question is worth 2 points.**

Aestheticians study the arts to serve many purposes.

-
-
-

Answer Choices
1. They aim to articulate what qualifies a piece of work as "art."
2. They want to persuade readers to reject certain art exhibits.
3. They aim to help viewers understand and evaluate art.
4. They want to explore the role of art in different societies.
5. They believe that they can decide what is "beautiful."
6. They mainly critique artists who create sensory experiences.

04

Hoover Dam

Time
00:20:00

Actual Practice

Hoover Dam is the second highest dam in the United States. The structure holds back the Colorado River in the Black Canyon, which is on the border between Arizona and Nevada, southeast of Las Vegas. The dam provides flood control, a steady water supply, electric power, and a lake for recreational use.

A Hoover Dam is an element of the Boulder Canyon Project, which includes a hydroelectric power plant. When the facility was being planned and built in the 1920s and 1930s, the monumental project was of a size that had never before been undertaken. **B** Engineers had not yet tackled the problems inherent in designing a dam of such **imposing** height and thickness, with such immense power units and welded pipes. **C** In the end, **they** were successful. The dam stands 221 meters high and is 379 meters long. **D**

Once the project was planned and approved, actual construction took only four years, ending in 1935. By the next year, the dam's generators began producing electricity. Although costs were considered expensive at the time of construction, the facility now provides economic benefits by preventing floods, and by providing water for 20 million people in the Southwest and for about 1 million square kilometers of farmland. The project's power plant is also one of the world's largest producers of electricity.

Starting in the late 1800s, settlers of the southwestern U.S. recognized that the area could support a larger population if there were some kind of water project. At the time, **farms and towns were springing up** in Southern California and elsewhere in the Southwest. **Engineers had diverted the Colorado River into canals to deliver water, but the river's unpredictability sprang from its natural cycle of flooding and drying out.**

By 1922, government officials including Herbert Hoover were planning the dam. Hoover later became the U.S. president, and the unfinished dam was named after him. But shortly thereafter, many Americans blamed Hoover for the economic woes of the **Great Depression** and therefore did not want the dam to be named in his honor. The next presidential administration called the structure the "Boulder Dam." However, in 1947 Congress made the name "Hoover Dam" official.

1) According to Paragraph 1, Hoover Dam fulfills all of the following purposes EXCEPT:
(A) It protects downstream areas from floods.
(B) It creates a lake for boating and swimming.
(C) It generates electricity.
(D) It protects canyon habitats.

2) Why is Las Vegas mentioned in Paragraph 1?
(A) It is where Hoover Dam is located.
(B) It is a location that readers may know.
(C) It receives the benefits of Hoover Dam.
(D) It developed in conjunction with the dam.

3) The word "**imposing**" in Paragraph 2 is closest in meaning to
(A) impressive
(B) frightening
(C) modest
(D) perfect

4) The word "**they**" in Paragraph 2 refers to
(A) engineers
(B) problems
(C) power units
(D) welded pipes

5) Look at the squares [■] that indicate where the following sentence could be added in Paragraph 2.

It is so thick that it contains enough concrete to build a road from one coast of the U.S. to the other.

Where would the sentence best fit?
Circle the square [■] to add the sentence.

6) Based on Paragraph 3, all of the following are true of Hoover Dam's construction EXCEPT:
   (A) It was constructed relatively speedily.
   (B) Millions of people rely on it for power and drinking water.
   (C) The project finished within its budget.
   (D) It provides water for agriculture in the Southwest.

7) Why does the author mention "**farms and towns were springing up**" in Paragraph 4?
   (A) To describe the enthusiastic nature of the people of the Southwest
   (B) To explain a motivation for building Hoover Dam
   (C) To emphasize the importance of population growth
   (D) To point out the urban goals of the Boulder Canyon Project

8) Which of the following best paraphrases the highlighted sentence in Paragraph 4?
   (A) Seasonal variances in water flow hindered the redistribution of the Colorado River.
   (B) The Colorado River, which comes from melting snow, floods and then trickles.
   (C) In order to tap the Colorado River, designers created a canal system.
   (D) The Colorado River is a mighty force now that its cycles are controlled.

9) What can be inferred about the Southwest from Paragraph 4?
   (A) It is the first region to use canals.
   (B) It has few water sources of its own.
   (C) It tends to have very hot weather.
   (D) It is a region that specializes in dams.

10) Why does the author mention the "**Great Depression**" in Paragraph 4?
    (A) To identify the difficult context in which the dam was built
    (B) To explain why Herbert Hoover wanted his name on the dam
    (C) To account for the initial public disdain for naming the dam after Hoover
    (D) To give an example of controversies about building the dam

11) According to Paragraph 5, who settled the question about the name of the dam?
    (A) Las Vegas residents
    (B) the president
    (C) the administration
    (D) a legislative body

12) What can be inferred about Herbert Hoover from Paragraph 5?
    (A) He did not care about the opinions of others.
    (B) People viewed him differently as time passed.
    (C) He created many successful economic policies.
    (D) People thought that he was honorable.

13) **Directions**: An introductory sentence relating to the passage is written below. Complete the exercise by choosing THREE answers that support the sentence. Some sentences do not belong because they do not support the sentence. **This question is worth 2 points.**

    The construction of Hoover Dam had several beneficial consequences.

    -
    -
    -

    Answer Choices
    1. It proved that dams of its size could be successfully engineered.
    2. It separated water into a host of canals for transportation.
    3. It played an important role in the Great Depression.
    4. It memorializes a president who was highly popular with the public.
    5. It made it possible to support population growth in a vast area.
    6. It prevents flooding in downstream communities.

The Exchange Rate

Consider two people meeting in a market, one selling bread and the other selling butter. If they both want buttered bread, the two people will have to negotiate how much a stick of butter is worth in terms of loaves of bread and vice versa. **In other words, they will have to settle on a *rate of exchange.***

The same principle is true when applied to money, or *currency*. When countries trade across borders, the market determines the ever-changing, or *floating*, value of each country's currency so that businesses know how to exchange it on any given day. For example, an American company that wants to import **coffee beans** from Guatemala will have to pay in the Guatemalan currency, the *quetzal* (Q). If Guatemalan coffee growers are selling beans for Q16 per pound, and on the morning of the purchase Q8 are worth $1, then the American company will have to pay $2 per pound. If many global companies make the same purchase on the same day, demand for the quetzal may drive up **its** value so that only Q7 can be purchased per dollar by afternoon. At that time, the American company will have to pay $2.29 per pound, even though the farmers have not changed the price. Thus, the American company will have to spend more dollars to purchase the same quantity of coffee beans.

In the 1970s, countries started letting their currencies float. **A** Before that time, countries agreed upon **fixed** exchange rates based on precious metals, or a *gold standard*. **B** Between 1946 and 1971, for example, the United States Treasury agreed to **redeem** approximately 4/5 of a gram of gold for each dollar. **C** Each country's currency had its own "worth in gold," and actual gold did not have to be exchanged. **D**

Although currency values float, governments sometimes **intervene** these days in order to keep their economies more stable. One way they do this is by buying and selling huge amounts of their own currencies, affecting the supply and demand for them.

1) In Paragraph 1, the author explains *rate of exchange* by
   (A) using a simplified example
   (B) describing its historical origins
   (C) contrasting it with local markets
   (D) pointing out its importance in daily life

2) Which sentence best paraphrases the highlighted sentence in Paragraph 1?
   (A) In summary, people who want to exchange goods will have to know the prices.
   (B) That is, the two will have to bargain until they agree upon the value of one item versus another.
   (C) In fact, the rate at which the two will have to come to an agreement will vary.
   (D) In another sense, the negotiators will be preparing for future exchanges.

3) In Paragraph 2, the author mentions "**coffee beans**" in order to
   (A) illustrate an important aspect of the trade between Central America and the U.S.
   (B) explain the significance of a product to the farmers who grow it
   (C) give an example of a commodity that is traded globally
   (D) persuade the reader of the importance of the quetzal in import-export figures

4) The word "**its**" in Paragraph 2 refers to
   (A) dollar
   (B) purchase
   (C) company
   (D) quetzal

5) Which of the following can be inferred from Paragraph 2?
   (A) The global coffee bean supply is dominated by one country.
   (B) All coffee bean trades are made using the quetzal.
   (C) Exchange rates are made public throughout the day.
   (D) Exchange rates tend to rise rather than fall.

6) Based on Paragraph 2, all of the following are true about global exchange EXCEPT:
(A) Producers usually receive payments in the currency of their own country.
(B) Buyers must exchange their own currency for the seller's currency.
(C) Buying a country's products makes the country's currency rise in value.
(D) Country's governments decide on the currency's exchange rate.

7) The word "**fixed**" in Paragraph 3 means
(A) repaired
(B) set
(C) flexible
(D) valuable

8) The word "**redeem**" in Paragraph 3 is closest in meaning to
(A) generate
(B) remove
(C) compensate
(D) forfeit

9) Look at the squares [■] that indicate where the following sentence could be added to Paragraph 3.

Each participating country agreed to consistently convert its currency to a rigidly fixed amount of gold or silver.

Where would the sentence best fit?
Circle the square [■] to add the sentence.

10) Based on Paragraph 3, why did the gold standard PROBABLY end?
(A) People were not trading enough.
(B) Too many people were finding their own gold by mining it.
(C) There was not enough gold.
(D) Governments wanted more economic flexibility.

11) The word "**intervene**" in Paragraph 4 is closest in meaning to
(A) step in
(B) call out
(C) reach out
(D) stand up

12) In Paragraph 4, what can be inferred about floating exchange rates?
(A) They do not need any management.
(B) They are unpopular in some countries.
(C) They do not depend on world demand.
(D) They may cause internal economic instability.

13) **Directions**: Select the sentences that most appropriately match the descriptions of each method of currency exchange. TWO of the answer choices will not be used. **This question is worth 3 points.**

Gold standard
•
•

Floating exchange rate
•
•
•

Answer Choices
1. It was based on values decided by different countries.
2. It uses more coins than paper money.
3. It requires governments to make promises about gold for money.
4. It changes on a daily basis.
5. It relies on supply and demand in the global marketplace.
6. It is used mostly for agricultural goods.
7. It is used by governments to buy or sell their own money.

Supernovas

Astronomers consider a supernova to be one of the most violent occurrences in the known universe. *Nova* means "new" in Latin, and a supernova appears to viewers on Earth to be a super-sized new star blazing into life. However, a *supernova* is actually a very old star dying by exploding, creating **fantastic** amounts of light until **it** fades a few months or years later. At its peak, a supernova might outshine its whole galaxy.

Supernovas occur in every galaxy. They create such a bright light that astronomers can detect some that are **10 billion light years** away. Studying supernovas allows research into how the universe has altered and is in the process of changing because supernovas **expel** elements that form new stars and planets.

There are different ways that supernovas develop. A Type 1 supernova starts with a *white dwarf*, or a star that has stopped burning and has shed its outer material. What is left is dense and hot, but the star normally cools off completely. However, the white dwarf's **gravity** is so strong that if the star comes near another star, the white dwarf can attract matter – usually hydrogen gas – from the other star. The extra "load" of matter creates pressure, and **the pressure in turn creates extremely hot temperatures that can lead to the atomic fusion of elements. The fusion then creates an explosion of released energy, as in a thermonuclear bomb.**

Type 2 supernovas occur when an especially massive star runs out of fuel. The energy that was resisting the pull of gravity decreases, so the star begins to **collapse** into its own center. The collapse raises the pressure and temperature at the center, causing iron atoms to begin fusing together, absorbing more energy. **A** The gravitational pressure builds, causing the star to explode, which may leave behind a small, dense neutron star or a white dwarf star. **B** If the original Type 2 star is at least five times as large as the Sun, it collapses into itself and becomes a *black hole* while the outside of the star explodes. **C** A black hole has such strong gravitational pull that even light cannot escape it. **D**

1) Paragraph 1 introduces a supernova by
   (A) describing its chemical processes
   (B) providing an example of one
   (C) persuading the reader to accept a theory about it
   (D) explaining why it was misnamed

2) The word "**fantastic**" in Paragraph 1 is closest in meaning to
   (A) moderate
   (B) unbelievable
   (C) imaginary
   (D) predictable

3) The word "**it**" in Paragraph 1 refers to
   (A) Earth
   (B) new star
   (C) supernova
   (D) peak

4) Why is the term "**10 billion light years**" mentioned in Paragraph 2?
   (A) To explain how powerful and how far away some observable supernovas are
   (B) To criticize astronomers for researching events that took place so long ago
   (C) To illustrate an important measurement in astronomy
   (D) To identify the farthest point in the universe that human researchers can observe

5) The word "**expel**" in Paragraph 2 is closest in meaning to
   (A) take in
   (B) burn off
   (C) force out
   (D) open up

6) What can be inferred from Paragraph 2?
(A) Astronomers know the history of the universe.
(B) Without supernovas, fewer stars and planets would form.
(C) Elements from supernovas burn up harmlessly.
(D) New suns and planets are more numerous than old ones.

7) According to Paragraph 3, a white dwarf star is
(A) a star with light that tends to be white
(B) a tiny, nuclear-fueled star
(C) the outer material of an old star
(D) the hot core of a cooling star

8) Paragraph 3 most likely mentions "**gravity**" to
(A) point out the force that attracts matter inward
(B) illustrate the behavior of hydrogen gas in space
(C) explain the process for supernovas
(D) emphasize the effect of heat and density

9) Which of the following best paraphrases the highlighted section in Paragraph 3?
(A) Pressure leads to heat and joining of atoms, which releases enormous energy.
(B) The star is so hot that it burns the hydrogen that it acquired from another star.
(C) Nuclear fuels creates a bomb-like effect on the surface of the star.
(D) Pressurized gas atoms explode because the star cannot become denser.

10) The word "**collapse**" in Paragraph 4 is closest in meaning to
(A) lean
(B) fall
(C) collect
(D) filter

11) According to Paragraph 4, all of the following are true about a star undergoing a Type 2 supernova EXCEPT:
(A) It is incredibly massive.
(B) It has used up its fuel.
(C) It bursts outward.
(D) Its iron atoms are split apart.

12) Look at the squares [■] that indicate where the following sentence could be added to Paragraph 4.

However, in some supernova explosions, matter disperses in space and no object of any kind remains behind.

Where would the sentence best fit?
Circle the square [■] to add the sentence.

13) **Directions**: Select the sentences that most appropriately match the descriptions of each type of supernova that a star undergoes. TWO of the answer choices will NOT be used. **This question is worth 3 points.**

A star undergoing a Type 1 supernova
●
●

A star undergoing a Type 2 supernova
●
●
●

Answer Choices
1. It can no longer resist its own gravity.
2. It constantly burns its outer material.
3. It attracts matter from another star.
4. It has extra pressure from hydrogen gas that leads to nuclear fusion.
5. It can expel elements that form new supernovas.
6. It may be so big that its gravity creates a black hole instead.
7. It sometimes becomes a white dwarf star.

The Short Story

Time
00:20:00

Short story authors have limited space to make an impression. As a result, they may start the story in the middle of some action rather than at the beginning and may attempt to surprise the reader by the end. There may be just one incident that takes place in one setting involving only a few characters over a short period of time. A famous short story **apocryphally* attributed to Ernest Hemingway** consists of just six words: *For sale: baby shoes, never worn.*

It is likely that people in prehistoric cultures told short stories in the forms of myths, fables, and folk tales. Perhaps the earliest story to be written down was *The Epic of Gilgamesh*, a Sumerian tale recorded on 12 clay tablets around 2500 BCE. Long epic tales, such as the ancient Greek *Odyssey*, may have been told first as short stories connected to an overall **narrative** because the saga* was too long to relate in one sitting. Once Europeans began publishing texts, novels or poems tended to be more popular than short stories. Thus, to appeal to a greater number of readers, some writers framed short stories in a larger story. For example, around 1350 CE, Italian author Giovanni Boccaccio wrote the *Decameron*. In it, 10 young people go to an abandoned country house to take refuge from the Black Death plague and make a plan to amuse each other with stories for 10 **consecutive** nights. This premise results in 100 tales.

A Market demand for modern short stories developed in the early 19th century with the popularity of published *gift books*. **B** These were meant to serve as holiday gifts, and **they** featured elaborate decorations, short fiction, essays, and poetry. **C** In 1837, novelist Nathaniel Hawthorne pioneered a new literary trend by gathering several stories that he had first published in gift books and published them together as *Twice-Told Tales*. **D**

When magazines began flourishing in the late 19th and early 20th centuries, modern short fiction found a perfect vehicle. In the United States, many famous writers, including Willa Cather, O. Henry, Edgar Allan Poe, and Mark Twain, published stories in magazines. Today, magazines still play an important role in short-story publishing.

*Apocryphally: well known but probably not true; of doubtful authenticity
*Saga: a long story, usually about a hero's adventures and achievements

1) Why does the author probably use the phrase **"apocryphally attributed to Ernest Hemingway"** in Paragraph 1?
   (A) To persuade the reader that the story is valuable because it is written by a great writer
   (B) To indicate that the story is widely said to have been written by him
   (C) To point out an important characteristic of Ernest Hemingway
   (D) To criticize the public for making assumptions without evidence

2) Based on Paragraph 1, short stories might feature all of these EXCEPT
   (A) few characters
   (B) limited settings
   (C) surprise endings
   (D) complex plots

3) In Paragraph 2, why does the author include the highlighted sentence?
   (A) To describe how people spent their time before they could read literature
   (B) To argue that the modern short story is just like ancient stories
   (C) To trace the origin of the modern short story
   (D) To identify the uses of myth and tradition in prehistory

4) According to Paragraph 2, the first written story may have been recorded
   (A) on sheets of papyrus
   (B) on bronze plates
   (C) on earthen panels
   (D) on stone walls

5) The word "**narrative**" in Paragraph 2 is closest in meaning to
(A) story
(B) character
(C) background
(D) conflict

6) In Paragraph 2, which of the following is true about *Decameron*?
(A) It focuses on the noble class.
(B) It is filled with entertaining tales.
(C) Its medieval stories are religious in nature.
(D) It is mainly about the Black Death.

7) The word "**consecutive**" in Paragraph 2 is closest in meaning to
(A) successful
(B) considerate
(C) successive
(D) contemporary

8) The word "**they**" in Paragraph 3 refers to
(A) modern short stories
(B) gift books
(C) decorations
(D) essays

9) Look at the squares [■] that indicate where the following sentence could be added to Paragraph 3.

Many well-known novelists turned to writing short stories for gift books.

Where would the sentence best fit?
Circle the square [■] to add the sentence.

10) From Paragraph 3, what can be inferred about Nathaniel Hawthorne's collection of *Twice-Told Tales*?
(A) It inspired other authors to publish short story collections.
(B) The stories that make it up had been told exactly twice.
(C) It was one of the last short story collections to be published.
(D) Its publishing marked the high point of the American gift book market.

11) Which of the following best paraphrases the highlighted sentence in Paragraph 4?
(A) The 19th and 20th centuries saw the rise of universal literacy and mass media.
(B) For around 150 years, magazines succeeded after they started publishing short fiction.
(C) The magazine publishers who began giving automobiles to their fiction writers became successful.
(D) The short story was especially suited to magazines, which started to boom in the late 1800s.

12) Based on Paragraph 4, which of the following is PROBABLY NOT true about magazines?
(A) They first became numerous in the late 1800s and early 1900s.
(B) They primarily consisted of nonfictional stories.
(C) They were popularized by prominent scribes.
(D) They created market demand for short stories.

13) **Directions**: An introductory sentence relating to the passage is written below. Complete the exercise by choosing THREE answers that support the sentence. Some sentences do not belong because they do not support the sentence. **This question is worth 2 points.**

Modern short stories were molded by both tradition and trends in publishing.

-
-
-

Answer Choices
1. Sumerian and Greek epics did not share characteristics of short stories.
2. Ancient tales were broken into segments to make storytelling easier.
3. Novels and poems were always popular in European history.
4. To reach more readers, a few medieval authors packaged short stories as episodes of a larger plot.
5. The popularity of magazines created demand for short fiction.
6. In a magazine, Ernest Hemingway published the shortest story on record.

Harvey Firestone

Harvey Samuel Firestone was one of the earliest **promoters** of America's "car culture." He had good reason to promote driving, as he was the **founder** and president of the Firestone Tire & Rubber Company, one of the leading tire manufacturers to this day.

Firestone was descended from French immigrants who had changed their name, *Feuerstein*, to Firestone. Born in Ohio in 1868, Firestone earned a high-school diploma and began working as a salesman for a "buggy," or carriage, company. **As a salesman, he became interested in gaining an advantage over his competition by improving carriage wheels for a smoother ride.** Firestone began experimenting with attaching rubber to metal carriage wheels. His experiments were a success, and he patented the process to manufacture his tires.

By 1900, Firestone had founded his own rubber-wheel sales company in Akron, Ohio, where rival Goodyear Tire & Rubber Company was also located. Within a few years, the Firestone Company began production of its own rubber tires for carriages. They were air-filled tires, which provided an even smoother ride than solid rubber tires.

In 1906, Firestone contacted his **acquaintance**, Henry Ford, about supplying tires for Ford's automobiles. Ford ordered 2,000 sets, an enormous number at the time. For many years, Firestone furnished half of the tires that Ford Motors used after it began mass-producing cars. Firestone and Ford became close friends and **collaborators** with each other and with **inventor Thomas Edison**.

A When the first Indianapolis 500 car race was held in 1911, the winner drove on Firestone tires, beginning a long association between Harvey Firestone and auto racing. **B** Firestone also became involved in America's Good Roads Movement, which advocated for the expansion of interstate highways and paved roads in rural areas. **C** His "Ship by Truck" campaign was aimed at the American business community. **It** urged delivering merchandise by truck rather than train or ship. **D**

1) The word "**promoters**" in Paragraph 1 is closest in meaning to
   (A) inventors
   (B) critics
   (C) advocates
   (D) programmers

2) The word "**founder**" in Paragraph 1 is closest in meaning to
   (A) creator
   (B) associate
   (C) genius
   (D) investor

3) What can be inferred about Harvey Firestone from Paragraph 1?
   (A) He faced many challenges as he worked to build his own company.
   (B) He was the only American tire-maker in the 1900s.
   (C) He promoted car culture to sell more tires.
   (D) He foresaw all the consequences of promoting car culture.

4) Why does the author PROBABLY mention "*Feuerstein*" in Paragraph 2?
   (A) To explain the background of an unusual name
   (B) To point out the difference between the Firestone and other tire companies
   (C) To criticize the Firestone family for rejecting its heritage
   (D) To describe an important influence on the tire company

5) According to Paragraph 2, how did Harvey Firestone get started in business?
   (A) He worked in his immigrant family's carriage business.
   (B) He worked as a carriage retailer.
   (C) He worked in a patent office.
   (D) He worked on an assembly line in Ohio.

6) Which of the following best paraphrases the
   highlighted sentence in Paragraph 2?
   (A) Selling buggies all day forced him to look more
       closely at their wheels.
   (B) He experimented with rubber materials for cars,
       starting with his first job.
   (C) He asked himself if there was a way to invent
       a more comfortable ride.
   (D) While selling carriages, he tried improving them
       so that he could sell more.

7) According to Paragraph 3, all of the following are true
   about the Firestone Company EXCEPT:
   (A) It was founded at the turn of the 20th century.
   (B) It was located in the same town as its main
       competitor at the time.
   (C) It started making its own tires immediately.
   (D) It manufactured air-filled tires rather than solid
       rubber tires.

8) The author uses the word "**acquaintance**" in
   Paragraph 4 in order to explain that
   (A) Firestone introduced himself to Ford by letter
   (B) the two men had met before at least once
   (C) the two men were close friends
   (D) Ford was already familiar with Firestone's
       product

9) The word "**collaborators**" in Paragraph 4 is closest in
   meaning to
   (A) managers
   (B) partners
   (C) manufacturers
   (D) specialists

10) What can be inferred about Firestone and Ford
    from the mention of "**inventor Thomas Edison**" in
    Paragraph 3?
    (A) They had a wide circle of good friends.
    (B) They helped Edison become famous and
        successful.
    (C) They shared Edison's interest in technical
        innovations.
    (D) They depended on Edison as their inventor.

11) Look at the squares [■] that indicate where the
    following sentence could be added to Paragraph 5.

    **Firestone understood the importance of the
    growing enthusiasm for driving.**

    Where would the sentence best fit?
    Circle the square [■] to add the sentence.

12) The word "**It**" in Paragraph 5 refers to
    (A) Good Roads Movement
    (B) "Ship by Truck" campaign
    (C) American business community
    (D) merchandise

13) **Directions**: An introductory sentence relating to the
    passage is written below. Complete the exercise by
    choosing THREE answers that support the sentence.
    Some sentences do not belong because they do not
    support the sentence. **This question is worth 2
    points.**

    **Harvey S. Firestone recognized profitable business
    opportunities.**

    ●

    ●

    ●

    Answer Choices
    1. He saw that carriages were too high-priced for the
       rural population.
    2. He thought that there might be an advantage to using
       air in rubber tires.
    3. He watched everything that the Goodyear company
       did and copied it.
    4. He provided parts for the first mass-produced
       automobiles.
    5. He realized that encouraging driving would increase
       demand for tires.
    6. He dedicated himself to winning at professional car
       racing.

Polystyrene

Polystyrene is a type of plastic made from petrochemicals. It makes up many of the hard plastic everyday objects that people use. **Although polystyrene creates environmental hazards, it is popular with manufacturers because it is tough, inexpensive, and easy to mold.** The plastic is used to make the outer casings of many appliances and computers as well as plastic drink cups, tableware, and toys, among other items. Polystyrene also can be made into insulating foam with the **brand name** *Styrofoam*, produced by the Dow Chemical company.

Polystyrene's molecular structure is a simple chain of repeating units of styrene, each consisting of eight carbon atoms and eight hydrogen atoms. **A** In 1839, German apothecary Eduard Simon discovered polystyrene by accidentally isolating it from a tree's resin, but he did not foresee its industrial uses. **B** Organic chemist Hermann Staudinger theorized in 1922 that liquid polystyrene's flexibility is due to **its** long chains of atoms. **C** Thus, the chains of atoms make the material moldable, but the strong atomic bonds within the chains also make the matter more durable than people may want. **D** Discarded polystyrene products make up much of the **litter** of the world, creating special hazards in oceans and rivers.

There are different ways to mold hard polystyrene products. *Injection molding* forces melted polystyrene into a **mold**; *vacuum molding* draws it in. Within the mold, the plastic cools and dries in the desired shape. *Blow molding* creates **a hollow interior** in an object by blasting air into a mold with the melted polystyrene, forcing the liquid plastic out to the edges of the mold.

Plastic foam is made in two ways. With *expanded* polystyrene, manufacturers mix the heated liquid polystyrene with a compound that will decompose and release gas bubbles into the mixture. The bubbles expand the plastic, leaving air-filled pockets as it hardens. Manufacturers also use a process called *extrusion*, in which they apply pressure to trap nonreactive gas bubbles in liquid polystyrene, and then let the mixture harden. Extrusion uses gases that contribute to global warming.

1) Which of the following best paraphrases the highlighted sentence in Paragraph 1?
   (A) Although environmental regulations should apply, businesses use polystyrene.
   (B) Polystyrene can easily be shaped into hard products, and it does not cost much.
   (C) Polystyrene is used despite its danger to the Earth because it is strong and cheap.
   (D) Big corporations favor polystyrene, while nature groups call it "dangerous."

2) According to Paragraph 1, which of the following statements about polystyrene is NOT true?
   (A) It is synthesized from petrochemicals.
   (B) It can be shaped into plastic forks or cups.
   (C) It can be made into packaging foam.
   (D) It is used in soft products such as plastic bags.

3) Why does the author PROBABLY mention "**brand name**" in Paragraph 1?
   (A) To identify polystyrene by a more familiar name
   (B) To categorize foamed polystyrene
   (C) To criticize Dow Chemical for making polystyrene foam
   (D) To explain how to find the best quality polystyrene

4) Based on the highlighted sentence in Paragraph 2,
   (A) Polystyrene monomer = 16 carbon-hydrogen polymers
   (B) Styrene = 8 carbon atoms + 8 hydrogen atoms
   (C) Carbon atoms + hydrogen atoms = 16 molecules
   (D) Polystyrene = chain-like molecule + carbon-hydrogen atoms

5) According to Paragraph 2, the first polystyrene was
(A) discovered after a purposeful search
(B) found in the thick liquid of a tree
(C) used in products right away
(D) thought to be rubber

6) The word "**its**" in Paragraph 2 refers to
(A) a tree
(B) chemist
(C) flexibility
(D) polystyrene

7) Look at the squares [■] that indicate where the following sentence could be added to Paragraph 2.

When heated, the chains are able to slide past each other, yet do not break apart themselves.

Where would the sentence best fit?
Circle the square [■] to add the sentence.

8) Which of the following can be inferred about polystyrene's molecules from Paragraph 2?
(A) They form a complicated material due to their atomic arrangement.
(B) Their long chain structures allow them to break down more easily.
(C) Their structure cannot be shaped easily.
(D) Their structure makes polystyrene both useful and problematic.

9) What can be inferred about polystyrene and "**litter**" in Paragraph 2?
(A) People throw out polystyrene products because they are impractical.
(B) People do not recycle polystyrene because doing so is a waste of time.
(C) Polystyrene breaks down on land but not in water.
(D) Polystyrene trash threatens the Earth's ocean species.

10) The word "**mold**" in Paragraph 3 means
(A) frame
(B) product
(C) foam
(D) cup

11) The phrase "**a hollow interior**" in Paragraph 3 is closest in meaning to
(A) an artificial shape
(B) a decorative touch
(C) a round opening
(D) an empty space

12) Based on Paragraph 4, all of the following are used to form polystyrene products EXCEPT
(A) flexibility
(B) gas bubbles
(C) pressure
(D) heat

13) **Directions**: Select the sentences that most appropriately match the descriptions of each plastic-molding method. TWO of the answer choices will NOT be used. **This question is worth 3 points.**

Hard plastic molding
-
-

Plastic foam molding
-
-
-

Answer Choices
1. It uses the breakdown of a compound to produce beads of air within the liquid plastic.
2. It sometimes makes use of atmosphere-harming gases as blowing agents.
3. It sometimes uses suction to pull liquid plastic into a mold.
4. It takes advantage of polystyrene's chain-like molecular structure.
5. It relies on freezing to harden materials into plastic solids.
6. It sometimes uses a blast of air to hollow out a product.
7. It forces a gas into liquid plastic as a way to trap bubbles.

Stoic Philosophy

Actual Practice

When people say that someone is *being stoic*, they often mean that someone is **suffering quietly** by suppressing emotions. However, this is not a completely accurate representation of the ancient Greek and Roman philosophy known as Stoicism.

The use of Stoicism as a guiding philosophy to life was first taught in Athens, Greece, around 300 BCE. It was popular for centuries, as was its main opposing philosophy, Epicureanism. Stoicism died out after 529 CE when the Roman emperor Justinian I suppressed all Greek philosophy in favor of Christianity.

Stoics taught that everything in the universe is **divine**. This divine essence is divided into two parts: natural matter and logos. *Logos* is a divine force that acts upon *natural matter*, which would otherwise remain inactive. In other words, if logos is the bowling ball, then natural matter is the pins. Because of logos, Stoics believed that people control very little beyond their own attitudes. Individuals are virtuous if **they** humbly accept reality as it is instead of reacting when reality is not as they would like it to be.

A Stoics believed that any person could become wise, good to others, and free of destructive emotions. Furthermore, they believed that a person could judge what was true about the natural order and then accept it in a selfless way. **B** Stoic philosopher Epictetus wrote, "Man is disturbed not by things, but by the views he takes of them." **C** This idea resembles ideas used in the current therapy called *cognitive-behavioral therapy*, which explores and revises irrational beliefs and expectations that may lead to fear, anxiety, and anger. **D**

One debate among modern scholars about the Stoics is whether they accepted slavery as part of the "natural order." This would conflict with their belief that **all people come from the same universal spirit and matter, in spite of apparent differences**. The Stoics said that slaves can be free in their minds. They also said that masters should be merciful to slaves. But apparently none of **them** spoke about abolishing slavery.

1) The author PROBABLY mentions "**suffering quietly**" in Paragraph 1 in order to
   (A) introduce the topics of thinking and feelings
   (B) point out the relationship between Stoicism and the people of today
   (C) persuade the reader that the term "stoic" has a positive meaning in English today
   (D) explain a common misperception about what Stoic philosophy is

2) What can be inferred about Emperor Justinian I from Paragraph 2?
   (A) He was an open-minded, accepting ruler.
   (B) He preferred Epicurean philosophy to Stoicism.
   (C) He thought that the Stoic teachings conflicted with Christian beliefs.
   (D) He was practical and did not want to have schools teaching philosophy.

3) The word "**divine**" in Paragraph 3 is closest in meaning to
   (A) godlike
   (B) dramatic
   (C) simple
   (D) special

4) According to Paragraph 3, Stoics believed that natural matter is
   (A) the entirety of the divine
   (B) a gift of the divine
   (C) meaningless to the divine
   (D) the passive part of the divine

5) The word "**they**" in Paragraph 3 refers to
   (A) natural matter and logos
   (B) Stoics
   (C) attitudes
   (D) Individuals

6) Look at the squares [■] that indicate where the following sentence could be added to Paragraph 4.

He did not want people to cover up their feelings but rather to *think* differently and *feel* differently as a result.

Where would the sentence best fit?
Circle the square [■] to add the sentence.

7) Why does the author mention "***cognitive-behavioral therapy***" in Paragraph 4?
(A) To explain how Stoicism can be misperceived by modern scholars
(B) To persuade the reader that the Stoics were correct about thoughts and emotions
(C) To describe a way that Stoic philosophy has influenced today's society
(D) To inform the reader about a current development in the field of psychology

8) Based on Paragraph 4, Stoics would PROBABLY agree with which of the following proverbs?
(A) "If life gives lemons, make lemonade."
(B) "The early bird gets the worm."
(C) "A rising tide lifts all boats."
(D) "Too many cooks spoil the broth."

9) According to Paragraphs 3 and 4, all of the following are part of Stoic philosophy EXCEPT:
(A) People cannot control much of what happens to them or around them.
(B) The natural order can be understood, which helps people become selfless.
(C) The universe is irrational, and people cannot make sense of it.
(D) People should adjust their attitudes to the real world.

10) Which of the following best paraphrases the highlighted phrase in Paragraph 5?
(A) People are all exactly the same.
(B) People are not fundamentally different.
(C) People are separate from the divine universe.
(D) People and their statuses are only illusions.

11) The word "**them**" in Paragraph 5 refers to
(A) Stoics
(B) minds
(C) slaves
(D) masters

12) Based on Paragraph 5, what is PROBABLY true about ancient Stoics?
(A) They often differed in their views on slavery.
(B) Some were slaves who wanted to know that freedom was possible.
(C) They believed that mental and physical freedom were different.
(D) They left behind much information on slavery.

13) **Directions**: An introductory sentence relating to the passage is written below. Complete the exercise by choosing THREE answers that support the sentence. Some sentences do not belong because they do not support the sentence. **This question is worth 2 points.**

Stoic philosophy stresses how a person should live.
-
-
-

Answer Choices
1. Individuals should accept whatever happens, even if it is bad for them personally.
2. People should focus on achieving their own happiness.
3. Retreating from the world to meditate is a good practice.
4. Some people are simply born better than others.
5. Perfection means freeing oneself from destructive emotions.
6. People should be treated as if they are made of the same divine ingredients.

Wounded Knee

Wounded Knee Creek on South Dakota's Pine Ridge Indian Reservation has a tragic history filled with death and violence. In 1890, the United States military **massacred** a group of Lakota Sioux people there. About 80 years later, armed Native Americans chose the site to protest federal policies toward tribes.

In 1890, there were rising tensions between the tribes of the Great Plains and European-American settlers. **The Native Americans had experienced decades of U.S. government mistreatment, including forced removal from their lands.** At the same time, a pacifist spiritual movement was sweeping through many tribes, focusing on bringing about peace through a ceremony called the Spirit Dance, which later was translated as "Ghost Dance." Some members of the Lakota Sioux believed that the Ghost Dance ceremony would lead to an end of the U.S. and a restoration of their lands and traditional way of life.

The U.S. military saw some Sioux Ghost Dancers as a threat and set out to arrest their leaders. On December 28, 1890, members of a *cavalry*, or military horseback unit, came across a Lakota Ghost Dance leader and about 350 of his followers, including elderly people, women, and children, trying to reach shelter. The soldiers forced **them** to stop and camp near Wounded Knee Creek. More U.S. troops arrived, numbering about 500. On the morning of December 29, the atmosphere was tense as the military tried to take away the Lakotas' guns. A shot rang out – it is still unclear who fired it – and in the **ensuing** chaos, the military began shooting at all of the Lakota in the camp, including unarmed women and children, as they tried to flee the conflict. It is believed that 150 to 300 Lakota were killed. Twenty-five U.S. soldiers died during the massacre, mostly from *friendly fire*, or accidental attacks from their own troops.

In 1973, a town near Wounded Knee became the site of a long-running political demonstration. About 200 armed people, including members of a Lakota tribe and some followers of the American Indian Movement, gathered there and refused to leave. **A** The demonstrators were surrounded by heavily armed law enforcement officers. **B** The two sides **exchanged fire** frequently, and there was a crush of media attention. **C** National opinion polls revealed widespread sympathy for the native occupiers. **D** After 71 days and the death of a U.S. Marshal as well as a young man of the tribe, the occupiers called off the protest and agreed to disarm.

1) The word "**massacred**" in Paragraph 1 is closest in meaning to
   (A) saved
   (B) captured
   (C) destroyed
   (D) slaughtered

2) In Paragraph 1, what can be inferred about the protestors choosing the Wounded Knee site?
   (A) They wanted to violently avenge the people who had been killed there once.
   (B) They wanted to take back ownership of the town and surrounding land.
   (C) They wanted to focus national attention on wrongdoings of the past and present.
   (D) They wanted to draw media attention to the creek and land and water issues.

3) Which of the following best paraphrases the highlighted sentence in Paragraph 2?
   (A) Over time, Native Americans had become angry as they received bad treatment.
   (B) For many years, Native Americans suffered from U.S. federal actions, including the seizure of their lands.
   (C) Native Americans and European Americans had experienced living near each other for many years, mostly with conflict.
   (D) For years, European Americans had treated tribes poorly and purchased much of the Great Plains.

4) According to Paragraph 2, all of the following are true about the Ghost Dance movement EXCEPT:
    (A) It encouraged followers to attack others.
    (B) It promoted dancing in a special way.
    (C) It promised the return of a vanishing lifestyle.
    (D) It attracted people from different tribes.

5) The word "**them**" in Paragraph 3 refers to
    (A) their leaders
    (B) members of a cavalry unit
    (C) soldiers
    (D) a Lakota leader and his followers

6) According to Paragraph 3, the goal of the U.S. military in 1890 was to
    (A) find travelers with its cavalry units
    (B) kill Native Americans because Americans felt threatened
    (C) keep disarmed people camped at a creek for safety
    (D) take into custody the leaders of a spiritual movement

7) According to Paragraph 3, which action incited the massacre of Lakotas?
    (A) U.S. soldiers forced the Lakota to stop their search for shelter.
    (B) The cavalry's friendly fire sparked panic among the Lakota.
    (C) U.S. soldiers attempted to disarm the Lakota, increasing tensions.
    (D) The cavalry unit arrested the Lakota Ghost Dance leader.

8) The word "**ensuing**" in Paragraph 3 means
    (A) following
    (B) devastating
    (C) maddening
    (D) ensuring

9) In Paragraphs 2 and 3, the author PROBABLY mentions the Ghost Dance spiritual movement to
    (A) describe a traditional Lakota belief system
    (B) explain why the U.S. military felt threatened
    (C) persuade the reader that the Native Americans were dangerous
    (D) illustrate how powerful and emotional some beliefs can be

10) The phrase "**exchanged fire**" in Paragraph 4 means
    (A) threw flames at each other
    (B) stole guns from each other
    (C) shouted angrily at each other
    (D) shot at each other

11) Look at the squares [■] that indicate where the following sentence could be added to Paragraph 4.

    They were outraged by the U.S. government breaking agreements with them, and by its support for a controversial Lakota tribal president.

    Where would the sentence best fit?
    Circle the square [■] to add the sentence.

12) According to the passage, the two incidents were alike in each of the following ways EXCEPT:
    (A) Both involved Lakota Sioux people.
    (B) Both ended with hundreds of deaths and injuries.
    (C) Both emerged from long-standing conflicts.
    (D) Both involved fear and anger on both sides.

13) **Directions**: Select the sentences that most appropriately match the descriptions of each Wounded Knee occurrence. TWO of the answer choices will NOT be used. **This question is worth 3 points.**

    1890 Wounded Knee Massacre
    ●
    ●
    ●

    1973 Wounded Knee Incident
    ●
    ●

    Answer Choices
    1. Reporters and photographers witnessed this event.
    2. It unfolded quickly after a mysterious gun shot.
    3. Many people attempted to escape this situation.
    4. It involved the interruption of a ceremonial dance.
    5. Firearms – rifles or handguns – did not contribute to the unfolding of events.
    6. It involved a standoff between the two sides lasting many days.
    7. Women and children were killed and injured during this event.

Social Darwinism

Time
00:20:00

When someone wants to cut government support for the poor or vulnerable, opponents may accuse that person of being a "Social Darwinist." **Today, the term is usually disparaging; it is not something one would call himself or herself.**

The term Social Darwinism came about some time after Charles Darwin published his 1859 book, *The Origin of Species*. **A** Darwin's theory describes the natural environment as a place where organisms must compete with each other to survive. **B** He said that the individuals who "win" the competition will survive longer. **C** Thus, winners will have more time to reproduce and pass on their winning traits to their offspring, also helping **them** survive. **D** Darwin called the process *natural selection*, and it has also been called "survival of the fittest."

During the late 1800s, a few British and American writers borrowed Darwin's biological theory and applied it to human social status – something Darwin had never done. They described the economy as a competitive arena. Those who are rich have "won" because they have the necessary qualities, while those who are poor have "lost" because they do not. Thus, a Social Darwinist may conclude that **poor people simply lack winning traits**, and helping them would **impede** society's overall progress. Social Darwinism ignores circumstances that are beyond an individual's control, such as inheritance of wealth.

By the turn of the century, Social Darwinism lost much of its influence as writers pointed out that, even among nonhuman species, cooperation within a species helps its members survive. However, in 1944 historian Richard Hofstadter **revived** the term "Social Darwinism" to refer to various extreme ideologies that led to fascism, brutality, and violence during the first part of the 20th century.

1) In Paragraph 1, how does the author introduce the term "Social Darwinist"?
   (A) by giving a definition of its meaning
   (B) by using another term that contrasts it
   (C) by using a metaphor that provides an image
   (D) by giving an example of how it might be used

2) Which of the following best paraphrases the highlighted sentence in Paragraph 1?
   (A) People do not associate themselves with Social Darwinists anymore.
   (B) The term is negative and used only by certain rude people.
   (C) Nowadays, no one seeks to be associated with the uncomplimentary label.
   (D) Social Darwinists call others by unflattering terms.

3) Look at the squares [■] that indicate where the following sentence could be added to Paragraph 2.

   Over many generations, a species becomes more adapted to its habitat with the winning traits that it inherits.

   Where would the sentence best fit?
   Circle the square [■] to add the sentence.

4) The word "**them**" in Paragraph 2 refers to
   (A) individuals
   (B) winners
   (C) traits
   (D) offspring

5) According to Paragraph 2, "*natural selection*" is a process of
   (A) successful organisms producing more young than other organisms produce
   (B) some individuals protecting their environment and others neglecting it
   (C) some organisms having more chances to live in wealthier environments than others do
   (D) rewarding the species that is able to limit the number of offspring to maximize resources

6) What can be inferred about Charles Darwin from Paragraph 2?
   (A) He was concerned primarily with biological processes.
   (B) He believed that natural selection affected a few species.
   (C) He was universally denounced for his social theories of natural selection.
   (D) He applied his theory to many aspects of human experience.

7) According to Paragraph 3, what is PROBABLY NOT a way a Social Darwinist would judge a person to be a winner?
   (A) Big house
   (B) Rigid moral code
   (C) Powerful friends
   (D) Plentiful leisure

8) According to Paragraph 3, Social Darwinism sees human society mostly as a
   (A) training ground for the affluent
   (B) set of resources
   (C) competition for wealth
   (D) pluralistic environment

9) Which of the following is the most similar in meaning to the highlighted phrase in Paragraph 3?
   (A) A person's poverty comes from not having qualities necessary for success.
   (B) People at the bottom of society's ladder do not have the education that they need.
   (C) Competitive disadvantages include not having certain survival traits.
   (D) The working classes do not have a history of winning.

10) The word "**impede**" in Paragraph 3 means
   (A) increase
   (B) delay
   (C) intensify
   (D) destroy

11) Why does the author mention "**revived**" in Paragraph 4?
   (A) To identify the way that the term came back into use
   (B) To explain why supporters of philosophy used the term
   (C) To describe a controversy about the term
   (D) To criticize a misuse of the term

12) What can be inferred about the term "Social Darwinism" in Paragraph 4?
   (A) Extremist groups used it to describe their own ideologies.
   (B) People changed their minds about it around 1944.
   (C) Darwin published material disproving the theory.
   (D) It was increasingly seen as a very negative term.

13) **Directions**: An introductory sentence relating to the passage is written below. Complete the exercise by choosing THREE answers that support the sentence. Some sentences do not belong because they do not support the sentence. **This question is worth 2 points.**

Social Darwinism attempts to explain unequal social structures.

   ●
   ●
   ●

Answer Choices
1. It was adapted from a theory focusing on differences in biological organisms.
2. It provides an intricate view of interactions among people.
3. It accounts for the average size of families in a given class.
4. It assumes that each individual has equal circumstances to begin with.
5. It may lead to the idea that helping the poor would be bad for society.
6. It is useful background for those who want to succeed in business.

Actual Test

Review   Help   Back   Next

Reading Section Directions

In this section, you will read three passages and answer reading comprehension questions about each passage. Most questions are worth one point, but the last question in each set is worth more than one point. The directions indicate how many points you may receive.

You will have 60 minutes to read all of the passages and answer the questions. Some passages include a word or phrase that is underlined and printed in blue. Click on the word or phrase to see a definition or an explanation.

When you want to move on to the next question, click on **Next**. You can skip questions and go back to them later as long as there is time remaining. If you want to return to previous questions, click on **Back**. You can click on **Review** at any time and the review screen will show you which questions you have answered and which you have not. From this review screen, you may go directly to any question that you have already seen in the reading section.

Confirm later after calculating....

	Very Poor	Poor	Good	Very Good	Excellent
Points	1 - 21	22 - 29	30 - 34	35 - 38	39 - 43
Scale	1 - 14	15 - 19	20 - 23	24 - 26	27 - 30
Your Score					

Time

00:20:00

Review Help Back Next

Questions 1 - 3

1) According to Paragraph 1, Spanish missions in California were places where all of the following occurred EXCEPT:
   (A) Spanish priests taught religion while being guarded by Spanish forces.
   (B) Native Americans were forced to raise crops and livestock.
   (C) Native Americans learned farming skills that helped sustain their own communities.
   (D) Native Californians from various tribes were forced to stay and learn Spanish.

2) Look at the four squares [■] that indicate where the following sentence could be added to Paragraph 1.

   Yet this oppression of native peoples, along with over taxation in Mexican and Californian colonies, led to a war between the Mexican colony and Spain.

   Where would the sentence best fit?
   Click on a square [■] to add the sentence to the passage.

3) According to Paragraph 2, when Mexico won independence from Spain, it
   (A) fought Native Americans who wanted independence
   (B) lost its territory in California to the U.S.
   (C) created a new constitution giving native peoples citizenship
   (D) closed the old institutions built by the Spanish

Ramona

A In the late 18th and early 19th centuries, Spain controlled current-day Mexico and much of the southwestern United States. Along the California coast, the Spanish established numerous missions, which served as church compounds and farms. **B** Spanish soldiers forced native Californian and Mexican tribes to work at the missions, learn the Spanish language, and practice the Spaniards' religion. **C** In 1821, after years of conflict, Mexico won independence from Spain, so California became part of the newly established Mexican government. **D**

The new Mexican government began closing the missions, and started processes that **culminated** in property being **granted** to some of the Mexican landowners who supported the government. The landowners created vast cattle and sheep ranches, or *ranchos*.

While the new class of landowners known as the *Califorñios* enjoyed a life of leisure, many Native Californians struggled to find work on the ranchos. **Yet in 1848, the natives' fate changed again when the U.S. won the Mexican-American War and took over the region.** Under American rule, most *Califorñio* ranches were reduced and many natives lost their ranch jobs. Also, because of the influx of American settlers, native tribes lost most of their hunting and gathering territory as well.

In 1884, author **Helen Hunt Jackson** published a romantic novel, *Ramona*, that she hoped would draw attention to the mistreatment of California native people. The novel follows an idealized half-native girl named Ramona, raised by her cruel *Califorñio* aunt on a *rancho*. Ramona falls in love with a Native-American ranch hand, and the two run away to get married. The couple experiences desperate poverty and harsh treatment, leading to the husband's death. Ramona becomes ill with grief, but then marries her kind cousin, who has inherited the *rancho*.

The **melodramatic novel** was a hit with the American public. *Ramona* may have helped native Californians, as the government set aside new reservations for "Mission Indians." But **its** immediate effect was a tourist craze for Spanish and Mexican settings. Soon California hoteliers **enthusiastically** marketed "Ramona's" world – romantic adobe buildings and courtyard gardens – to guests.

4) The word "**culminated**" in Paragraph 2 is closest in meaning to
   (A) featured
   (B) excelled
   (C) resulted
   (D) specialized

5) The word "**granted**" in Paragraph 2 is closest in meaning to
   (A) awarded
   (B) sold
   (C) marketed
   (D) leased

6) Which of the following best paraphrases the highlighted sentence in Paragraph 3?
   (A) However, in 1848, an American victory in the Mexican-American War enabled the U.S. to improve the quality of life of many Native Californians.
   (B) As a result, California's native tribes were destroyed after the U.S. won the Mexican-American War in 1848.
   (C) Moreover, the history of the U.S. was changed forever when it won the Mexican-American War in 1848 and took over Mexico.
   (D) But in 1848, after winning the Mexican-American War, the U.S. assumed control of California, changing the native people's lives again.

Ramona

A In the late 18th and early 19th centuries, Spain controlled current-day Mexico and much of the southwestern United States. Along the California coast, the Spanish established numerous missions, which served as church compounds and farms. **B** Spanish soldiers forced native Californian and Mexican tribes to work at the missions, learn the Spanish language, and practice the Spaniards' religion. **C** In 1821, after years of conflict, Mexico won independence from Spain, so California became part of the newly established Mexican government. **D**

The new Mexican government began closing the missions, and started processes that **culminated** in property being **granted** to some of the Mexican landowners who supported the government. The landowners created vast cattle and sheep ranches, or *ranchos*.

While the new class of landowners known as the *Californios* enjoyed a life of leisure, many Native Californians struggled to find work on the ranchos. **Yet in 1848, the natives' fate changed again when the U.S. won the Mexican-American War and took over the region.** Under American rule, most *Californio* ranches were reduced and many natives lost their ranch jobs. Also, because of the influx of American settlers, native tribes lost most of their hunting and gathering territory as well.

In 1884, author **Helen Hunt Jackson** published a romantic novel, *Ramona*, that she hoped would draw attention to the mistreatment of California native people. The novel follows an idealized half-native girl named Ramona, raised by her cruel *Californio* aunt on a *rancho*. Ramona falls in love with a Native-American ranch hand, and the two run away to get married. The couple experiences desperate poverty and harsh treatment, leading to the husband's death. Ramona becomes ill with grief, but then marries her kind cousin, who has inherited the *rancho*.

The **melodramatic novel** was a hit with the American public. *Ramona* may have helped native Californians, as the government set aside new reservations for "Mission Indians." But **its** immediate effect was a tourist craze for Spanish and Mexican settings. Soon California hoteliers **enthusiastically** marketed "Ramona's" world – romantic adobe buildings and courtyard gardens – to guests.

Review   Help   Back   Next

Time

00:12:00

Questions 7 - 9

7) In Paragraph 3, what can be inferred about California after 1848?
   (A) Mexicans began immigrating to the state from Mexico.
   (B) Americans began moving in and enslaved the natives.
   (C) Californios immediately left their property.
   (D) Many Native Americans had no way to earn a living.

8) Why does the author mention "**Helen Hunt Jackson**" in Paragraph 4?
   (A) To identify someone who wanted to publicize an injustice
   (B) To discuss the works of an important writer during the late 19th century
   (C) To introduce a Native American who achieved fame
   (D) To acknowledge the person who inspired the creation of *Ramona*

9) In Paragraph 4, what can be inferred about the plot of *Ramona*?
   (A) Ramona's husband continues to work on her family's *rancho*.
   (B) Ramona and her first husband become successful rancho owners.
   (C) Ramona regrets her decision to marry a California native.
   (D) Ramona's aunt does not want her to marry a Native American.

Ramona

A In the late 18th and early 19th centuries, Spain controlled current-day Mexico and much of the southwestern United States. Along the California coast, the Spanish established numerous missions, which served as church compounds and farms. **B** Spanish soldiers forced native Californian and Mexican tribes to work at the missions, learn the Spanish language, and practice the Spaniards' religion. **C** In 1821, after years of conflict, Mexico won independence from Spain, so California became part of the newly established Mexican government. **D**

The new Mexican government began closing the missions, and started processes that **culminated** in property being **granted** to some of the Mexican landowners who supported the government. The landowners created vast cattle and sheep ranches, or *ranchos*.

While the new class of landowners known as the *Californios* enjoyed a life of leisure, many Native Californians struggled to find work on the ranchos. **Yet in 1848, the natives' fate changed again when the U.S. won the Mexican-American War and took over the region.** Under American rule, most *Californio* ranches were reduced and many natives lost their ranch jobs. Also, because of the influx of American settlers, native tribes lost most of their hunting and gathering territory as well.

In 1884, author **Helen Hunt Jackson** published a romantic novel, *Ramona*, that she hoped would draw attention to the mistreatment of California native people. The novel follows an idealized half-native girl named Ramona, raised by her cruel *Californio* aunt on a *rancho*. Ramona falls in love with a Native-American ranch hand, and the two run away to get married. The couple experiences desperate poverty and harsh treatment, leading to the husband's death. Ramona becomes ill with grief, but then marries her kind cousin, who has inherited the *rancho*.

The **melodramatic novel** was a hit with the American public. *Ramona* may have helped native Californians, as the government set aside new reservations for "Mission Indians." But **its** immediate effect was a tourist craze for Spanish and Mexican settings. Soon California hoteliers **enthusiastically** marketed "Ramona's" world – romantic adobe buildings and courtyard gardens – to guests.

Time

00:08:00

Review Help Back Next

Questions 10 - 12

10) The phrase "**melodramatic novel**" in Paragraph 5 is closest in meaning to
   (A) novel that could easily be acted out on stage or screen
   (B) story whose characters and actions are exaggerated
   (C) book with a calm tone and sensitive topics
   (D) fiction book with many plot lines

11) The word "**its**" in Paragraph 5 refers to
   (A) American public
   (B) *Ramona*
   (C) government
   (D) tourist craze

12) Why does the author use the word "**enthusiastically**" in Paragraph 5?
   (A) To emphasize that hotel owners were eager to profit from tourists' interest in California
   (B) To criticize the exploitation of hotel guests in many California towns and cities
   (C) To point out that California hoteliers provided optimal service to their guests
   (D) To contrast the attitudes of "Mission Indians" with the attitudes of California hoteliers

Ramona

A In the late 18th and early 19th centuries, Spain controlled current-day Mexico and much of the southwestern United States. Along the California coast, the Spanish established numerous missions, which served as church compounds and farms. **B** Spanish soldiers forced native Californian and Mexican tribes to work at the missions, learn the Spanish language, and practice the Spaniards' religion. **C** In 1821, after years of conflict, Mexico won independence from Spain, so California became part of the newly established Mexican government. **D**

The new Mexican government began closing the missions, and started processes that **culminated** in property being **granted** to some of the Mexican landowners who supported the government. The landowners created vast cattle and sheep ranches, or *ranchos*.

While the new class of landowners known as the *Californios* enjoyed a life of leisure, many Native Californians struggled to find work on the ranchos. **Yet in 1848, the natives' fate changed again when the U.S. won the Mexican-American War and took over the region.** Under American rule, most *Californio* ranches were reduced and many natives lost their ranch jobs. Also, because of the influx of American settlers, native tribes lost most of their hunting and gathering territory as well.

In 1884, author **Helen Hunt Jackson** published a romantic novel, *Ramona*, that she hoped would draw attention to the mistreatment of California native people. The novel follows an idealized half-native girl named Ramona, raised by her cruel *Californio* aunt on a *rancho*. Ramona falls in love with a Native-American ranch hand, and the two run away to get married. The couple experiences desperate poverty and harsh treatment, leading to the husband's death. Ramona becomes ill with grief, but then marries her kind cousin, who has inherited the *rancho*.

The **melodramatic novel** was a hit with the American public. *Ramona* may have helped native Californians, as the government set aside new reservations for "Mission Indians." But **its** immediate effect was a tourist craze for Spanish and Mexican settings. Soon California hoteliers **enthusiastically** marketed "Ramona's" world – romantic adobe buildings and courtyard gardens – to guests.

Review   Help   Back   Next

Question 13

13) **Directions**: An introductory sentence is written below. Choose THREE answers from the passage that support the sentence. Some sentences do not belong. **This question is worth 2 points.**

The novel *Ramona* depicted consequences of colonial attitudes toward California native tribes.

-
-
-

Answer Choices

1. The Spanish mission system started the process of dislodging Native Californians from their land.

2. Native tribes worked as laborers on the ranchos of wealthy Mexicans.

3. Native cultures in California developed differently in deserts, forests, grasslands, and coastal areas.

4. When the U.S. took over California, new immigrants settled in many former tribal territories.

5. Native tribes who had been forced to move to the missions were later called "Mission Indians."

6. Public support of California native people changed dramatically after the novel's publication.

Ramona

A In the late 18th and early 19th centuries, Spain controlled current-day Mexico and much of the southwestern United States. Along the California coast, the Spanish established numerous missions, which served as church compounds and farms. **B** Spanish soldiers forced native Californian and Mexican tribes to work at the missions, learn the Spanish language, and practice the Spaniards' religion. **C** In 1821, after years of conflict, Mexico won independence from Spain, so California became part of the newly established Mexican government. **D**

The new Mexican government began closing the missions, and started processes that **culminated** in property being **granted** to some of the Mexican landowners who supported the government. The landowners created vast cattle and sheep ranches, or *ranchos*.

While the new class of landowners known as the *Californios* enjoyed a life of leisure, many Native Californians struggled to find work on the ranchos. **Yet in 1848, the natives' fate changed again when the U.S. won the Mexican-American War and took over the region.** Under American rule, most *Californio* ranches were reduced and many natives lost their ranch jobs. Also, because of the influx of American settlers, native tribes lost most of their hunting and gathering territory as well.

In 1884, author **Helen Hunt Jackson** published a romantic novel, *Ramona*, that she hoped would draw attention to the mistreatment of California native people. The novel follows an idealized half-native girl named Ramona, raised by her cruel *Californio* aunt on a *rancho*. Ramona falls in love with a Native-American ranch hand, and the two run away to get married. The couple experiences desperate poverty and harsh treatment, leading to the husband's death. Ramona becomes ill with grief, but then marries her kind cousin, who has inherited the *rancho*.

The **melodramatic novel** was a hit with the American public. *Ramona* may have helped native Californians, as the government set aside new reservations for "Mission Indians." But **its** immediate effect was a tourist craze for Spanish and Mexican settings. Soon California hoteliers **enthusiastically** marketed "Ramona's" world – romantic adobe buildings and courtyard gardens – to guests.

Time

00:20:00

Review Help Back Next

Questions 14 - 17

14) The author describes the nickname "Yankee" in Paragraph 1 by
   (A) illustrating debates about it with specific evidence
   (B) explaining analysts' interpretation of its meaning
   (C) describing controversy over its initial uses
   (D) introducing one theory about its origin

15) The word "**disputed**" in Paragraph 1 is closest in meaning to
   (A) revised
   (B) waived
   (C) debated
   (D) supported

16) According to Paragraph 2, most linguists think that the term "Yankee" originally
   (A) started out as a term to tease people about their appearance
   (B) started as a misunderstanding about settlers having the same name
   (C) tended to be people who enjoyed eating cheese
   (D) referred to some non-English settlers in areas along the East Coast of the United States

17) The word "**anglicized**" in Paragraph 2 is closest in meaning to
   (A) made English
   (B) changed often
   (C) spread abruptly
   (D) used religiously

Yankee: An American Nickname

People from the United States often have been referred to as "Yankees." While the nickname is well known, no one is certain of its origins. Many theories have been proposed and mostly **disputed** by linguists. Currently, it is widely accepted that the term probably came about in relation to Dutch settlers from the Netherlands.

In the 1700s, many Dutch colonists lived in the areas that are now New York, New Jersey, Delaware, and Connecticut. **A** Two common Dutch names are *Jan*, pronounced "Yawn," and *Kees*. Sometimes, they were combined for the given name *Jan Kees*. **B** Yet another possibility is that "Yankee" originated from a derisive term for Dutch people, who famously made good cheese; *Jan Kaas* meant "John Cheese." **C** Whatever its exact source, the name "Yankee" appears to have been **anglicized** over time and applied to all colonists, including English **ones**. **D**

British soldiers began to use "Yankee" as a term for colonists in the late 1700s. **As the British tried to suppress the rising colonial revolt, the term became a way to make fun of their foes.** One popular song went:

Yankee Doodle went to town/A-riding on a pony,

Stuck a feather in his hat/And called it Macaroni.

A "doodle" was a fool, and a "Macaroni" was a type of man who dressed too stylishly. After Americans won battles against Britain, the colonists sang the song about themselves because they were proud to have beaten their better-supplied, better-dressed foes.

The term "Yankee" continues to vary in **connotation**. In the U.S., Southerners have used the term to describe all Northerners, especially those from New England. During the American Civil War (1861-1865) between northern and southern territories, Southerners called the northern troops "Yankees." During World War I and II, people in the Allied countries used "Yankee" as a friendly nickname for American soldiers. **In the latter half of the 20th century, as the U.S. continued its involvement in conflicts abroad, people were more likely to use the term in an unfriendly way, as in, "Yankee, go home!"** Most Americans, however, probably associate the name with the professional baseball team, the New York Yankees.

Time

00:16:00

Review Help Back Next

Questions 18 - 20

18) The word "**ones**" in Paragraph 2 refers to
(A) New York, New Jersey, Delaware, and Connecticut
(B) Dutch names
(C) Jan Kees
(D) colonists

19) Look at the squares [■] that indicate where the following sentence could be added to Paragraph 2.

Alternatively, the nickname could have stemmed from the nickname for Jan, *Janeke*.

Where would the sentence best fit? Click on a square [■] to add the sentence to the passage.

20) Which of the following best paraphrases the highlighted sentence in Paragraph 3?
(A) The nickname was a way to have fun during the stress of fighting.
(B) British troops used the term to belittle their enemies as they tried to maintain British rule.
(C) The rebels surprised the British with rising up in more force than expected.
(D) While controlling the colonies, British troops used the nickname to amuse the colonists.

Yankee: An American Nickname

People from the United States often have been referred to as "Yankees." While the nickname is well known, no one is certain of its origins. Many theories have been proposed and mostly **disputed** by linguists. Currently, it is widely accepted that the term probably came about in relation to Dutch settlers from the Netherlands.

In the 1700s, many Dutch colonists lived in the areas that are now New York, New Jersey, Delaware, and Connecticut. **A** Two common Dutch names are *Jan*, pronounced "Yawn," and *Kees*. Sometimes, they were combined for the given name *Jan Kees*. **B** Yet another possibility is that "Yankee" originated from a derisive term for Dutch people, who famously made good cheese; *Jan Kaas* meant "John Cheese." **C** Whatever its exact source, the name "Yankee" appears to have been **anglicized** over time and applied to all colonists, including English **ones**. **D**

British soldiers began to use "Yankee" as a term for colonists in the late 1700s. **As the British tried to suppress the rising colonial revolt, the term became a way to make fun of their foes.** One popular song went:

Yankee Doodle went to town/A-riding on a pony,

Stuck a feather in his hat/And called it Macaroni.

A "doodle" was a fool, and a "Macaroni" was a type of man who dressed too stylishly. After Americans won battles against Britain, the colonists sang the song about themselves because they were proud to have beaten their better-supplied, better-dressed foes.

The term "Yankee" continues to vary in **connotation**. In the U.S., Southerners have used the term to describe all Northerners, especially those from New England. During the American Civil War (1861-1865) between northern and southern territories, Southerners called the northern troops "Yankees." During World War I and II, people in the Allied countries used "Yankee" as a friendly nickname for American soldiers. **In the latter half of the 20th century, as the U.S. continued its involvement in conflicts abroad, people were more likely to use the term in an unfriendly way, as in, "Yankee, go home!"** Most Americans, however, probably associate the name with the professional baseball team, the New York Yankees.

Time

00:12:00

Questions 21 - 23

21) In Paragraph 3, what can be inferred about the British from their song "Yankee Doodle"?
   (A) They were implying that rebels were overconfident and undersupplied.
   (B) They wanted to focus attention on the colonists' unsophisticated hats and dressing style.
   (C) They wanted to scare and threaten their opponents.
   (D) They wanted to persuade rebels to switch over to their side.

22) The word "**connotation**" in Paragraph 4 is closest in meaning to
   (A) implication
   (B) explanation
   (C) diction
   (D) organization

23) Which of the following statements is PROBABLY true based on the highlighted sentence in Paragraph 4?
   (A) People outside of the U.S. made up new songs about "Yankees."
   (B) Protestors in some countries did not want U.S. forces there.
   (C) "Yankee" was applied to soldiers who were outside their base.
   (D) The U.S. became involved in conflicts from the 1950s onward.

Yankee: An American Nickname

People from the United States often have been referred to as "Yankees." While the nickname is well known, no one is certain of its origins. Many theories have been proposed and mostly **disputed** by linguists. Currently, it is widely accepted that the term probably came about in relation to Dutch settlers from the Netherlands.

In the 1700s, many Dutch colonists lived in the areas that are now New York, New Jersey, Delaware, and Connecticut. **A** Two common Dutch names are *Jan*, pronounced "Yawn," and *Kees*. Sometimes, they were combined for the given name *Jan Kees*. **B** Yet another possibility is that "Yankee" originated from a derisive term for Dutch people, who famously made good cheese; *Jan Kaas* meant "John Cheese." **C** Whatever its exact source, the name "Yankee" appears to have been **anglicized** over time and applied to all colonists, including English **ones**. **D**

British soldiers began to use "Yankee" as a term for colonists in the late 1700s. **As the British tried to suppress the rising colonial revolt, the term became a way to make fun of their foes.** One popular song went:

Yankee Doodle went to town/A-riding on a pony,

Stuck a feather in his hat/And called it Macaroni.

A "doodle" was a fool, and a "Macaroni" was a type of man who dressed too stylishly. After Americans won battles against Britain, the colonists sang the song about themselves because they were proud to have beaten their better-supplied, better-dressed foes.

The term "Yankee" continues to vary in **connotation**. In the U.S., Southerners have used the term to describe all Northerners, especially those from New England. During the American Civil War (1861-1865) between northern and southern territories, Southerners called the northern troops "Yankees." During World War I and II, people in the Allied countries used "Yankee" as a friendly nickname for American soldiers. **In the latter half of the 20th century, as the U.S. continued its involvement in conflicts abroad, people were more likely to use the term in an unfriendly way, as in, "Yankee, go home!"** Most Americans, however, probably associate the name with the professional baseball team, the New York Yankees.

Time

00:08:00

Review   Help   Back   Next

Questions 24 - 25

24) All of the following are true about the nickname "Yankee" EXCEPT:
   (A) It has been used for more than two centuries.
   (B) It can mean "Northerner" or "American."
   (C) Its use became problematic during the U.S. Civil War.
   (D) It was first used widely outside of the U.S. during global conflicts of the 20th century.

25) Based on Paragraph 4, during the U.S. Civil War, a Southerner would MOST LIKELY use the term "Yankee" as
   (A) a way to compliment a fellow Southerner
   (B) a way to show respect to a Northerner
   (C) a way to insult a Northerner
   (D) a way to secretly communicate with a fellow Southerner

Yankee: An American Nickname

People from the United States often have been referred to as "Yankees." While the nickname is well known, no one is certain of its origins. Many theories have been proposed and mostly **disputed** by linguists. Currently, it is widely accepted that the term probably came about in relation to Dutch settlers from the Netherlands.

In the 1700s, many Dutch colonists lived in the areas that are now New York, New Jersey, Delaware, and Connecticut. **A** Two common Dutch names are *Jan*, pronounced "Yawn," and *Kees*. Sometimes, they were combined for the given name *Jan Kees*. **B** Yet another possibility is that "Yankee" originated from a derisive term for Dutch people, who famously made good cheese; *Jan Kaas* meant "John Cheese." **C** Whatever its exact source, the name "Yankee" appears to have been **anglicized** over time and applied to all colonists, including English *ones*. **D**

British soldiers began to use "Yankee" as a term for colonists in the late 1700s. **As the British tried to suppress the rising colonial revolt, the term became a way to make fun of their foes.** One popular song went:

Yankee Doodle went to town/A-riding on a pony,

Stuck a feather in his hat/And called it Macaroni.

A "doodle" was a fool, and a "Macaroni" was a type of man who dressed too stylishly. After Americans won battles against Britain, the colonists sang the song about themselves because they were proud to have beaten their better-supplied, better-dressed foes.

The term "Yankee" continues to vary in **connotation**. In the U.S., Southerners have used the term to describe all Northerners, especially those from New England. During the American Civil War (1861-1865) between northern and southern territories, Southerners called the northern troops "Yankees." During World War I and II, people in the Allied countries used "Yankee" as a friendly nickname for American soldiers. **In the latter half of the 20th century, as the U.S. continued its involvement in conflicts abroad, people were more likely to use the term in an unfriendly way, as in, "Yankee, go home!"** Most Americans, however, probably associate the name with the professional baseball team, the New York Yankees.

Question 26

26) **Directions**: Select the sentences that most appropriately match the descriptions of each way that the term "Yankee" is used. TWO of the answer choices will NOT be used. **This question is worth 3 points.**

"Yankee" – Positive Tone

●

●

"Yankee" – Negative Tone

●

●

●

Answer Choices

1. American fighters eventually became proud of this name.
2. This may have been used to deride "cheese-makers."
3. This may have been applied to all settlers, whether Dutch or English.
4. The Allied Forces used this for Americans during World War II.
5. British troops used this during the Revolutionary War.
6. All Americans used this for themselves during the Civil War.
7. This has been used to criticize U.S. activity in foreign conflicts.

Yankee: An American Nickname

People from the United States often have been referred to as "Yankees." While the nickname is well known, no one is certain of its origins. Many theories have been proposed and mostly **disputed** by linguists. Currently, it is widely accepted that the term probably came about in relation to Dutch settlers from the Netherlands.

In the 1700s, many Dutch colonists lived in the areas that are now New York, New Jersey, Delaware, and Connecticut. **A** Two common Dutch names are *Jan*, pronounced "Yawn," and *Kees*. Sometimes, they were combined for the given name *Jan Kees*. **B** Yet another possibility is that "Yankee" originated from a derisive term for Dutch people, who famously made good cheese; *Jan Kaas* meant "John Cheese." **C** Whatever its exact source, the name "Yankee" appears to have been **anglicized** over time and applied to all colonists, including English **ones**. **D**

British soldiers began to use "Yankee" as a term for colonists in the late 1700s. **As the British tried to suppress the rising colonial revolt, the term became a way to make fun of their foes.** One popular song went:

Yankee Doodle went to town/A-riding on a pony,

Stuck a feather in his hat/And called it Macaroni.

A "doodle" was a fool, and a "Macaroni" was a type of man who dressed too stylishly. After Americans won battles against Britain, the colonists sang the song about themselves because they were proud to have beaten their better-supplied, better-dressed foes.

The term "Yankee" continues to vary in **connotation**. In the U.S., Southerners have used the term to describe all Northerners, especially those from New England. During the American Civil War (1861-1865) between northern and southern territories, Southerners called the northern troops "Yankees." During World War I and II, people in the Allied countries used "Yankee" as a friendly nickname for American soldiers. **In the latter half of the 20th century, as the U.S. continued its involvement in conflicts abroad, people were more likely to use the term in an unfriendly way, as in, "Yankee, go home!"** Most Americans, however, probably associate the name with the professional baseball team, the New York Yankees.

Time

00:20:00

Review Help Back Next

Questions 27 - 29

27) How does the author introduce hummingbirds in Paragraph 1?
   (A) By explaining details about their coloring
   (B) By contrasting their size and weight to other birds
   (C) By describing their unique flight characteristics
   (D) By giving a history of their name

28) Based on Paragraph 1, hummingbirds do NOT
   (A) make quick flying movements to drive away other birds
   (B) fly upside-down
   (C) fly in one place without moving in any direction
   (D) soar on drafts of air

29) According to Paragraph 1, why would it PROBABLY be difficult to distinguish markings on a hummingbird's wings?
   (A) The bird is too small.
   (B) The wings are too colorful.
   (C) The bird flaps its wings too fast.
   (D) The bird flies around too quickly.

Hummingbirds

The hummingbird is the smallest warm-blooded *vertebrate*, or animal with a spinal column, in the world. These amazing creatures are like tiny, colorful helicopters. They can fly forward, backward, and upside down, or they can hover in one place. Hummingbirds beat their wings from 12 to 200 times a second, so fast that the motion is a blur to human eyes. Their name refers to the sound that their wings make as they fly: a buzzing or "humming" sound. To protect their territories, hummingbirds can zoom and dart at other birds, even large ones, and chase them away.

A Everything about a hummingbird's anatomy helps the bird obtain flower nectar and small insects. Its **miniscule** size and wings that can rotate in all directions allow the bird to hover in the air in front of flowers while it sips nectar from them. **B** The hummingbird's eyes can see a wider spectrum of hues, including ultraviolet shades, than the spectrum visible to humans. **C** Its brain is **relatively large**, so the bird is able to sample hundreds of flowers and remember which ones provide the most nectar. **D**

Some hummingbird species have coevolved with particular species of flowers. **Many flowers that have evolved to rely on hummingbirds for pollination are tube-shaped; thus, they are well matched to the bird's long, thin beak.** These flowers are often red because hummingbirds prefer the color. Researchers have theorized that hummingbirds choose red flowers for **a practical reason**. **Bees** compete with hummingbirds for nectar, and bees do not see red very well. Therefore, when hummingbirds spot a red flower, they know that they are more likely to have it all to themselves. Access to enough nectar is critical because **it is imperative that hummingbirds take in 12 times their body weight in nectar each day.**

In all, there are over 320 different species of hummingbirds. A majority of the species live in tropical areas of Central and South America, but a few of them migrate to North America during the spring and summer.

Review　Help　Back　Next

Questions 30 - 32

30) Look at the four squares [■] that indicate where the following sentence could be added to Paragraph 2.

Another beneficial sense is the hummingbird's acute hearing, which the hummingbird uses to pick up the high-pitched buzzing of edible insects.

Where would the sentence best fit?
Click on a square [■] to add the sentence to the passage.

31) The word "**miniscule**" in Paragraph 2 is closest in meaning to
(A) diminutive
(B) unnoticeable
(C) natural
(D) gigantic

32) According to Paragraph 2, what is PROBABLY true about a hummingbird's vision compared to a person's vision?
(A) It sees plants that humans cannot.
(B) It can see more colors in its habitat.
(C) It integrates information better.
(D) It has less depth perception.

Hummingbirds

The hummingbird is the smallest warm-blooded *vertebrate*, or animal with a spinal column, in the world. These amazing creatures are like tiny, colorful helicopters. They can fly forward, backward, and upside down, or they can hover in one place. Hummingbirds beat their wings from 12 to 200 times a second, so fast that the motion is a blur to human eyes. Their name refers to the sound that their wings make as they fly: a buzzing or "humming" sound. To protect their territories, hummingbirds can zoom and dart at other birds, even large ones, and chase them away.

A Everything about a hummingbird's anatomy helps the bird obtain flower nectar and small insects. Its **miniscule** size and wings that can rotate in all directions allow the bird to hover in the air in front of flowers while it sips nectar from them. **B** The hummingbird's eyes can see a wider spectrum of hues, including ultraviolet shades, than the spectrum visible to humans. **C** Its brain is **relatively large**, so the bird is able to sample hundreds of flowers and remember which ones provide the most nectar. **D**

Some hummingbird species have coevolved with particular species of flowers. **Many flowers that have evolved to rely on hummingbirds for pollination are tube-shaped; thus, they are well matched to the bird's long, thin beak.** These flowers are often red because hummingbirds prefer the color. Researchers have theorized that hummingbirds choose red flowers for **a practical reason**. **Bees** compete with hummingbirds for nectar, and bees do not see red very well. Therefore, when hummingbirds spot a red flower, they know that they are more likely to have it all to themselves. Access to enough nectar is critical because **it is imperative that hummingbirds take in 12 times their body weight in nectar each day.**

In all, there are over 320 different species of hummingbirds. A majority of the species live in tropical areas of Central and South America, but a few of them migrate to North America during the spring and summer.

Review Help Back Next

Questions 33 - 35

33) The phrase "**relatively large**" in Paragraph 2 means
   (A) big, but not always
   (B) big, considering the animal's size
   (C) big, but only in some species
   (D) big, compared to its closest relative

34) Which of the following best paraphrases the first highlighted sentence in Paragraph 3?
   (A) Flowers that depend on hummingbirds for exchanging pollen adapted to be tubular.
   (B) Certain flowers specifically rely on hummingbirds to cross-pollinate the species.
   (C) Hummingbirds' mouths are best suited to flowers that have adapted to them.
   (D) Long flowers grow only in places where hummingbirds with special beaks exist.

35) The phrase "**a practical reason**" in Paragraph 3 refers to
   (A) providing the most nectar
   (B) having a tubular shape
   (C) matching the birds' long, thin beaks
   (D) being less distinct to bees

Hummingbirds

The hummingbird is the smallest warm-blooded *vertebrate*, or animal with a spinal column, in the world. These amazing creatures are like tiny, colorful helicopters. They can fly forward, backward, and upside down, or they can hover in one place. Hummingbirds beat their wings from 12 to 200 times a second, so fast that the motion is a blur to human eyes. Their name refers to the sound that their wings make as they fly: a buzzing or "humming" sound. To protect their territories, hummingbirds can zoom and dart at other birds, even large ones, and chase them away.

A Everything about a hummingbird's anatomy helps the bird obtain flower nectar and small insects. Its **miniscule** size and wings that can rotate in all directions allow the bird to hover in the air in front of flowers while it sips nectar from them. **B** The hummingbird's eyes can see a wider spectrum of hues, including ultraviolet shades, than the spectrum visible to humans. **C** Its brain is **relatively large**, so the bird is able to sample hundreds of flowers and remember which ones provide the most nectar. **D**

Some hummingbird species have coevolved with particular species of flowers. **Many flowers that have evolved to rely on hummingbirds for pollination are tube-shaped; thus, they are well matched to the bird's long, thin beak.** These flowers are often red because hummingbirds prefer the color. Researchers have theorized that hummingbirds choose red flowers for **a practical reason**. **Bees** compete with hummingbirds for nectar, and bees do not see red very well. Therefore, when hummingbirds spot a red flower, they know that they are more likely to have it all to themselves. Access to enough nectar is critical because **it is imperative that hummingbirds take in 12 times their body weight in nectar each day.**

In all, there are over 320 different species of hummingbirds. A majority of the species live in tropical areas of Central and South America, but a few of them migrate to North America during the spring and summer.

36) Why does the author mention "**Bees**" in Paragraph 3?
 (A) To discuss how bees see the world around them
 (B) To describe how competition for resources affects bees
 (C) To illustrate something about an important insect pollinator
 (D) To explain why hummingbirds might make certain choices

37) What can be inferred about hummingbirds from the second highlighted clause in Paragraph 3?
 (A) They expend little energy daily.
 (B) If nectar is unavailable, they cannot survive for long.
 (C) They have an excessive love for nectar.
 (D) In spite of their small size, they often become fat.

38) Based on Paragraph 4, which of the following is true about MOST hummingbird species?
 (A) They fly long distances.
 (B) They live in the United States.
 (C) They thrive in warmer climates.
 (D) They are tenacious survivors.

Hummingbirds

The hummingbird is the smallest warm-blooded *vertebrate*, or animal with a spinal column, in the world. These amazing creatures are like tiny, colorful helicopters. They can fly forward, backward, and upside down, or they can hover in one place. Hummingbirds beat their wings from 12 to 200 times a second, so fast that the motion is a blur to human eyes. Their name refers to the sound that their wings make as they fly: a buzzing or "humming" sound. To protect their territories, hummingbirds can zoom and dart at other birds, even large ones, and chase them away.

A Everything about a hummingbird's anatomy helps the bird obtain flower nectar and small insects. Its **miniscule** size and wings that can rotate in all directions allow the bird to hover in the air in front of flowers while it sips nectar from them. **B** The hummingbird's eyes can see a wider spectrum of hues, including ultraviolet shades, than the spectrum visible to humans. **C** Its brain is **relatively large**, so the bird is able to sample hundreds of flowers and remember which ones provide the most nectar. **D**

Some hummingbird species have coevolved with particular species of flowers. **Many flowers that have evolved to rely on hummingbirds for pollination are tube-shaped; thus, they are well matched to the bird's long, thin beak.** These flowers are often red because hummingbirds prefer the color. Researchers have theorized that hummingbirds choose red flowers for **a practical reason**. **Bees** compete with hummingbirds for nectar, and bees do not see red very well. Therefore, when hummingbirds spot a red flower, they know that they are more likely to have it all to themselves. Access to enough nectar is critical because **it is imperative that hummingbirds take in 12 times their body weight in nectar each day.**

In all, there are over 320 different species of hummingbirds. A majority of the species live in tropical areas of Central and South America, but a few of them migrate to North America during the spring and summer.

Question 39

39) **Directions**: An introductory sentence is written below. Choose the THREE answers that support the sentence. Some sentences do not belong. **This question is worth 2 points.**

Hummingbirds have adapted to their habitats in many specialized ways.

- ●
- ●
- ●

Answer Choices

1. Their flying abilities help them protect "their" territories and drink without landing.
2. Their small size allows them to hover while they feed.
3. Their eyes, narrow beaks, and good memories help them access good nectar sources.
4. Their name comes from the sound of their flying, which is one way to notice them.
5. The exact number of hummingbird species is unclear.
6. Hummingbirds must compete with bees for the nectar of red flowers.

Hummingbirds

The hummingbird is the smallest warm-blooded *vertebrate*, or animal with a spinal column, in the world. These amazing creatures are like tiny, colorful helicopters. They can fly forward, backward, and upside down, or they can hover in one place. Hummingbirds beat their wings from 12 to 200 times a second, so fast that the motion is a blur to human eyes. Their name refers to the sound that their wings make as they fly: a buzzing or "humming" sound. To protect their territories, hummingbirds can zoom and dart at other birds, even large ones, and chase them away.

A Everything about a hummingbird's anatomy helps the bird obtain flower nectar and small insects. Its **miniscule** size and wings that can rotate in all directions allow the bird to hover in the air in front of flowers while it sips nectar from them. **B** The hummingbird's eyes can see a wider spectrum of hues, including ultraviolet shades, than the spectrum visible to humans. **C** Its brain is **relatively large**, so the bird is able to sample hundreds of flowers and remember which ones provide the most nectar. **D**

Some hummingbird species have coevolved with particular species of flowers. **Many flowers that have evolved to rely on hummingbirds for pollination are tube-shaped; thus, they are well matched to the bird's long, thin beak.** These flowers are often red because hummingbirds prefer the color. Researchers have theorized that hummingbirds choose red flowers for **a practical reason**. **Bees** compete with hummingbirds for nectar, and bees do not see red very well. Therefore, when hummingbirds spot a red flower, they know that they are more likely to have it all to themselves. Access to enough nectar is critical because **it is imperative that hummingbirds take in 12 times their body weight in nectar each day.**

In all, there are over 320 different species of hummingbirds. A majority of the species live in tropical areas of Central and South America, but a few of them migrate to North America during the spring and summer.

ACTUAL TOEFL
VOCABULARY

Select the vocabulary word or phrase that has the closest meaning.

1. **relatively**
   A. accurately
   B. comparatively
   C. doubtfully
   D. skeptically

2. **vibrant**
   A. dim
   B. vivid
   C. serious
   D. happy

3. **depend on**
   A. rely on
   B. settle on
   C. focus on
   D. take on

4. **assure**
   A. contradict
   B. guarantee
   C. discourage
   D. condemn

5. **afford**
   A. conceal
   B. refrain
   C. oppose
   D. provide

6. **mandate**
   A. order
   B. denial
   C. refusal
   D. answer

7. **repercussion**
   A. cause
   B. failure
   C. effect
   D. hatred

8. **feat**
   A. achievement
   B. failure
   C. fatigue
   D. excess

9. **figure out**
   A. doubt
   B. determine
   C. allure
   D. follow

10. **primary**
    A. fundamental
    B. additional
    C. informal
    D. secondary

11. **enhance**
    A. impair
    B. worsen
    C. assure
    D. improve

12. **brittle**
    A. easily seen
    B. easily fixed
    C. easily learned
    D. easily broken

13. **annihilate**
    A. revive
    B. animate
    C. enjoy
    D. destroy

14. **luminous**
    A. obscure
    B. gloomy
    C. brilliant
    D. famous

15. **presumably**
    A. exactly
    B. unlikely
    C. supposedly
    D. doubtfully

16. **appreciate**
    A. assist
    B. confuse
    C. understand
    D. apply

17. **endorse**
    A. advance
    B. repel
    C. support
    D. compromise

18. **approach**
    A. effect
    B. section
    C. influence
    D. method

19. **at the urging of**
    A. in opposition to
    B. with the disapproval of
    C. at the insistence of
    D. in reference to

20. **emit**
    A. consider
    B. evolve
    C. accomplish
    D. discharge

21. **prevalent**
    A. widespread
    B. isolated
    C. heartening
    D. ranked

22. **handle**
    A. ease
    B. repose
    C. rest
    D. manage

23. **sole**
    A. proud
    B. only
    C. safe
    D. careful

24. **conserve**
    A. convert
    B. save
    C. present
    D. produce

25. **belch**
    A. suddenly emit
    B. suddenly absorb
    C. suddenly withhold
    D. suddenly depart

26. **boon**
    A. great protest
    B. great benefit
    C. great harm
    D. great increase

27. **allocate**
    A. condemn
    B. retract
    C. keep
    D. designate

28. **provided**
    A. or
    B. and
    C. if
    D. so

29. **flow**
    A. obstruction
    B. movement
    C. countless
    D. tributary

30. **devastation**
    A. preservation
    B. conservation
    C. destruction
    D. description

31. **mechanism for**
    A. payment for
    B. reason for
    C. explanation for
    D. method for

32. **allude**
    A. suggest
    B. allow
    C. oppose
    D. conceal

33. **restricted**
A. caused
B. limited
C. effected
D. altered

34. **enact**
A. establish
B. destroy
C. abolish
D. correct

35. **unaccounted for**
A. unavailable
B. unexplained
C. undecided
D. understood

36. **unique**
A. common
B. distinct
C. similar
D. unclear

37. **terrain**
A. scenery
B. land
C. ocean
D. atmosphere

38. **cluster**
A. clarity
B. claim
C. group
D. awe

39. **equilibrium**
A. imbalance
B. space
C. balance
D. heavy

40. **retain**
A. resume
B. release
C. bend
D. maintain

41. **retard**
A. delay
B. finish
C. lose
D. save

42. **ruthlessly**
A. mercifully
B. heartlessly
C. eventually
D. constantly

43. **invariably**
A. nearly
B. irregularly
C. constantly
D. briefly

44. **attribute A to B**
A. move A to B
B. ascribe A to B
C. bring A to B
D. recommend A to B

45. **coincidentally**
A. separately
B. simultaneously
C. subsequently
D. speedily

46. **abandon**
A. give as
B. give up
C. give out
D. give to

47. **arduous**
A. passionate
B. difficult
C. clever
D. unknown

48. **give rise to**
A. interfere
B. revise
C. cause
D. discover

49. **relic**
A. content
B. unity
C. whole
D. artifact

50. **miniature**
A. huge
B. small
C. important
D. worthless

51. **convey**
A. retain
B. communicate
C. construct
D. translate

52. **perpetually**
A. originally
B. continually
C. surprisingly
D. directly

53. **contiguous**
A. precious
B. complex
C. neighboring
D. replaced

54. **compel**
A. conduct
B. hinder
C. allow
D. force

55. **viable**
A. able to survive
B. able to feel
C. able to resist
D. able to move

56. **concede**
A. conceal
B. dismiss
C. admit
D. reject

57. **concentrate on**
A. done with
B. focus on
C. skim through
D. start on

58. **allegedly**
A. questionably
B. supposedly
C. doubtfully
D. accordingly

59. **expandable**
A. flexible
B. rigid
C. separate
D. unbending

60. **exceedingly**
A. roughly
B. mildly
C. highly
D. actually

61. **allocation**
A. alliance
B. rejection
C. assignment
D. collection

62. **contraction**
A. construction
B. expansion
C. prediction
D. reduction

63. **comprehensive**
A. through
B. slight
C. thorough
D. exclusive

64. **emphasize**
A. stress
B. distribute
C. mislead
D. dispersed

65. **hint**
A. specialty
B. clue
C. statement
D. recognition

66. **evaluate**
A. focus
B. assess
C. create
D. invent

67. **vulnerable**
A. probable
B. defenseless
C. viable
D. protected

68. **innovation**
A. old development
B. new development
C. current development
D. no development

69. countering
A. opposing
B. cooperative
C. accommodating
D. cautious

70. conquer
A. battle
B. construct
C. defeat
D. surrender

71. remarkable
A. notable
B. native
C. normal
D. natural

72. pertinent
A. inappropriate
B. relevant
C. mistaken
D. various

73. appreciable
A. unnoticed
B. necessary
C. significant
D. appropriate

74. cumbersome
A. graceful
B. wholesome
C. resourceful
D. burdensome

75. constitute
A. command
B. confirm
C. connect
D. comprise

76. colonize
A. destroy
B. inhabit
C. remodel
D. transfer

77. devour
A. invent
B. consume
C. engineer
D. develop

78. dense
A. abnormal
B. thick
C. pure
D. actual

79. deceiving
A. transparent
B. apparent
C. decaying
D. misleading

80. traumatic
A. pleasing
B. upsetting
C. tiring
D. calming

81. successive
A. interrupted
B. causal
C. in sequence
D. leading

82. embodiment
A. description
B. submission
C. representation
D. statement

83. decline
A. weaken
B. debate
C. strengthen
D. wander

84. demise
A. creation
B. birth
C. end
D. belief

85. deem
A. define
B. consider
C. measure
D. evolve

86. rudimentary
A. basic
B. rude
C. impressive
D. respectful

87. master
A. bind
B. release
C. unleash
D. learn

88. incompatible
A. constant
B. consistent
C. conflicting
D. conventional

89. barren
A. agile
B. fertile
C. busy
D. lifeless

90. embody
A. assure
B. represent
C. trust
D. produce

91. impart
A. settle
B. observe
C. take
D. provide

92. fashion
A. caution
B. sentiment
C. performance
D. style

93. sophisticated
A. highly refined
B. highly trusted
C. highly interested
D. highly supported

94. commonly
A. generally
B. occasionally
C. rarely
D. specially

95. furnish
A. distinguish
B. impede
C. utilize
D. provide

96. absurd
A. reasonable
B. rational
C. ridiculous
D. reflective

97. palatial
A. practical
B. forbidden
C. frightening
D. magnificent

98. discrete
A. united
B. disturbing
C. distant
D. separate

99. anchor
A. remove
B. fasten
C. locate
D. discuss

100. dominate
A. surpass
B. control
C. follow
D. precede

101. intrinsic
A. interesting
B. learned
C. inherent
D. popular

102. fuse
A. banish
B. detach
C. combine
D. protect

103. disintegrate
A. break down
B. build up
C. blow up
D. give in

104. adopt
A. begin to amaze
B. begin to help
C. begin to realize
D. begin to use

88C 89D 90B 91D 92D 93A 94A 95D 96C 97D 98D 99B 100B 101C 102C 103A 104D
69A 70C 71A 72B 73C 74D 75D 76B 77B 78B 79D 80B 81C 82C 83A 84C 85B 86A 87D

206 | iBT TOEFL® PATTERN Reading II

105. **concern**
A. ignorance
B. interest
C. popularity
D. specialty

106. **reluctant**
A. reliable
B. distrust
C. mysterious
D. unwilling

107. **generate**
A. destroy
B. abandon
C. produce
D. guide

108. **dramatically**
A. unskillfully
B. easily
C. expertly
D. greatly

109. **hazard**
A. humor
B. respect
C. safety
D. danger

110. **bustling**
A. loud
B. lethargic
C. lively
D. languid

111. **prosperous**
A. unsuccessful
B. flourishing
C. relieving
D. proper

112. **approximate**
A. close to
B. native to
C. far from
D. different from

113. **eclectic**
A. various
B. simple
C. same
D. boring

114. **erratic**
A. consistent
B. unpredictable
C. natural
D. enthusiastic

115. **resilient**
A. slow to recover
B. quick to recover
C. do not recover
D. will recover

116. **enactment**
A. argument
B. establishment
C. destruction
D. correction

117. **obvious**
A. unclear
B. opposite
C. evident
D. optional

118. **presume**
A. assure
B. disbelieve
C. reserve
D. assume

119. **justify**
A. support
B. signify
C. oppose
D. judge

120. **fabricate**
A. destroy
B. connect
C. produce
D. finalize

121. **imply**
A. demonstrate
B. explicate
C. illustrate
D. indicate

122. **swift**
A. quick
B. smart
C. slow
D. mute

123. **subsequent**
A. following
B. including
C. generating
D. preceding

124. **durable**
A. temporary
B. doable
C. short-lived
D. long-lasting

125. **thus**
A. consequently
B. clearly
C. commonly
D. obviously

126. **ultimately**
A. finally
B. previously
C. deadly
D. originally

127. **confines**
A. boundaries
B. locations
C. buildings
D. conditions

128. **contemporary**
A. attentive
B. current
C. old-fashioned
D. temporary

129. **disperse**
A. arrange
B. disturb
C. continue
D. spread

130. **bulk**
A. majority
B. priority
C. minority
D. loyalty

131. **account for**
A. complicate
B. explain
C. write
D. confuse

132. **exert**
A. drop
B. find
C. apply
D. lose

133. **foster**
A. encourage
B. discourage
C. accept
D. decline

134. **vigor**
A. variety
B. difference
C. attraction
D. energy

135. **initial**
A. original
B. final
C. literate
D. instructed

136. **furthermore**
A. initially
B. additionally
C. accordingly
D. finally

137. **attainment**
A. failure
B. acquirement
C. achievement
D. rejection

138. **substantial**
A. unimportant
B. significant
C. independent
D. intelligent

139. **initiate**
A. increase
B. finish
C. free
D. begin

140. **cope with**
A. struggle with
B. compare with
C. deal with
D. cover with

141. **prevailing**
A. widespread
B. minor
C. unknown
D. familiar

142. **abruptly**
A. occasionally
B. suddenly
C. steadily
D. usually

143. **attributable to**
A. repulsed by
B. appealed by
C. affected by
D. caused by

144. **intriguing**
A. inspiring
B. encouraging
C. interesting
D. boring

145. **contend**
A. honor
B. retreat
C. argue
D. disrespect

146. **confine**
A. discredit
B. restrict
C. confuse
D. prove

147. **inducement**
A. introduction
B. hindrance
C. incentive
D. process

148. **potent**
A. fragile
B. breakable
C. powerful
D. unable

149. **distinction**
A. difference
B. obedience
C. similarity
D. rebellion

150. **consequent**
A. original
B. resultant
C. conditional
D. objective

151. **impetus**
A. challenge
B. stimulus
C. collapse
D. inspiration

152. **impose**
A. detach
B. exist
C. force
D. relax

153. **alteration**
A. loss
B. remain
C. modification
D. accident

154. **phenomenal**
A. normal
B. refused
C. extraordinary
D. approved

155. **fragment**
A. take up
B. break up
C. bring out
D. pull out

156. **massive**
A. enormous
B. sensitive
C. cruel
D. minute

157. **essential**
A. true
B. minor
C. vital
D. false

158. **vastly**
A. mildly
B. roughly
C. greatly
D. precisely

159. **consumption**
A. completion
B. utilization
C. stability
D. scarcity

160. **uniquely**
A. commonly
B. exceptionally
C. hardly
D. occasionally

161. **aggregate**
A. collect
B. control
C. plan
D. forget

162. **inevitable**
A. inexpensive
B. unnecessary
C. unavoidable
D. countable

163. **extended**
A. reduced
B. experienced
C. affected
D. lengthened

164. **refine**
A. decline
B. improve
C. learn
D. suggest

165. **persist**
A. continue
B. leave
C. stop
D. accelerate

166. **skeptical**
A. believable
B. dishonest
C. dispirited
D. doubtful

167. **abound in**
A. be plentiful
B. be limited
C. be careful
D. be effective

168. **persistent**
A. short-lived
B. long-lasting
C. pleasing
D. annoying

169. **consent**
A. agree
B. disapprove
C. affect
D. contain

170. **minute**
A. tiny
B. huge
C. great
D. poor

171. **inadvertently**
A. unintentionally
B. deliberately
C. knowingly
D. identically

172. **abundance**
A. plenty
B. deficiency
C. absence
D. existence

173. **fragmented**
A. completed
B. divided
C. weakened
D. strengthened

174. **distinct**
A. careful
B. distant
C. capable
D. noticeable

175. **disseminate**
A. disagree
B. collect
C. spread
D. prove

176. **modest**
A. complex
B. upset
C. simple
D. proud

159B 160B 161A 162C 163D 164B 165A 166D 167A 168A 169A 170A 171A 172A 173B 174D 175C 176C
141A 142B 143D 144C 145C 146B 147C 148C 149A 150B 151B 152C 153C 154C 155B 156A 157C 158C

208 | iBT TOEFL® PATTERN Reading II

177. contentious
A. terrible
B. effective
C. argumentative
D. controversial

178. refinement
A. small improvement
B. small invention
C. small argument
D. small interest

179. adjacent
A. neighboring
B. considering
C. linking
D. connecting

180. embark on
A. discourage
B. start
C. finish
D. challenge

181. imposing
A. impressive
B. attentive
C. unimportant
D. repulsive

182. distinctive
A. abnormal
B. characteristic
C. controversial
D. unclear

183. evident
A. apparent
B. uncertain
C. mistaken
D. capable

184. encompass
A. include
B. join
C. exclude
D. direct

185. conspicuous
A. unseen
B. familiar
C. mysterious
D. obvious

186. detect
A. destroy
B. manage
C. discover
D. delete

187. sequentially
A. consecutively
B. secularly
C. suddenly
D. abruptly

188. astonishing
A. boring
B. amazing
C. interesting
D. annoying

189. exhausted
A. taken off
B. used up
C. covered by
D. brought in

190. deliberate
A. harmful
B. unwilling
C. helpful
D. intentional

191. exceptionally
A. mildly
B. initially
C. excitingly
D. distinctively

192. harness
A. utilize
B. produce
C. complete
D. harden

193. offset
A. understand
B. operate
C. destroy
D. balance

194. assume
A. know
B. consume
C. release
D. suppose

195. onset
A. invention
B. attraction
C. interest
D. beginning

196. prolonged
A. reduced
B. bonded
C. lengthened
D. provided

197. radically
A. subsequently
B. additionally
C. apparently
D. drastically

198. obscured
A. exposed
B. hidden
C. offensive
D. obvious

199. conjecture
A. surprise
B. prove
C. close
D. guess

200. conclusive
A. adequate
B. definitive
C. unequal
D. strange

201. comprise
A. include
B. confirm
C. destroy
D. exclude

202. virtually
A. artificially
B. nearly
C. differently
D. importantly

203. eventually
A. in fact
B. at least
C. in the end
D. in the middle

204. optimize
A. make the best use of
B. make the worst use of
C. make the least use of
D. make no use of

205. subsequently
A. unfamiliarly
B. previously
C. lower
D. later

206. fragmentation
A. creation
B. conclusion
C. deprivation
D. destruction

207. potential
A. probable
B. unavailable
C. conceptual
D. impossible

208. notable
A. insignificant
B. unable
C. outstanding
D. conclusive

209. prominence
A. insignificance
B. intelligence
C. ignorance
D. importance

210. deliberation
A. discussion
B. destruction
C. unwillingness
D. instruction

211. predominantly
A. mainly
B. certainly
C. approximately
D. questionably

212. integrate
A. segregate
B. switch
C. divide
D. combine

213. **contention**
A. conflict
B. effect
C. challenge
D. disrespect

214. **forage**
A. search for food
B. drop food
C. grow food
D. eat food

215. **exclusively**
A. solely
B. partially
C. approximately
D. hardly

216. **ingenious**
A. very honest
B. very deceitful
C. very clever
D. very awkward

217. **assess**
A. evaluate
B. begin
C. finish
D. access

218. **intrigue**
A. bore
B. warn
C. reject
D. fascinate

219. **obscure**
A. extreme
B. perfect
C. careless
D. unclear

220. **decimate**
A. rule
B. destroy
C. create
D. yield

221. **entire**
A. whole
B. incomplete
C. halfway
D. clear

222. **analogous**
A. passionate
B. different
C. analyzed
D. similar

223. **prevail**
A. be mature
B. be dominant
C. be weak
D. be afraid

224. **precise**
A. vague
B. steep
C. exact
D. gradual

225. **intense**
A. silent
B. calm
C. noisy
D. extreme

226. **roughly**
A. approximately
B. greatly
C. precisely
D. specifically

227. **inherent**
A. unable
B. capable
C. additional
D. essential

228. **elaborate**
A. immense
B. creative
C. complicated
D. simple

229. **merely**
A. definitely
B. continually
C. completely
D. only

230. **prominent**
A. outstanding
B. alluring
C. different
D. imminent

231. **considerably**
A. calmly
B. greatly
C. lightly
D. unknowingly

232. **notably**
A. particularly
B. approximately
C. generally
D. rarely

233. **readily**
A. narrowly
B. willingly
C. widely
D. fairly

234. **justly**
A. wrongly
B. rightfully
C. unfairly
D. automatically

235. **lethal**
A. dangerous
B. safe
C. harmless
D. reachable

236. **predominant**
A. historic
B. willing
C. principal
D. minor

237. **barely**
A. altogether
B. just
C. always
D. quite

238. **immensely**
A. certainly
B. extremely
C. doubtfully
D. moderately

239. **proliferation**
A. growth
B. reduction
C. excellence
D. production

240. **ample**
A. scarce
B. plentiful
C. incomplete
D. whole

241. **eventual**
A. first
B. final
C. early
D. proper

242. **configuration**
A. significance
B. arrangement
C. agreement
D. definition

243. **optimum**
A. most current
B. most promising
C. most dangerous
D. most favorable

244. **execute**
A. perform
B. explain
C. exercise
D. blame

245. **consequence**
A. cause
B. trouble
C. agreement
D. outcome

246. **profound**
A. possible
B. impossible
C. significant
D. trivial

247. **proliferate**
A. lessen
B. multiply
C. decrease
D. agree

248. **convention**
A. theory
B. invention
C. exclusive
D. conference

249. aggregated
A. dispersed
B. exported
C. imported
D. combined

250. ultimate
A. additional
B. extra
C. eventual
D. unnecessary

251. consume
A. collect from
B. share with
C. use up
D. divide by

252. vast
A. narrow
B. enormous
C. insignificant
D. precise

253. phenomenon
A. regularity
B. tradition
C. refusal
D. occurrence

254. modify
A. change
B. remain
C. design
D. create

255. accumulate
A. order
B. correct
C. collect
D. consider

256. compelling
A. convincing
B. computing
C. increasing
D. producing

257. advent
A. improvement
B. advancement
C. certainty
D. beginning

258. initially
A. at last
B. in the end
C. at first
D. in time

259. consequently
A. almost
B. therefore
C. always
D. sometimes

260. striking
A. typical
B. remarkable
C. influential
D. enormous

261. pose
A. present
B. gather
C. reject
D. accept

262. component
A. factor
B. potential
C. comfort
D. collection

263. immense
A. large
B. little
C. intense
D. delicate

264. abundant
A. scarce
B. limited
C. numerous
D. unbounded

265. prolong
A. extend
B. shorten
C. produce
D. remove

266. postulate
A. possess
B. claim
C. instruct
D. pretend

267. potentially
A. unlikely
B. strongly
C. possibly
D. greatly

268. principal
A. standard
B. minor
C. main
D. different

269. pronounced
A. indistinct
B. notable
C. ordinary
D. upright

270. extensive
A. widespread
B. expensive
C. restricted
D. precious

271. plausible
A. incredible
B. believable
C. unlikely
D. worthy

272. severe
A. various
B. extreme
C. moderate
D. individual

273. decimation
A. creation
B. domination
C. destruction
D. submission

274. unprecedented
A. new
B. outdated
C. common
D. alternative

275. amplify
A. increase
B. complete
C. decrease
D. empty

276. intact
A. separated
B. unaffected
C. combined
D. damaged

277. integration
A. union
B. collection
C. donation
D. division

278. marked
A. vague
B. ambiguous
C. obvious
D. obscure

279. considerable
A. insignificant
B. dependent
C. moderate
D. significant

280. conjecture
A. fact
B. doubt
C. assumption
D. collection

281. lucrative
A. vague
B. clear
C. profitable
D. unprofessional

282. significantly
A. unwillingly
B. carefully
C. considerably
D. expensively

283. attain
A. assure
B. lose
C. retain
D. reach

284. flourish
A. appear
B. lose
C. fail
D. prosper

285. **remnant**
A. remains
B. remembrances
C. alterations
D. difficulties

286. **significant**
A. simple
B. serious
C. important
D. unnecessary

287. **crucial**
A. effective
B. insignificant
C. efficient
D. important

288. **sequence**
A. disorder
B. order
C. confusion
D. origin

289. **consensus**
A. continuity
B. argument
C. suspension
D. approval

290. **sustained**
A. abundant
B. constant
C. continental
D. multiple

291. **exploitation**
A. use
B. rejection
C. start
D. exploration

292. **fragmentary**
A. forgetful
B. pleasant
C. incomplete
D. conclusive

293. **fluctuation**
A. change
B. uniformity
C. relaxation
D. easiness

294. **induce**
A. bring about
B. focus on
C. take from
D. introduce to

295. **critical**
A. important
B. unnecessary
C. possible
D. clinical

296. **conventional**
A. traditional
B. competitive
C. inconsistent
D. significant

297. **minutely**
A. in order
B. in detail
C. in absence
D. in danger

298. **crude**
A. cruel
B. primitive
C. polished
D. current

299. **exceptional**
A. effortless
B. widespread
C. reasonable
D. extraordinary

300. **sustain**
A. take
B. assume
C. support
D. bring

301. **inherent in**
A. characteristic of
B. knowledge of
C. critical of
D. inside of

302. **particular**
A. public
B. specific
C. general
D. familiar

303. **exploit**
A. take off
B. take care of
C. take advantage of
D. take away

304. **substantially**
A. correctly
B. insignificantly
C. inadequately
D. considerably

305. **predominated**
A. most controversial
B. most dangerous
C. most helpful
D. most important

306. **intermittently**
A. intentionally
B. secretly
C. knowingly
D. periodically

307. **simultaneously**
A. at different times
B. at the same time
C. at the end
D. at the most

308. **stipulate**
A. acquire
B. excite
C. imply
D. require

309. **account**
A. amount
B. report
C. result
D. addition

310. **indispensable**
A. independent
B. unnecessary
C. essential
D. healthy

311. **markedly**
A. noticeably
B. slightly
C. extremely
D. mildly

312. **mimic**
A. control
B. imitate
C. differ
D. oppose

313. **radical**
A. extreme
B. advanced
C. superficial
D. analytical

314. **vigorous**
A. various
B. horrible
C. strong
D. weak

315. **severity**
A. standard
B. seriousness
C. movement
D. fairness

316. **albeit**
A. while
B. although
C. since
D. whether

317. **ingenuity**
A. honesty
B. denseness
C. ignorance
D. intelligence

318. **alter**
A. change
B. manage
C. turn
D. repair

319. **entirely**
A. clearly
B. completely
C. separately
D. inadequately

320 **optimal**
A. flawed
B. absent
C. ideal
D. present

321. **advocate**
A. oppose
B. compete
C. support
D. clash

322. **manipulate**
A. generate
B. create
C. control
D. ruin

323. **fundamental**
A. different
B. efficient
C. difficult
D. basic

324. **promote**
A. behave
B. encourage
C. process
D. divide

325. **enigma**
A. knowledge
B. advancement
C. mystery
D. energy

326. **expansion**
A. reduction
B. concentration
C. growth
D. difficulty

327. **frigid**
A. cold
B. fresh
C. clean
D. particular

328. **excavate**
A. uncover
B. exist
C. conceal
D. influence

329. **application**
A. starvation
B. utilization
C. satisfaction
D. redemption

330. **intrusive**
A. inattentive
B. indifferent
C. intentional
D. interfering

331. **prolific**
A. fertile
B. barren
C. famous
D. unpopular

332. **subject to**
A. relevant to
B. unlikely to
C. susceptible to
D. forced to

333. **compacted**
A. compressed
B. flexible
C. inflated
D. comprising

334. **abandoned**
A. accepted
B. supported
C. deserted
D. provided

335. **rigid**
A. patient
B. flexible
C. kind
D. strict

336. **deviation**
A. reflection
B. conversation
C. departure
D. development

337. **deposit**
A. recall
B. delete
C. place
D. lower

338. **broadly**
A. locally
B. rarely
C. generally
D. exactly

339. **probe**
A. investigate
B. command
C. warrant
D. breach

340. **assimilate**
A. absorb
B. reject
C. mistake
D. differ

341. **succession**
A. decline
B. sequence
C. damage
D. mischief

342. **facilitate**
A. make hard
B. make easy
C. make known
D. make unknown

343. **strategy**
A. plan
B. account
C. rally
D. mystery

344. **momentous**
A. reliable
B. thrust
C. significant
D. pull

345. **hazardous**
A. trivial
B. predictable
C. dangerous
D. undecided

346. **concern**
A. contain
B. deliver
C. accept
D. worry

347. **erect**
A. erase
B. delay
C. escape
D. raise

348. **uniformly**
A. consistently
B. unnaturally
C. roughly
D. unevenly

349. **impede**
A. facilitate
B. initiate
C. attract
D. inhibit

350. **epitomize**
A. rushing
B. tangled
C. corrupt
D. exemplify

351. **transitory**
A. brief
B. lengthy
C. boring
D. quick

352. **consistently**
A. slowly
B. rarely
C. early
D. regularly

353. **be accustomed to**
A. be saved from
B. be increased to
C. be known for
D. be used to

354. **pinpoint**
A. locate directly
B. locate inexactly
C. locate exactly
D. locate early

355. **invariable**
A. changeable
B. constant
C. convertible
D. careless

356. **secrete**
A. report
B. reveal
C. review
D. release

357. inflation
A. distinction
B. compression
C. connection
D. expansion

358. justified
A. exclusive
B. right
C. extreme
D. wrong

359. grasp
A. unleash
B. understand
C. grow
D. establish

360. successively
A. one coming later
B. two at a time
C. one before the other
D. one after another

361. found
A. organize
B. institute
C. establish
D. finish

362. rebound
A. collapse
B. merit
C. recover
D. create

363. diffuse
A. discuss
B. determine
C. distribute
D. discover

364. prosperity
A. economic well-being
B. economic disadvantage
C. economic struggle
D. economic battle

365. enigmatic
A. known
B. clear
C. energetic
D. puzzling

366. ambiguous
A. predictable
B. accurate
C. obvious
D. uncertain

367. enormous
A. quiet
B. loud
C. small
D. huge

368. embed
A. find
B. implant
C. emphasize
D. excite

369. extant
A. existing
B. misplaced
C. bemused
D. found

370. subtle
A. hard to recognize
B. hard to recommend
C. hard to resist
D. hard to react

371. broaden
A. widen
B. consume
C. compress
D. lower

372. precarious
A. pointed
B. fast
C. strong
D. unstable

373. celebrated
A. unknown
B. famous
C. typical
D. rare

374. now and then
A. occasionally
B. seemingly
C. presently
D. ultimately

375. feasible
A. achievable
B. available
C. agreeable
D. arguable

376. hinder
A. consider
B. explore
C. prevent
D. determine

377. correspondingly
A. unfairly
B. extremely
C. accordingly
D. unsuitably

378. cling to
A. stick to
B. remove from
C. add to
D. take with

379. staple
A. minor item
B. exciting item
C. basic item
D. extreme item

380. ritual
A. informal
B. uncustomary
C. ceremonial
D. bizarre

381. rigorous
A. mild
B. severe
C. special
D. kind

382. transform
A. simplify
B. preserve
C. transfer
D. change

383. utterly
A. talkatively
B. partially
C. personally
D. completely

384. integral
A. supplemental
B. useless
C. essential
D. voluntary

385. exhibit
A. conceal
B. veil
C. show
D. disguise

386. breakthrough
A. sudden advance
B. delayed advance
C. no advance
D. timely advance

387. key
A. promising
B. insignificant
C. professional
D. important

388. speculation
A. fabrication
B. prevention
C. information
D. supposition

389. apparent
A. frequent
B. negligible
C. evident
D. occasional

390. remarkably
A. unknowingly
B. surprisingly
C. commonly
D. usually

391. magnify
A. acclaim
B. lower
C. diminish
D. enlarge

392. extract
A. wait
B. combine
C. remove
D. guess

357D 358B 359B 360D 361C 362C 363C 364A 365D 366D 367D 368B 369A 370A 371A 372D 373B 374A
375A 376C 377C 378A 379C 380C 381B 382D 383D 384C 385C 386A 387D 388D 389C 390B 391D 392C

393. formidable
A. intimidating
B. insignificant
C. relevant
D. specific

394. objective
A. purpose
B. experience
C. observation
D. source

395. innovative
A. original
B. traditional
C. inept
D. skillful

396. tend
A. care for
B. live for
C. long for
D. build for

397. converge
A. come together
B. break apart
C. come forward
D. spread out

398. criterion
A. creativity
B. alternative
C. standard
D. criticism

399. provoke
A. doubt
B. believe
C. prevent
D. incite

400. manifest
A. embody
B. comply
C. resist
D. maintain

401. fragile
A. strong
B. decorative
C. sturdy
D. delicate

402. inordinate
A. moderate
B. excessive
C. ordinary
D. generous

403. perpetuate
A. continue
B. cease
C. care
D. concern

404. anxious
A. happy
B. fearless
C. content
D. worried

405. arid
A. wet
B. rigid
C. dry
D. heavy

406. rigor
A. mildness
B. kindness
C. closeness
D. harshness

407. moreover
A. separately
B. additionally
C. independently
D. unintentionally

408. strew
A. gather
B. scatter
C. receive
D. order

409. tremendous
A. minute
B. trendy
C. huge
D. minimal

410. prestige
A. timidity
B. lowliness
C. faith
D. status

411. inflate
A. insert
B. anger
C. enlarge
D. compress

412. consistent with
A. in cooperation with
B. in trouble with
C. in contrast with
D. in agreement with

413. peril
A. comfort
B. safety
C. danger
D. pleasure

414. contract
A. condense
B. predict
C. stretch
D. contain

415. anarchy
A. disorder
B. analysis
C. harmony
D. method

416. devise
A. create
B. destroy
C. control
D. balance

417. likewise
A. vastly
B. chiefly
C. officially
D. similarly

418. complex
A. portion
B. respect
C. facility
D. comment

419. solely
A. truly
B. warmly
C. only
D. richly

420. objective
A. unknown
B. unfair
C. unbiased
D. unjust

421. allegiance
A. knowledge
B. development
C. loyalty
D. experience

422. trauma
A. damage
B. calm
C. relief
D. shape

423. ephemeral
A. hidden
B. permanent
C. temporary
D. excellent

424. adequate
A. disturbing
B. inferior
C. helpful
D. suitable

425. disband
A. distract
B. dismiss
C. repress
D. design

426. expansive
A. liberal
B. spacious
C. significant
D. reserved

427. dramatic
A. dull
B. sharp
C. ordinary
D. significant

428. complex
A. proper
B. complicated
C. relative
D. dependent

429. restrict
A. break
B. expand
C. prohibit
D. fix

430. mounting
A. speeding up
B. slowing down
C. decreasing
D. increasing

431. dependable
A. sensitive
B. interested
C. misleading
D. reliable

432. anticipate
A. overlook
B. continue
C. expect
D. allow

433. shatter
A. destroy
B. fix
C. deflate
D. attach

434. attribute
A. clarity
B. attraction
C. characteristic
D. praise

435. revise
A. change
B. continue
C. corrupt
D. control

436. copious
A. meager
B. abundant
C. scarce
D. thin

437. anxiety
A. noise
B. ease
C. comfort
D. worry

438. comparable
A. competitive
B. incoherent
C. equivalent
D. balanced

439. explicit
A. obscure
B. obvious
C. observant
D. obsessive

440. essentially
A. unintentionally
B. apparently
C. basically
D. additionally

441. thrive
A. throw away
B. take back
C. do well
D. bring up

442. subjected to
A. limited to
B. guarded with
C. covered with
D. exposed to

443. detrimental
A. beneficial
B. harmful
C. favorable
D. valuable

444. negligible
A. major
B. insignificant
C. frequent
D. standard

445. collaborate
A. cooperate
B. disturb
C. follow
D. manage

446. indigenous
A. poor
B. rich
C. foreign
D. native

447. engraved
A. carved
B. buried
C. engaged
D. sharpened

448. trigger
A. block
B. transport
C. take
D. activate

449. embellish
A. decorate
B. enable
C. progress
D. recover

450. current
A. straight
B. present
C. curly
D. past

451. retrieve
A. give back
B. talk back
C. bring back
D. hold back

452. conversely
A. slightly
B. favorably
C. contrastingly
D. equally

453. hypothetical
A. supposed
B. authentic
C. genuine
D. evident

454. nevertheless
A. ever
B. never
C. forever
D. however

455. assert
A. deny
B. debate
C. declare
D. delude

456. commission
A. revoke
B. order
C. tailor
D. settle

457. hamper
A. manage
B. represent
C. understand
D. obstruct

458. decline
A. decrease
B. return
C. use
D. save

459. enduring
A. short-lived
B. lasting
C. momentary
D. fleeting

460. frankly
A. fluently
B. frequently
C. honestly
D. unfortunately

461. compensate
A. reimburse
B. compute
C. expand
D. concentrate

462. bombard
A. begin
B. attack
C. assist
D. protect

463. alternative
A. assistance
B. substitute
C. necessity
D. exception

464. intimate with
A. regardless of
B. enemy of
C. unfamiliar with
D. affectionate toward

447A 448D 449A 450B 451C 452C 453A 454D 455C 456B 457D 458A 459B 460C 461A 462B 463B 464D

429C 430D 431D 432C 433A 434C 435A 436B 437D 438C 439B 440C 441C 442D 443B 444B 445A 446D

465. eccentric
A. elegant
B. unusual
C. insignificant
D. careful

466. merge
A. combine
B. divide
C. carry
D. remove

467. immune
A. immense
B. reliable
C. invulnerable
D. favorable

468. drastically
A. slightly
B. faintly
C. severely
D. clearly

469. excessive
A. moderate
B. reasonable
C. accessible
D. extreme

470. viability
A. complexity
B. modesty
C. vanity
D. feasibility

471. continuous
A. ongoing
B. outgoing
C. regular
D. disturbed

472. continual
A. temporary
B. constant
C. fleeting
D. eternal

473. thriving
A. impaired
B. scarce
C. failing
D. successful

474. prime
A. unworthy
B. inferior
C. superior
D. respectable

475. decisive
A. definitive
B. uncertain
C. problematic
D. extreme

476. hence
A. unnecessarily
B. subsequently
C. consequently
D. importantly

477. speculate
A. neglect
B. disregard
C. specialize
D. hypothesize

478. uniform
A. imbalanced
B. inconsistent
C. invariable
D. imperfect

479. primarily
A. additionally
B. mainly
C. secondarily
D. informally

480. exceed
A. surpass
B. follow
C. precede
D. acquire

481. chancy
A. careful
B. certain
C. risky
D. safe

482. counterpart
A. contrast
B. opposite
C. stranger
D. equivalent

483. evoke
A. conclude
B. arouse
C. result
D. unsettle

484. requisite
A. essential
B. unnecessary
C. optional
D. beneficial

485. dissipated
A. dispersed
B. attached
C. isolated
D. detached

486. cite
A. mention
B. bring
C. perform
D. withdraw

487. obtain
A. discredit
B. sacrifice
C. predict
D. acquire

488. halt
A. stop
B. begin
C. learn
D. affect

489. heritage
A. expression
B. limitation
C. hesitation
D. tradition

490. appreciably
A. appropriately
B. insignificantly
C. noticeably
D. briefly

491. duplicate
A. support
B. deliver
C. reproduce
D. indicate

492. reasonable
A. intolerable
B. sensible
C. accountable
D. unbearable

493. pristine
A. guilty
B. pure
C. stiff
D. alert

494. elongate
A. lengthen
B. shorten
C. command
D. request

495. link
A. allow
B. detach
C. connect
D. restart

496. facet
A. fact
B. center
C. branch
D. aspect

497. deviate
A. go straight
B. turn aside
C. move forward
D. travel far

498. assorted
A. broken
B. similar
C. alert
D. various

499. camouflage
A. uncover
B. hide
C. disclose
D. bare

500. presumable
A. apparent
B. extreme
C. impossible
D. uncertain

Answer Keys

Chapter 1 Vocabulary

Warm Up   p. 7

1) metropolis   11) thermometer
2) solitude   12) antislavery
3) intercept   13) supervise
4) satisfying   14) suggest
5) abstain   15) propel
6) extraordinary 16) multilingual
7) monologue   17) minor
8) benefactor   18) manuscript
9) equidistant   19) uniforms
10) microscope 20) megaphone

Quick Practice   p. 8

1) Ⓐ An *exposition* is generally a large meeting or show meant to advertise manufactured products, and an *exhibition* is a public display of artisanal work or craft works, such as model railroads.

2) Ⓒ Since a *spur* is a pointed wheel affixed to the heel of a boot used to urge a horse to action, the word *spurred* is metaphorically close in meaning to *encouraged* or urged.

3) Ⓑ A *kit* is a *set* of parts that are used for a specific purpose, so *sets* is closest in meaning. Moreover, "*kits* and parts" go together in the sentence, and a *set* is simply a series of parts, so one can infer that *sets* can logically replace *kits*.

4) Ⓒ If two objects are *uniform*, they are identical to one another or *consistent* with each other. Manufacturing standards are generally created to ensure that all parts are *consistent*.

5) Ⓓ When something is *even*, it is distributed *equally* over all surfaces. The following sentence also clarifies the statement that rainfall is not *even*, or *equal*, in all areas.

6) Ⓑ To *drench* something is to cover it completely, usually with water or some other liquid. Thus, *drenches* means *exces-*

sively wets in regards to rain's effect on forests.

7) Ⓐ A *descent* is a movement downward, so *descends* means *falls*, which fits in the sentence since "rain," the noun that *descends*, infrequently *falls* "on desert areas."

8) Ⓒ If something that is even is distributed equally over all surfaces, something *uneven* has the opposite meaning, which is indicated by the prefix *un-*, meaning "not." Thus, *uneven* is closest in meaning to *unbalanced*.

9) Ⓑ A *swift* person is able to move with great speed. A messenger would have to run *rapidly* to deliver important, urgent, or warning messages across great distances.

10) Ⓒ To *announce* something is to have it *made known* officially to an audience. This makes sense in context since a messenger's job is to deliver announcements on important issues.

11) Ⓒ To *declare* something is to announce it, so a *declaration* is a way to notify people about important news. Thus, *declaration* is closest in meaning to *notification*.

12) Ⓐ To *derive* means to trace something back to where it began. Where something begins is known as its *origin*, so *derive* means *originate*.

13) Ⓑ When something is *exemplary*, it is *praiseworthy* because it acts as the ideal example. If "Critics have praised *High Noon*," it must be a *praiseworthy* film.

14) Ⓐ To *depict* something is to *portray* it using images or words. Thus, a *depiction* is a *portrayal*, which is hinted at when the author describes the image of "a bleak, empty landscape."

15) Ⓓ When it is used to describe a landscape, *bleak* means *bare* and desolate, and it is often used to describe uninhabited or inhospitable areas, such as a desert or large plain. When the author describes a "*bleak*, empty landscape," the descriptor "empty" clarifies the meaning of "*bleak*."

16) Ⓐ *Breaks with* is an idiomatic phrase that means to *abandon* or end a relationship with someone. *High Noon* goes against, or *abandons*, traditional cowboy film stereotypes.

17) Ⓓ The word *barren* describes land that is agriculturally unproductive and therefore likely uninhabited and *empty*.

18) Ⓒ When something is *appointed*, it is designated to a certain position. Therefore, *appointed* is closest in meaning to *selected*.

19) Ⓐ Something that is *astonishing* is often said to be surprising or *amazing*.

20) Ⓑ To *conquer* is to gain a victory over something or someone. When one empire *conquers* another, the defeated lands are *taken over*.

21) Ⓓ *Intuition* is untaught, inborn knowledge. Thus, when the baby turtles crawl *intuitively*, they do so without thinking, or *naturally*.

22) Ⓒ When something is *generated*, it is created or *produced*. We can find this definition using context since a stimulus *produces* animal behavior.

23) Ⓑ When used as a verb, to *cue* means to provide a *signal* or indication. Moreover, when we plug the answer choices into the place of *cues*, only *signals* makes sense in context.

24) Ⓐ The adjective *belligerent* is used to describe warlike

action. The sentence states that the fish "attacks anything red," which indicates that the stickleback has *aggressive* behavior.

25) Ⓓ When something is *wide*, it is expansive or broad, and the verb *spread* means distributed. Thus, *widespread* means distributed expansively, which means cuneiform was *common* to many places.

26) Ⓐ *Copious* is a synonym of *plentiful*, and both mean numerous or high in quantity. One would need *plentiful* wedge-shaped marks to be able to convey the complexity of meaning in a language.

27) Ⓓ The verb to *cease* means to *stop*. One can determine that *stopped* is appropriate since "more efficient writing systems" would cause cuneiform to *stop* existing.

28) Ⓒ Someone who is *efficient* is very capable at a given task. Thus, *efficient* is a synonym for *effective*. This makes sense since cuneiform would likely be replaced by a "more *effective* writing system."

29) Ⓒ When something is *intricate*, it is complicated or difficult to understand, so *intricate* means *complex*. Moreover, *Rube Goldberg* means "ridiculously *complex*" in regards to the *intricacy* of his machines.

30) Ⓑ The *lexicon* of a language is all the words that comprise that language. Thus, *lexicon* means *vocabulary*. The mention of "synonym" after *lexicon* also indicates that the answer has to do with language, which helps determine the correct answer.

31) Ⓑ A *gadget* is any sort of mechanical *device*. Since Professor Butts was an "inventor," it makes sense that he created *devices*.

32) Ⓐ If something is *absurd*,

it goes against logic and common sense. Therefore, cartoons that present "intricate devices designed to accomplish simple tasks" are absurd because they make no sense, or are *nonsensical*.

33) (D) A *predecessor* is something or someone that comes before. The prefix *pre-* means "before." Simply by breaking down *predecessor*, we can determine that it is the *forerunner* since the prefix *fore-* also means "before."

34) (B) Because the prefix *pro-* means "forward," one can determine that *proceeded* has to do with going in a forward direction. Though Leonardo designed the parachute, he "never *continued* to make such a device."

35) (D) To *fabricate* something means to *make* something by fitting parts together. Furthermore, since the sentence focuses on the creation of the parachute, the verb *made* fits well in context.

36) (C) To *utilize* something is to make *use* of it. The sentence discusses the emergency escape of Blanchard in which he had to *use* his parachute prototype.

37) (A) When something is *asserted*, it is *claimed* with conviction. Since the entire passage centers on claims of the Bermuda Triangle's mysteries, *claimed* fits well in context.

38) (B) Something that is *eerie* is said to inspire suspicion or fear. The word "dangerous," which is used in the same sentence, also indicates that the adverb *eerily* means fearfully or *frighteningly*.

39) (B) The prefix *in-* means "not," and something *explicable* can be explained. Therefore, *inexplicable* means "not explainable," which is a synonym for *mysterious*. Since the Bermuda Triangle is eerie, which means feared, we can use context to determine that the area is likely *mysterious*.

40) (C) An *anomaly* is a deviation from what is considered normal; thus, it is an *irregularity*. Throughout the passage, the Bermuda Triangle is described as *inexplicable* or *eerie*, so one can determine that it would also be described as *irregular*.

Chapter 2 Referent

1) neither
2) it
3) one
4) it
5) both
6) its
7) it
8) a few
9) it
10) their
11) our
12) your
13) the first
14) one
15) others
16) her
17) the latter
18) he
19) their
20) a little

1) (D) The pronoun *him* must be referring to a masculine noun, and *father* is the nearest usable masculine referent. When *father* is put in place of *him*, it makes the sentence clear and logical.

2) (C) The passage states that it is used "to illustrate Washington's character," and a *story* is often used to tell, or illustrate, a point. Moreover, *this story* is the nearest referent preceding *it* and is therefore the correct answer.

3) (C) *These* refers to *great skills in calligraphy*. Since *They*, the first word of the sentence, refers to "educated government employees," the answer cannot be [B]. Also, it makes sense that "They [employees] used *these* [*great skills*] to create...."

4) (D) Though all the answers work to some degree when plugged in for the pronoun *Some*, *highly diverse works* is the best referent because *literati painters* cannot "consist of older men" since that is illogical. Also, [A] and [C] fall under the larger category of *highly diverse works*, so [D] is most appropriate.

5) (B) *These* must refer to Nepal's *three main regions* because, as is indicated by the sentence, *These* encompasses all three remaining answer choices, so the answer cannot be any of the regions individually and must be referring to all three regions at once.

6) (D) Since the mountain called Mount Everest is one example of *them*, one can conclude that *them* must refer to a group of mountains. Therefore, the answer must be *Himalayas*.

7) (D) When the phrase "reacts to" appears before the pronoun *them*, we can determine that *them* refers to *allergens* because the second sentence is simply supporting the idea presented in the first sentence.

8) (A) *One* is an indefinite pronoun, which means that its referent will often have to be inferred. When we plug the answer choices into the sentence, only *an individual* would "develop asthma when exposed to pollen."

9) (C) The passage states that "U.S. doctors commonly recommend" aspirin; therefore, it makes sense that those same *U.S. doctors* would "claim that…daily use of aspirin" may have health benefits.

10) (C) "Heartburn and stomach irritation" are neither *certain benefits* nor *leading causes of death*. Therefore, the referent of *these* must be the preceding noun *side effects*.

11) (C) *His* refers to *Virgil's* because *Virgil* is the subject of the sentence and the only singular masculine noun present within the same sentence as *his*.

12) (C) Though the *Idylls* is mentioned two sentences previous to the pronoun *it*, the *Idylls* remains the focus of the remainder of the passage. Thus, *it* must refer to the *Idylls* because it is the nearest applicable noun.

13) (D) *Machines and gadgets* is the referent for *they* because they are the nearest plural nouns. Moreover, [D] makes sense in the context of the passage since the focus of the passage is on industrial designers making manufacturers' *machines and gadgets* more appealing.

14) (C) Since *their* is possessive and shows ownership over "products," one must determine who owns the products. Since the passage focuses on *businesses* trying to improve their products, answer [C] is most logical.

15) (D) *Its* shows possession over "borders," so one can determine that *its* must refer to one of the two nations – the U.S. or Mexico. Since *United States* is the nearest applicable noun, it must be the appropriate referent for *its*.

16) (C) *It* is used to describe a referent that "was forced to give up a vast territory" after losing a war. *It* must be referring to *Mexico* because *Mexico* lost the war and had to give up territories.

17) (A) When the answer choices are plugged into the sentence, only *many changes* is logical since odorizers are examples of the changes made to prevent explosions.

18) (C) *It* must refer to a *gas leak* because the sentence states that *it* can be detected by a strong odor for safety.

19) (C) Though the nearest preceding noun to *they* is *muscles*, one must use the context of the first sentence and realize that the word *muscles* functions to describe what *hearts* actually consist of. Since *muscles* refers back to *hearts*, and *hearts* are said to "get broken," *they* logically refers to *hearts*.

20) (B) In the passage, "*It*… holds the heart," and the primary structure that holds the heart in the passage is the *pericardium*. Thus, *pericardium* must be the referent of *it*.

1) (C) Though the films listed in answer choice [D] immediately precede the pronoun *these*, they are examples of the larger category of *many movies in the film noir style*. Since *these* discusses general characteristics of *film noir*, [C] is a better choice.

2) (A) Someone who is *solitary* is *alone* or without companionship. Though *lonely* may also seem like a reasonable answer, *lonely* carries the connotation that a person is alone yet desires companionship, which is something not implied by *solitary*.

3) (A) To *lure* someone is to attract or *entice* him or her. We can determine this using context since "beautiful women" may *entice* men to do foolish things, such as become involved in bad situations.

4) (B) The adjective *grim* is often used to describe situations that have no positive outcomes. Thus, *grim* is closest in meaning to *hopeless*, which fits the "world of moral corruption" in *film noirs*.

5) (C) The pronoun *it* acts as the subject of the sentence, and since the main focus of the latter half of the passage is on the plot and *action of film noirs*, we can conclude that *it* refers to *action* so that the main idea remains consistent.

6) Ⓒ Within the passage, examples of "*dingy* settings" include "rundown offices or hotel rooms." Thus, the adjective *dingy* corresponds with the adjective rundown, or *dreary*.

7) Ⓓ *Film noirs* take place at night in dingy settings, so one can infer that a *rundown* building is related to the dingy, night-time atmosphere. The word that is closest in meaning to *rundown* is *deteriorating*, or falling apart.

8) Ⓑ *Anxiety* is a feeling of *uneasiness* or distress. Because the genre of *film noir* contains grim situations and characters are not "able to escape their fate," we can determine that a sense of *uneasiness* is present in the films.

9) Ⓐ The final two sentences of the passage tell the reader how a *sense of anxiety* is depicted in *film noirs*. Thus, *this* refers to the *sense of anxiety* since the details following *this* tell the reader more about how this *anxiety* is achieved.

10) Ⓓ *Edgy* is an adjective that describes a feeling of *tension* or anxiety. The definition can be determined using context since "*edgy* music and deep shadows" describes how the "sense of anxiety" is achieved in *film noirs*.

11) Ⓒ To *deem* is to *consider* or have an opinion. One can determine this answer using the context of the sentence because the sentence discusses how "buyers of fine art" viewed, or *considered*, women painters.

12) Ⓐ Someone who is *proficient* is relatively skilled, or *capable*, in a certain subject. The meaning of *proficient* can be determined using the passage since one can determine the "buyers of fine art" did not consider women particularly *capable* of painting.

13) Ⓒ A person who is *brilliant* shows great talent in a particular area and is therefore *exceptional*. The words proficient and *brilliant* work together in the first sentence of the passage to show qualities usually desired in *exceptional*

artists.

14) Ⓒ Though there are several singular nouns that precede *its* in the sentence, only *a story* fits because *its* shows possession over a "most dramatic moment." Of all the answer choices, only *a story* is likely to have a "most dramatic moment."

15) Ⓑ A person who is *adept* shows a high level of *skill* at a given task. Since the passage states that Gentileschi was able to paint for powerful families, we can determine that she must have been *skilled*.

16) Ⓓ One who is *commissioned* is commanded or *hired* to accomplish a certain task. Because Gentileschi was a skilled artist, we can infer that she would be *hired* to paint for others.

17) Ⓓ The pronoun *they* refers back to the nearest plural noun phrase, which is *women*. Though *subjects* also makes sense when it replaces the pronoun, *women* provides more specific information and is a closer referent to *they*.

18) Ⓐ Something that is *sensational* will produce a strong reaction. Since Gentileschi's paintings depict suffering and violence, it can be inferred that her paintings are *dramatic*.

19) Ⓒ The sentence containing *them* continues to focus on *Gentileschi's sensational paintings* by describing their contents; therefore, *Gentileschi's sensational paintings* is the best referent because it precedes *them* and agrees with the pronoun in terms of number.

20) Ⓒ Beheading someone is an extreme, bloody way to take revenge. Therefore, we can conclude that *ruthlessly* describes the *brutal* way in which Judith decided to take revenge, so *ruthlessly* is closest in meaning to *brutally*.

21) Ⓐ The word *undergone* refers to bird's "development of special beaks and feet." Thus, if something *undergoes* development, we can infer that it goes through a process of development, or *experiences* development.

22) Ⓒ An *adaptation* is a modification or a *change*. The sentence lists *changes* that water

fowl have undergone, such as the development of "special beaks and feet."

23) Ⓓ Something that is *edible* is something that is *ingestible*. This makes sense in context since water fowl would likely adapt "special beaks and feet" that would help them find food that they can ingest.

24) Ⓐ Since the passage discusses the adaptations of water fowl, and since flamingos are a type of water fowl, the reader can determine that *these* refers to *water fowl*. The sentence implies that *these* refers to the larger category of birds to which flamingos belong.

25) Ⓐ A *characteristic* is a trait or *feature*. We can determine this definition from context since the first sentence implies all water fowl have adaptations specific to their environment, and *features* is closest in meaning to both adaptations and *characteristics*.

26) Ⓓ The phrase "To help *them* walk in deeper water" explains why flamingos have such long legs. Therefore, *flamingos* is the referent to *them* even though *them* comes after the pronoun.

27) Ⓓ When it refers to water, *shallow* means *not deep*. [D] is the only logical choice since lagoons are always salty and coastal, and *not favored* makes no sense in context.

28) Ⓑ Based on the information in the passage, we can infer that a *foraging* flamingo will "gaze into the water" and "scoop up food." Therefore, a *foraging* animal is *searching* for food.

29) Ⓒ The pronoun *they* refers to birds that "hang their heads down." Since *flamingos* is the nearest noun that possesses a head, we can infer that *flamingos* is the referent.

30) Ⓒ When something is *arduous*, it requires much work and is therefore *difficult*. Since they have specialized necks and beaks, flamingos do not have a *difficult* time looking in the water. Thus, they can do it "without *difficult* effort."

31) Ⓐ To *confront* is to *encounter* someone or something that may have hostile intentions. Since the "fight-or-flight re-

sponse" is a customary response to conflict, we can use context to determine that *confront* means *encounter*.

32) Ⓑ According to Paragraph 1, a "fight-or-flight response is *triggered* in the body," and it also "occurs when humans… are angered." Hence, there is a relationship between the words *triggered* and "occurs," and the answer choice with the closest meaning to "occurs" is *initiated*, which means to cause something to begin.

33) Ⓑ *It* refers to *anger*. The pronoun *it* is described as something that "motivates people to challenge wrongdoing," and since the author mentions that "Anger can be useful," we can infer that "*Anger* can be useful if anger motivates people…."

34) Ⓐ *Hostile* is an adjective that describes behavior related to unprovoked attacks. Similarly, *combative* describes excessive aggression. The meaning of *hostile* is determined from the passage since it is associated with anger that "is uncontrolled."

35) Ⓐ When used as a verb, to *cover* can mean to extend or go over something. To *comprise* means to include or contain.

36) Ⓓ Anger management classes aim to achieve results, and a *strategy* is a tactic, or a planned series of steps meant to achieve a certain result.

37) Ⓐ The use of the word "also" following *They* indicates that this sentence is continuing the discussion on what people learn in *anger management classes*. Thus, *They* refers back to *anger management classes*.

38) Ⓓ The sentence states that *cognitive* restructuring changes "irrational and negative thinking." Therefore, we can determine that *cognitive* is related to "thinking," and these two words are closest in meaning to *mental*, or occurring in the brain.

39) Ⓒ The meaning of *irrational* can be determined by breaking the word down. The prefix *ir-* means "not," and *rational* means reasonable. Therefore, *irrational* means *unreasonable*.

40) Ⓐ The pronoun *this* is being used to replace a noun phrase that

"teaches more positive 'self-talk.'" Therefore, *this* must be related to something positive, and *cognitive restructuring* aims to achieve positive results.

Chapter 3 Fact & Detail

Warm Up   p. 33

1) F   6) O   11) F   16) O
2) F   7) O   12) O   17) O
3) O   8) F   13) F   18) O
4) O   9) O   14) F   19) F
5) F   10) O   15) F   20) F

Quick Practice   p. 34

1) (A) The passage states that "the peasants that lived and worked on a lord's estate could not expect to be granted such a license," so the *hunters given permission to enter the royal forests were not peasants.*

2) (B) Paragraph 1 indicates that nobles claiming private forests and restricting access to these forests "caused great public resentment." The public's displeasure demonstrates that *many people thought that hunting rules were unfair.*

3) (C) Since hunting in the forests "helped them [nobles] maintain fitness for war," one benefit of hunting was that *nobles sharpened their skills for battle.*

4) (D) Paragraph 2 states that falcons and hawks helped in the hunt, so *birds of prey were trained to help hunters acquire meat.*

5) (B) Since a "solvent dissolving a solute creates a solution," we can determine that *a solute is dissolved*, and *a solvent* does the dissolving. Only (B) properly explains this relationship since the other choices either reverse this process or exclude mention of the solute.

6) (A) In a solution, two molecules "are attracted to areas of negative and positive charges in each other's structures." Therefore, claiming the solute and solvent *react to each other's charges* is an accurate simplification of this process.

7) (C) According to Paragraph 2, oil molecules are said to be *alike and therefore* "oils...form a solution because their molecules are similar."

8) (B) The passage states that "solutes are not always solid or liquid; a gas can be dissolved into water," so *liquids, solids, and gases can act as solutes.*

9) (C) Claiming that Meucci *conveyed verbal messages by using his device in his residence* is a summary of the passage's statement that he used his device to communicate with his wife on the second floor of his house while he remained on the ground floor.

10) (D) Since Meucci claimed "he was not able to get funding to develop his [telephone] prototype," we can conclude that he lacked *money to move it beyond the early stage* of development.

11) (A) Though Bell was challenged in court, Paragraph 2 reveals that he was granted the U.S. patent for the telephone. This patent insured that no one else could copy or steal his invention; therefore, Bell had the *sole rights to the invention of the telephone.*

12) (B) "Meucci's device had been based on simpler acoustic principles," so *Meucci's invention used different technology than Bell's.*

13) (B) "Two European factions fought for their proposed successors" to the throne of Spain, so we can determine that *Two rival groups wanted different princes to succeed to the throne of Charles II.*

14) (C) One faction supported "a French prince" while an Austrian prince was "supported by England." Therefore, the two factions were *France vs. Austria* and *England.* The other nations mentioned were parts of these larger conflicting factions.

15) (B) Both factions' choices for a successor were cousins of Charles II and from either France or Austria. Thus, *Charles II's two potential successors belonged to different European kingdoms.*

16) (A) Paragraph 3 states that "the French prince...was removed from French succession" in order to *limit the French prince's power* and ensure that he could not rule both France and Spain.

17) (B) Since "The public can tour these locations [the Philadel-

phia and Denver Mints] and learn how coins are manufactured," it makes sense that mints *offer tours at sites where regular coins are produced.*

18) (D) Since "proof" coins are primarily "samples created to ensure quality before the large-scale production," we can also describe them as a *preliminary set of coins to check quality.*

19) (C) The factories in both New York and San Francisco produce "proof" coins, which are "samples created to ensure quality," but they are not meant for circulation. Therefore, New York and San Francisco produce *coins that probably will not be used as money.*

20) (B) In Paragraph 3, the process for minting "punches out blank coins," which are then heated "before the *washer-and-dryer stage.*" Then the coins "go through an *upsetting mill*" and "are stamped with designs."

21) (A) The passage indicates that DJs in New York City, which is an *urban center*, began making music that eventually led to the formation of breakdancing, which was a "sidewalk phenomenon" that was witnessed *outdoors.*

22) (C) When DJs isolated "the rhythmic 'breakdown' sections of dance records," they "helped create a sidewalk phenomenon" known as breakdancing. Thus, we can trace breakdancing to the *rhythmic sections of dance records.*

23) (A) Paragraph 2 indicates that breakdancing includes "spinning...on one's head" and "various handstands." These acts demonstrate that dancers *invert their bodies by using upper-body strength and balance.*

24) (D) The author states that "any type of music with a fast tempo can serve" as breakdance music and that "the activity has gained worldwide popularity," so we can conclude that breakdancing *has adapted to newer styles of music and different places.*

25) (D) Since the statue "holds up a lighted torch," we can determine that it "enlightens" the world by *carrying a lighting device.*

26) (C) Paragraph 1 states that

the statue is modeled after "the Roman goddess... associated with freed Roman slaves." The quote is restated in the answer choice as a *goddess connected with liberation of slaves.*

27) (C) Paragraph 2 indicates that the creation of the statue was inspired by the end of slavery in the U.S., and it is modeled after a goddess associated with freedom. Putting these pieces of information together, we can conclude that *the pursuit of freedom and democracy affected many lives.*

28) (B) Because the arm, torch, and head were shown at various expositions, we can conclude that the statue *was shown to the public in segments.*

29) (C) Presley bought Graceland "in 1957 when he was at the height of his popularity." Thus, *he purchased a residence* is the only answer choice supported by the passage since Grace was not Presley's aunt and there is no mention of a Presley family home or farmhouse.

30) (C) Paragraph 1 explains that Presley purchased Graceland because he "hoped to find quiet and privacy there." Therefore, it makes sense that Graceland *tended to be a quiet place where Presley could take a break from the pressures of fame.*

31) (C) Much of Paragraph 2 is devoted to describing Graceland's *variety of recreation facilities* including "a racquetball court, a TV room with three TVs" and a variety of other amenities.

32) (B) Though Graceland *was purchased to provide isolation*, which is clarified in Paragraph 1 since "Presley hoped to find quiet and privacy there," the estate "has become one of the most-visited private homes...." Thus, it *now draws many tourists.*

33) (C) Imprinting is described as "learning a behavior quickly and permanently." Since this process is permanent, imprinting allows for lessons *that once learned, the brain never needs to learn again.*

34) (C) Paragraph 1 states that newborns imprint upon "what they assume is their mother" immediately after birth. Thus, the object of imprinting is *whoever*

or whatever the newborn thinks *is its parent*. [A] is not correct because sometimes newborns will imprint on human owners or animals other than a parent.

35) Ⓐ Imprinting allows infants to "recognize their own kind." Therefore, it makes sense that a benefit of imprinting is that *newborns know which group they belong to and who is not like them*.

36) Ⓑ Paragraph 2 states that "Imprinting is easy to identify in bird species." Hence, *newly hatched birds* is the best answer supported by the passage.

37) Ⓓ The passage states that Webster "labored…to produce a dictionary" by learning 26 languages, and he "added technological and scientific words" to the American vocabulary.

38) Ⓓ Since Webster "wanted to standardize regional usage, pronunciation, and spelling within the relatively new United States," we can determine that *he wanted to unify the new nation's language*.

39) Ⓒ "Because the skunk inhabits the Americas," one can conclude that it is not an animal that would have been named by the British since they would not have seen it. Thus, *skunk is a word that did not have British origins*.

40) Ⓒ Critics claimed "that Webster had included too many common words" in his dictionary, and thus *it included some words that seemed to not belong in a dictionary* because they were informal or improper.

Chapter 4 Negative Fact

Warm Up   p. 49

1) C	6) D	11) E	16) A
2) D	7) E	12) D	17) A
3) E	8) B	13) E	18) D
4) B	9) A	14) E	19) C
5) E	10) C	15) C	20) C

Quick Practice   p. 50

1) Ⓑ According to the passage, the CEA "offers unbiased advice…on domestic and international economic affairs." Hence, the CEA does not *only give advice on domestic economic affairs* since it also advises on

international affairs.

2) Ⓑ Because "The CEA is made up of a chairperson and two members, who are appointed by the president," it is false that *the U.S. Senate selects the members of the CEA*.

3) Ⓒ The passage states that backgammon "was played around 3000 BCE," which means it's been around for *about 5,000 years*; it is one of the "most popular two-player board games," so *it requires a game board and two players*; and it was present in the *four ancient civilizations* of Mesopotamia, Egypt, Rome, and Persia. Thus, [C] is the only unmentioned choice.

4) Ⓐ The author never mentions backgammon falling out of popularity since "it is one of the oldest and most popular two-player board games in the world," so backgammon was not *rediscovered in the 20th century*.

5) Ⓒ Though community colleges "offer the choice of [easier] remedial classes," the passage does not indicate that all of a community college's *lower-division courses are easier than… elsewhere*.

6) Ⓓ Although one can attain "career training certificates" at a community college, the passage never states that *the campuses offer numerous career opportunities for students*.

7) Ⓑ According to the passage, Gandhi lived in South Africa for two decades, which is much less than *most of his life*. Moreover, the passage does not indicate that he *grew up in South Africa* since he studied law in London.

8) Ⓐ One of Gandhi's first jobs after college was "at a law office in South Africa." Furthermore, "over two decades there [in Africa], he became committed to social justice." Thus, we can conclude that he was *committed to social causes* from early in his career.

9) Ⓓ It is impossible that painters *knew that mixing oil with pigment produced a better paint* before 1500 CE because painters did not learn "about oil paint until around 1500 CE."

10) Ⓐ Although egg yolk was used to make tempera, the pas-

sage states that tempera "cannot be applied thickly." Therefore, we cannot conclude that egg yolk make tempera *soft and flexible on canvas surfaces*.

11) Ⓐ Since "*pop music* refers to an identifiable genre, not just any music that is well liked," it makes sense that pop music does not *refer to whatever type of music that is popular*.

12) Ⓑ Pop music "aims to have a broad appeal," so it features *the kinds of songs that most people enjoy*; the "lyrics usually focus on love and romance," which means pop is *focused on romantic relationships*; and pop music has a "catchy" and "repeating" chorus. However, *lyrics being complex and irregular* is not mentioned.

13) Ⓑ The passage states that Day wanted "to fight the tough economic times" by producing "an inexpensive, simple, and vividly written newspaper to sell...." Therefore, his goal was to make money, not *start a charitable institution*.

14) Ⓒ Though the *Sun* "provided 'human interest' stories" and "was published until 1950," we cannot assume that it *printed only "human interest" stories until 1950*.

15) Ⓒ Even though Brook Farm was located in West Roxbury, the passage never states that the farm's goal was to *alter the structure of West Roxbury farms*. In fact, there is no mention of Brook Farm interacting with other farms in the area at all.

16) Ⓐ According to the passage, many residents of Brook Farm "had academic or religious backgrounds," but no mention is made that *the atmosphere at Brook Farm was based on religious philosophy*.

17) Ⓑ The last sentence of the passage indicates that "the Kuba kingdom was colonized by Belgians starting in 1885," but there is no mention of a Belgian presence when the kingdom was formed 260 years later.

18) Ⓓ Even though the Kuba kingdom fell into decline when it "was colonized…in 1885," more recently "the kingdom has been revived and exists today." Thus, it is false to claim that the Kuba

kingdom *is now only a part of history*.

19) Ⓒ The passage states that "Vikings were northern Germanic people," but ancestral homes are never mentioned in the passage, so it is never stated that they *always went back to their ancestral homes in the north*.

20) Ⓐ Though a retreat is never explicitly mentioned, the passage states that Vikings "could reverse direction without turning around," so [B] is supported. And though Vikings "were expert sea travelers," the passage does not state they *were the only people in Europe…who know how to master the waves*.

Exercises Ch. 3-4   p. 57

1) Ⓑ According to Paragraph 1, dopamine is something that "can create a feeling of pleasure" and motivate "a person to repeat behaviors that resulted in… pleasure. Since it creates such a feeling, dopamine cannot be *a feeling of motivation* itself.

2) Ⓑ Because "dopamine can create a feeling of pleasure and helps the brain retain memories of rewarding experiences," it makes sense that dopamine *causes the brain to store memories of positive experiences*.

3) Ⓒ The passage speculates that dopamine motivates "a person to repeat behaviors that resulted in a sense of pleasure" and "may have developed to reinforce healthy learned behaviors." Claiming that dopamine *creates a reward-based learning system* is an accurate restatement of these ideas.

4) Ⓓ Since "it takes time for these memories [of drug use] to fade," it is not true that *people can recover from substance abuse fairly quickly*.

5) Ⓑ The passage introduces groundwater as "stored in millions of tiny spaces between particles of rock and sand." Thus, groundwater is *in the spaces between underground rocks*.

6) Ⓒ According to Paragraph 2, "roads and concrete" cause rainwater to run "off the surface before it can sink in," and some regions "have overdrawn and depleted the groundwater." Thus,

run-off and over-pumping cause groundwater depletion.

7) D Since groundwater depletion involves the lack of water in an area, it makes sense that *disasters such as flooding* are not a consequence of this depletion.

8) B Although "roots and wetlands help...replenish groundwater," the passage does not claim that groundwater *is more unpolluted, fresh, and pure than above-ground water*.

9) C The passage defines a *gold rush* as "a period of time when thousands of people flock to areas where gold has been discovered." Hence, a gold rush can be summarized as *when people hurry to find gold*.

10) D Paragraph 1 states that "a worker found a nugget in a stream" in California "just as the United States was taking over the territory." Soon, "the secret [of gold] was out." This summary coincides exactly with the events in choice [D].

11) A Paragraph 2 does not discuss the duration of the gold rush, so it is not supported that the gold rush *lasted many years*. Also, California's change from territory to state took one year, which does not indicate a *long push for statehood*.

12) C Even though Paragraph 1 states that "the United States was taking over the territory from Mexico," Paragraph 2 does not mention that the gold rushes *influenced the territorial outcome of the Mexican-American War*.

13) D Paragraph 1 claims that the play "premiered in 1959 in a Broadway theater," and then goes onto to say this "was the first time a play by an African-American woman had ever opened a play on Broadway."

14) C Paragraph 2 discusses the significance of the play's title, explaining that the title was inspired by a poem about "dreams that are...put off." Hence, the title is part of *a metaphor about not being able to achieve dreams*.

15) B Though Paragraph 2 indicates that the play is about an African-American family that buys a home "in an all-white neighborhood," there is no indication that they *do not realize* that the neighborhood is all-white.

16) A The plot involves an African-American family with white neighbors who "try to pay them to back out of the deal" to purchase a new house. Thus, the protagonist's family *experiences racism and hostility* in their new, rich neighborhood, not *in their poor neighborhood*.

Chapter 5 Coherence

Warm Up p. 65

1) 3-1-2	6) 2-1-3
2) 2-1-3	7) 1-2-3
3) 3-1-2	8) 1-2-3
4) 3-1-2	9) 2-1-3
5) 1-2-3	10) 2-3-1

Quick Practice p. 67

1) B The added sentence provides the origin of *etiquette's* relationship with cards and labels. Thus, this new information should be added directly after the sentence that introduces the origin of the word *etiquette* since it elaborates on that origin.

2) A The primary focus of the passage is ghost stories. The added sentence provides a definition of *ghost stories*, and definitions precede details in an explanation, so the added sentence should be placed at [A].

3) C The passage mentions that "shyness is often influenced by heredity" and provides an example of this, yet the final sentence presents an example that shows shyness develops because of learning. Thus, a word that indicates contrast, such as *However*, is necessary to transition between the opposing examples.

4) B The added sentence mentions that *Dipteran insects have a special characteristic*, but it does not mention what that characteristic is. Because the sentence following [B] tells us that Dipteran's special characteristic is having "a single pair of wings," we can determine that the added sentence should precede it.

5) B Since the sentence following [B] provides the example of a three-part name, *Gaius Julius Caesar*, we can determine that a basic explanation should precede this example. Since the added sentence provides a basic

explanation of the Roman naming system (*method divided people's names into three sections*), this sentence should be placed at [B].

6) C The added sentence states that mescaline is illegal except *for very specific purposes*. The final sentence claims that a very specific group (the Native American Church) "is allowed to use peyote." Thus, the final sentence provides an example of a *specific purpose*, so the added sentence should come before the final sentence.

7) A The first sentence of the passage provides a definition of a metaphor. Since the added sentence restates this definition in simpler terms, this sentence should come after the first sentence and be placed at [A].

8) C In the added sentence, *this situation* describes a time of economic growth, as indicated by the mention of *pay more for employees' labor*. Thus, the added sentence should come after the mention of economic growth and be placed at letter [C].

9) B The sentence that follows [B] explains the merits of Democritus' work even though he had not been introduced in the passage. Since the added sentence introduces Democritus' relationship to Leucippus, it should be placed at [B].

10) D This passage explains Louisiana's history in chronological order. Thus, the added sentence must be placed at [D] since it discusses the years 1763 – 1800. The preceding sentence mentions 1718 (an earlier time) and the following sentence discusses 1800 onward.

Chapter 6 Inference

Warm Up p. 77

1) A	2) A	3) B	4) B	5) A
6) A	7) B	8) A	9) A	10) B

Quick Practice p. 78

1) B The passage states that Cosell's "questions were blunt and analytical rather than admiring." Since Cosell was not always admiring of the athletes, we can safely infer that *he was not embarrassed to ask athletes about mistakes*.

2) C Although "not all viewers liked Cosell because...his questions were blunt and analytical," the passage also states he was "the best-known sports broadcaster in" the U.S. Since "not all viewers" means that some did not like his honesty, we can infer *many viewers liked Cosell's honesty* and blunt questions.

3) D Because alchemy "was studied for more than four millennia across three different continents," thousands of students must have studied it. However, the goals of alchemy are eternal life and limitless wealth, which are both unattainable. Thus, it is likely that *many studied it and met only with frustration*.

4) A According to the passage, the two goals of alchemy were "to turn any metal into gold or silver" (*riches*) and to give people "eternal youth" (*immortality*), which we can infer are long-sought, deep-seated human desires.

5) B Since Samhain followed the annual cattle slaughter, we can infer that the festival *coincided with a time of plentiful meat* from the cows that provided food for the Samhain feasts.

6) B If "the barrier between the living and the dead became thin on the night of Samhain," and people set places at the table for "deceased loved ones," then we can infer that the Gaelic people held a belief that *people's souls stayed around their families for a while after death*.

7) D The early folk musicians were regarded as "unsophisticated" and "socialistic" and "did not sell huge numbers of records." Therefore, it is reasonable to infer that their music *did not appeal to wealthier, conservative listeners*.

8) B Folk music in the 1940s did not sell well, but in the 1950s the folk-singing "Kingston Trio achieved commercial success." The only way a genre can go from unsuccessful to successful is if *dismissive customers changed their minds*.

9) B Because the author claims that "each student has a preferred style of focusing on, processing, and retaining information," we can infer that every student learns differently. Thus, *if information is only presented in one way, some students will struggle.*

10) Ⓐ Gardner's argument agrees with the author's by claiming that "each student has a preferred" style of learning. Thus, Gardner would likely approve of having students learn through different types of learning presented in [A] since this method would address many different learning styles.

11) Ⓓ Since Evans "admitted her identity" after achieving critical acclaim, we can infer that she originally used a male name to increase her chances of success and that *she did not want readers and critics to be biased against her* simply because of her gender.

12) Ⓒ Because Rowling's "male name" was created "so that boys would be more likely to read the books," we can infer her publisher believed that boys prefer books written by men, which means it is likely that *boys think of books written by women as "girls' books."*

13) Ⓓ The passage states that bioluminescence "creates cold light" within a firefly. Using this statement, we can determine that the light *does not generate heat.*

14) Ⓑ The passage states that fireflies "send signals to potential mates by emitting a flashing light," which is a result of their bioluminescence. Since sending signals is the only use of the lights mentioned in the passage, we can infer that *they developed bioluminescence as an adaptation to allow communication.*

15) Ⓑ According to the passage, Egypt is located near the Nile River, which means the kingdom had *available water.* Moreover, Egyptians used bathing as a "break from the desert heat," which means there was *hot weather.* Since they "bathed daily," we can infer the Egyptians had *a cultural value of cleanliness.*

16) Ⓐ Since Egyptians were willing to invest in soaps and cleansing creams, and spent the time to "bathe daily" and shave their entire bodies, it is safe to assume that *they spent a fair amount of time and resources* on bathing.

17) Ⓒ The passage makes no mention of Greco-Finnish trade, so [A] can be eliminated. There is no indication of a Finnish written record, so we cannot assume its existence and therefore, [B] can be eliminated. [D] is irrelevant and can be eliminated. Thus, process of elimination indicates that [C] is the safest inference since *preserved chewed gum* would be compelling archaeological evidence.

18) Ⓓ Though [C] may seem like a reasonable inference, it is too large an assumption to say that tree names have *always* been used for gum naming. Thus, claiming that *the origins of gum have had lasting linguistic influences* is the best inference since the passage presents multiple examples of gum-producing trees influencing modern languages.

19) Ⓐ The passage begins by claiming that "Many tourists visit General Sherman." Since the rest of the passage is devoted to presenting examples of other large, popular trees, we can infer that *people are fascinated by trees of extreme size and age.*

20) Ⓑ Since General Sherman has "stood for more than 2,000 years," it is likely that trees like General Sherman are *highly resistant to stressors in the environment.*

Exercises Ch. 5-6   p. 84

1) Ⓐ The sentences that come before and after [A] both mention Jacob Davis' idea, but neither sentence mentions what this idea consists of. Thus, the added sentence should be placed at [A] because the sentence clarifies that *His idea was to sew copper rivets* on the pockets.

2) Ⓓ Since jeans became associated with "rebellious protagonists" and "synonymous with youthful nonconformity" in the 1950s, we can infer that they largely *appealed to people who wanted to appear daring.*

3) Ⓑ The use of *Hence* in the added sentence indicates that this sentence provides a consequence for a previous sentence. Thus, the added sentence should be placed at [B] since *they decided to play a trick on…Max Harris* is a consequence of despising "the modern style of poetry" that Harris promoted.

4) Ⓑ The end of the passage justifies Harris' appreciation of the joke poetry by stating "recent critics and writers have agreed" with his assessment of the poetry. Thus, we can infer that Harris' analysis has become more appreciated and that he *may have been better at recognizing good poetry than people realized.*

5) Ⓐ The added sentence uses the pronoun *these* to refer to "*if-then* statements." Therefore, we want to place this sentence at [A] since it refers to the first mention of "*if-then*" statements and provides a name for the terms that are discussed throughout the passage.

6) Ⓒ The final sentence provides an example of a three-part conditional statement that is more complex than the previous example. It is reasonable to assume that more conditional statements make a program more precise.

7) Ⓑ The added sentence addresses a reader's possible objection to the statement made in the first sentence that "children learn through play" by elaborating upon and reaffirming the statement made in the first sentence. Thus, the best place for the added sentence is directly after the first sentence, so [B] is the correct answer.

8) Ⓑ When children at play "talk with other children or adults about what they are doing," they are *building conversational skills,* which are *crucial to childhood development.*

9) Ⓐ If the teacher mentioned in Paragraph 1 was *aware of others' cultural expectations,* then she might not misinterpret the child's body language as disrespect and would *help prevent conflict* as a result of her understanding.

10) Ⓒ The main idea of the added sentence is that *enculturation* applies to all ages. The final sentence of the paragraph elaborates upon this idea by providing an example of an older person being enculturated by younger people. Since a statement should precede elaborations upon that statement, [C] is the correct answer choice.

11) Ⓑ Since Astley created a business out of horse riding, it makes sense that "he and other riders exhibited their own trick riding at night" in order to increase business and *promote his daytime riding classes.*

12) Ⓓ The added sentence provides the final step to Astley's creation of the modern circus by placing his trick riding and other entertainments in an *Amphitheatre…to showcase his exhibit.* Because the added sentence provides this final step, it should be placed at [D].

13) Ⓒ The use of the phrase *To prevent this* in the added sentence indicates that this sentence should come after something that concerns *farmers in many places.* Since "hungry birds" are the only problem faced by farmers mentioned in the passage, we can determine that the added sentence should be placed at [B].

14) Ⓓ The final sentence of the passage mentions that updated "bird scarers include loud recorded noises or metallic ribbons that shimmer." Since none of these things are truly threatening or frightening, we can infer that *birds notice when conditions in an environment are unusual,* which often scares them away.

15) Ⓑ Even though "Freud experienced criticism" for his approach to psychology, Paragraph 1 states that the basic idea that there are "unconscious causes for…distress and anxiety" was "revolutionary."

16) Ⓓ The author spends much of Paragraph 2 discussing Horney's interpretation of neuroses. Since the added sentence provides a counterexample to neuroses sufferers, it should be placed at [D] so it comes after the discussion of neuroses.

Chapter 7 Purpose

Warm Up	p. 95
1) DES	6) CR
2) CR	7) DES
3) PER	8) PER
4) DES	9) DES
5) DES	10) CR

Quick Practice   p. 96

1) Ⓑ The highlighted portion introduces us to the purpose of zoos and aquariums, which includes animal breeding and reintroduction. Thus, the highlighted portion tells us how *zoos and aquariums are helping* different animal species.

2) Ⓓ The California condor is mentioned as an example of a "nearly extinct species" that was reintroduced to the wild. Therefore, the condor is mentioned as it *can be found in nature because of zoo programs.*

3) Ⓓ In the passage, *eternal* is an adjective that describes classicists' views on "facts and ideals," so the purpose of *eternal* is to *explain the classicist view of ideals.*

4) Ⓐ If "Romanticism…emphasized originality," we can conclude that "originality" is included to *describe what Romantics aimed for* (or emphasized) *in the arts.*

5) Ⓒ The first sentence of the passage mentions that *60 Minutes* is a "long-running" program, so we can determine that the highlighted portion *provides a detail* about the show's longevity mentioned earlier.

6) Ⓑ The mention of a "ticking stopwatch" coincides with the focus of the rest of the passage, which is on what makes *60 Minutes* a unique news show. Using this main idea, we can conclude the *stopwatch* is mentioned *to describe…the show's format.*

7) Ⓓ The passage's main focus is on similarities between a computer and a brain. Thus, the first mention of the computer (the highlighted portion) serves *to introduce a comparison used throughout the passage* between a computer and a brain.

8) Ⓒ The second sentence indicates that both nerve cells in the brain and electrical wires in the computer help send signals. Hence, "signals" helps link brains and computers, identifying *something that* they *have in common.*

9) Ⓒ The highlighted portion helps the reader understand who Demosthenes was and how he relates to history, and it introduces the main idea of the passage,

which is Demosthenes' work in public speaking. Overall, the highlighted passage explains *the significance* of Demosthenes as *a historical figure.*

10) Ⓐ The highlighted portion adds a detail about how Demosthenes practiced to become an orator. Since the method described is unconventional and was likely quite uncomfortable, we can conclude that it shows *how motivated Demosthenes was to become an orator.*

11) Ⓒ Because the main focus of the passage is the goals of the Great Society to improve life, "introduced reforms" describes *Johnson's efforts to make changes* through the Great Society.

12) Ⓐ The highlighted portion provides an example of a part of Johnson's life that "motivated him to improve societal conditions" using the Great Society. In other words, the highlighted portion explains *one reason that* he *wanted the Great Society.*

13) Ⓓ The author puts *eating insects* into historical context by mentioning how ancient and widespread the practice is. Clearly the author wants readers to see that the practice *is not only a modern culinary trend.*

14) Ⓒ Claiming that insects may be able to serve as *mini-livestock* implies that insects could be raised like traditional livestock for human consumption, but it also addresses their smaller size. Since the idea is elaborated upon in the following sentence, we can deduce that *mini-livestock* is mentioned to *introduce and explain* how insects can be used.

15) Ⓓ Though the story is not relayed until later in the passage, the mention of "filial piety" in the first sentence provides the reader with a common theme in Korean folktales, and therefore gives *an interpretation of the story's message.*

16) Ⓑ Shim Chung's sacrifice for her father shows her "respect and care" for her parent. Furthermore, even the Sea Dragon King values "her act of selflessness" for her father and decides to save her life. Hence, it shows her commitment to and the *importance of filial piety.*

17) Ⓐ Without the contributions of Goodyear, there would have been no improved rubber with which to make dolls. Therefore, the purpose of mentioning Goodyear is to *explain* the origins of the doll makers' *new material.*

18) Ⓒ The highlighted portion provides a detail about the rubber dolls produced during the 1800s. Hence, the only clear purpose of this quote is *to provide an interesting fact about dolls.*

19) Ⓑ Since history depends largely on written records of events, the highlighted portion tells us *the written origins of Holy Grail stories* since it provides a period for when concrete records of the stories begin.

20) Ⓒ The passage states that written Holy Grail stories "may have been based on the Celtic people's earlier tales," which indicates that the Celts provide *a possible root of the Holy Grail theme.*

Chapter 8 Paraphrase

Warm Up   p. 107

1) A   2) B   3) B   4) A   5) B
6) B   7) A   8) A   9) B   10) B

Quick Practice   p. 109

1) Ⓒ The statement that Hamilton "helped shape the current U.S. economy" is synonymous with *Hamilton helped create the foundation for the U.S. economy.*

2) Ⓓ Since Hamilton tried to "maintain national economic stability," we know that he wanted a bank that would *stabilize the U.S. economy.*

3) Ⓓ Choice [D] contains the same information as the highlighted portion, but reverses the order of the clauses. [D] best summarizes the difference between *instinctive* and *learned* behaviors.

4) Ⓒ If "behaviors are mostly a combination of" instinct and learning, then we can rephrase the highlighted portion to read that *behaviors are not based only on instinct or learning.*

5) Ⓐ The passage states that absorbers are made from numerous materials and are "usually painted black." The answer choice that best summarizes

these key pieces of information describes these features as *black-painted substances, such as metal or ceramic.*

6) Ⓑ The only answer choice that states that an absorber "collects 95 percent or more of the solar radiation" without including false or irrelevant information simplifies the statistic to say that an *absorber gathers almost 100 percent of the Sun's energy.* Approximations are acceptable in paraphrased statements.

7) Ⓑ The main idea of the highlighted portion is that the spoils system is "reasonable when a party appoints capable individuals…." The most concise rewording of this states the system *is acceptable if qualified individuals are chosen to make policy.*

8) Ⓒ A key idea of this highlighted portion is that the spoils system is unacceptable when "able employees" are dismissed "from government jobs." The only choice that accurately rewords this crucial statement claims many reject the system when it leads to *firing qualified workers.*

9) Ⓓ Since the highlighted portion focuses on what "Plautus added" to Greek comedy, the best paraphrase states *Plautus added his own twist to Greek New Comedy.*

10) Ⓐ From the highlighted portion, we learn that Plautus valued comedy over plot; the answer choice that best paraphrases this claims that *a good time was more important…than the intricate aspects of playwriting.*

11) Ⓒ Because it is "possible to make a distinction between" oxygen and steam, the best paraphrase claims that they *are technically both vapors,* but that *they can also be differentiated.*

12) Ⓐ Choice [A] reverses the order that the highlighted information is presented in, but it is the only answer that correctly differentiates vapors from gases.

13) Ⓑ The highlighted portion provides a definition for the game "peek-a-boo." Only Choice [B] correctly paraphrases this definition without adding unnecessary commentary.

14) Ⓒ Since the game "helps

babies learn that objects...are permanent," we can determine that they *are pleasantly surprised* (or enjoy) the game *before they learn of object permanence.*

15) Ⓐ The key facts of the highlighted portion are that the crash 1) caused a 25 percent unemployment rate in America and 2) caused 40 percent of the banks to shut down. Though [A] uses approximations, it provides the most concise summary of these key events.

16) Ⓓ The most concise paraphrase of "Banks had no money" because "their customers began withdrawing all of the money..." mentions the key ideas that *customers were depleting their... accounts* so that *banks no longer had enough money.*

17) Ⓓ The phrase "independent thinking" can be described as the ability for *people to think for themselves.* Thus, [D] provides the most direct rephrasing of the highlighted portion.

18) Ⓐ The phrase "everyone has access to it [philosophy] at any time" is synonymous with the statement that *philosophical thinking was available to all people.*

19) Ⓒ The primary purpose of the highlighted portion is to explain that Franklin expected that electricity could travel from one medium to another. The answer choice that most accurately summarizes this information claims that *negative electrical charges could probably flow through wet material and metal.*

20) Ⓑ This answer choice contains identical information to the highlighted portion, but it reverses the clauses.

Exercises Ch. 7-8   p. 117

1) Ⓑ Since Coolidge was made president in the "early morning" following Harding's death, we can infer that the purpose of the highlighted portion was *to emphasize how urgent it was* that the country should have a president.

2) Ⓐ The mention of "public confidence in the White House" shows that Coolidge's successful racial and economic policies *earned the trust of the Americans.*

3) Ⓒ Harding's presidency is described as "scandal-driven" *to contrast* with Coolidge's status as "a popular president."

4) Ⓒ The purpose of mentioning that Coolidge "won a second term" and was "in office until 1929" is to *provide evidence that Coolidge was popular* since only a popular president is likely to serve two terms.

5) Ⓓ The passage states Impressionist music "sought to create a mood or feeling" (*a sensation* and *an atmosphere*) and that "it attempted to evoke a place or a natural phenomenon" (*a setting or an image*).

6) Ⓓ According to the passage, Debussy's *Nocturnes*, or "Nights," conveyed "nighttime clouds" (*natural*), "brightly lit festivals" (*social*), "and the mythical Sirens" (*mystical*). All these describe various *aspects of night.*

7) Ⓓ In the passage, "Zeus" is mentioned, and then he is immediately compared to an "early king of Crete, for whom people felt great awe." Since Zeus is not mentioned again until the end of the passage, he serves *to compare a god to a real ancient ruler.*

8) Ⓒ Since "modern scholars usually have no evidence" for Euhemerus' origin stories, the highlighted portion is mentioned *to point out a weakness in using Euhemerus' theory.*

9) Ⓓ Studying the "*Vedas*" caused Müller to realize that "the gods seemed like forces of nature," and thus the "*Vedas*" provided the basis for his theory.

10) Ⓑ Zeus' name means ""shining" or "radiance,"" which are also qualities attributed to the Sun. Therefore, the highlighted portion shows *how a natural force* (the Sun) *may have been personified as a god* (Zeus).

11) Ⓑ According to the passage, Aristotle studied "animals in their habitats" (*watching creatures' ordinary lives*), and "dissected (*cutting some open*) some animals to learn more," during his studies "As a natural historian."

12) Ⓒ The key pieces of information from the highlighted portion claim that Aristotle created an animal-rating "scale from simple to complex," and the scale was "based on their physiology and behavior." Only [C] addresses all these points.

13) Ⓑ The main focus of the passage is on the Liberian women's peace movement. The highlighted portion, then, emphasizes this main idea by showing why *women risked their safety for peace* from such a long civil war.

14) Ⓐ Since demonstrations can be violent or nonviolent, the highlighted portion tells us *an important characteristic of the Liberian peace protests* and illustrates what made this protest unique.

15) Ⓓ Since the civil war lasted 14 years, we can determine that "negotiators could not come to an agreement" because they showed an *unwillingness to compromise.*

16) Ⓑ The highly valued Nobel Peace Prize is awarded to individuals who make great humanitarian efforts, so it is mentioned in the passage to implicitly *show that the global community admired the...movement.*

17) Ⓓ The two key ideas of the highlighted portion are that the book "caught the public's imagination" (*many people have enjoyed it*), and that "the source of Defoe's ideas is still a mystery" (*whether the novel is based on true stories*).

18) Ⓐ The key plot point to be taken from the mention of *Hayy ibn Yaqdhan* is that it is the tale of *a boy on a deserted island* who may have inspired Defoe. The other choices contain incorrect or irrelevant information.

19) Ⓑ Since the plant is "Originally from the Andes Mountains," we can assume the plant grows best there, so these mountains are *the conditions to which the plant is...adapted.*

20) Ⓐ The highlighted portion mentions an unusual characteristic of the nasturtium, so its purpose must be *to point out one of the flower's identifying features.*

21) Ⓒ Though larvae may eat the nasturtium, the flower may also help attract butterflies, which many people enjoy viewing. Thus, the mention of the highlighted portion could convey good or bad news to a gardener, and it shows *a characteristic... that gardeners may or may not like.*

22) Ⓒ If the nasturtium has "crowded out" other species, it has pushed other plants from an area, causing them to die off. Thus, the purpose of the highlighted portion shows how the plant is *invasive in a natural area.*

23) Ⓐ In Paragraph 1, the first calculating device was "invented around 2000 BCE," and the most recent one mentioned is from the 1970s. Therefore, we can summarize this chronology and say that *humans have used tools to calculate numbers for at least four millennia.*

24) Ⓒ The highlighted sentence focuses on the "expanding needs of the consumer," which is best paraphrased by the phrase, *respond to the needs of the public.*

Chapter 9 Summary

Warm Up   p. 129

1) 2   2) 3   3) 1   4) 3   5) 2
6) 1   7) 2   8) 2   9) 1   10) 3

Quick Practice   p. 131

1) 1, 4, 6 The correct answers support Shakespeare being a great dramatist. The passage states that Shakespeare's characters "make audiences laugh, cry, and gasp" (they appeal *to the audience's emotions*), "cope with timeless themes" (*audiences... relate to the basic problems*), and "contributed greatly to the... English language" (*influenced modern English*).

2) 1, 4, 6 The correct answers explain the benefits of pets. According to the passage, pets can potentially reduce "an owner's anxiety" (*a soothing effect*), "perform very specific tasks" (*fulfill a particular function*), and help children "learn empathy and accountability" (*children can learn about work and compassion*).

3) 2, 5, 6 The correct answers focus on human curiosity about Mars. From the passage, we can determine that Mars "reminded them [Romans] of blood" (*people associated the planet*

with bloodshed). Moreover, "Recent robotic rovers" are an example of humans examining *Mars in many ways*. Finally, Mars' proximity "has long caused people to wonder about it," so *it was scrutinized long before there were telescopes*.

4) 2, 3, 4 The correct answers focus on the benefits of sleep. From the research on sleep, we know that sleep maintains "immune systems," so it *helps the body...fight sickness*. During sleep, brain is "busy sorting, storing, and discarding information," which means that it *preserves meaningful new concepts*. While the brain is sorting information, the body is "repairing cells," or restoring *itself on a cellular level*.

5) 1, 5, 6 The correct answers focus on why beavers were trapped. The passage states that beaver fur was "made into felt for warm hats and coats" (used as *outerwear for chilly places*). It also states that beavers were trapped to "trade the furs for supplies" (the *skins served as a kind of currency*) and used *for culinary and mercantile purposes* since "Native Americans and early settlers also consumed beaver meat."

6) 1, 2, 4 "Negative aspects" of modeling include that models "must apply for each modeling assignment separately" (*continually compete for work*), "possess the 'look' that the industry is seeking" (*be favored inconsistently*), and "suffer from eating disorders, anxiety, or depression" (*experience mood disorders and lose too much weight*).

7) 1, 4, 5 The correct answers describe the interesting characteristics of Hawaiian language. According to the passage, in the Hawaiian language the meaning "of a word depends on the situation," so they *have a precise meaning only when used in a sentence*. Furthermore, it "consists of only five vowels and eight consonants," so *its syllables are formed with a relatively small number of consonants and vowels*. Finally, "some Hawaiian words have multiple meanings," so Hawaiian *uses many inferences*.

8) 2, 3, 4 The correct answers

describe reasons for homeschooling. The passage states that some families home-school because they "live too far away from any schools" (*schools may be too remote*), "feel critical of the quality of public schools" (*are critical of government-funded education*), or "feel that children will learn best when...[they] are allowed to make more decisions" (*if they are allowed to be more autonomous*).

9) 2, 4, 5 The correct answers describe either the support for or the criticism of fluoridation. The supporters of fluoridation claim it "slows down the loss of tooth enamel," so *it helps prevent tooth decay for everyone*. However, detractors cite "rare cases of excessive fluoride causing harm to bones" (*fluoridation has damaged health on occasion*) and that "more research is needed to justify public water fluoridation" (*more research about fluoride is necessary*).

10) 2, 3, 6 The correct answers provide reasons why slang exists. The passage states that slang develops "to express concepts brought about by new technology" (*Newly invented tools often require...new words*), "to express a sense of shared identity" (*to feel more connected to each other*), and because "People also borrow foreign words as slang" (*other languages contribute slang words*).

Chapter 10 Organization

Warm Up   **p. 143**

1) Train: 1, 4, 5   Plane: 3, 6, 8
2) Play: 1, 5, 6   Movie: 2, 3, 7
3) Whale: 1, 7, 8   Shark: 3, 5, 6
4) Brain: 2, 5, 6   Computer: 1, 3, 8
5) Golf: 1, 7, 8   Tennis: 3, 5, 6
6) Italy: 2, 4, 7   Egypt: 1, 5, 8
7) Ocean: 1, 7, 8   Lake: 2, 4, 6
8) Comedy: 2, 4, 7   Tragedy: 1, 5, 6
9) Chemist: 1, 5, 8   Psychologist: 2, 3, 6
10) Energy: 2, 6, 8   Fatigue: 3, 4, 5

Quick Practice   **p. 147**
1) Adolescent brain: 3, 6
    Adult brain: 2, 4, 7
According to the passage, adolescents are "more likely to take risks for...social rewards" (*social rewards especially affect it*), and use "more basic and impulsive

parts of the brain" (are *open to taking risks*). Adults, on the other hand, rely "on memories, experience, and reasoning" (*more active...at the strategizing level* and *experience* dictates *decisions*), and "make wiser decisions that support stability" (*choose to be stable*).

2) Shield volcanos: 4, 7
    Stratovolcanos: 2, 3, 6
A shield volcano is a volcano that "resembles a warrior's 'shield'" (*named after something used in ancient battles*), and spews "fiery liquid rock" when it erupts. Stratovolcanos are named after "strata," or *the materials that form the volcano*. They "are the most common (*prevalent*) type of volcano," and they "emit...solid debris" (*solid material comes out when these erupt*).

3) Folk dances: 1, 3
    Social dances: 4, 6, 7
The passage states that folk dances "developed among common people in villages" (*small, rural communities*) and were performed for "religious rituals" (*for religious purposes*). However, social dancing is "with a partner at a social event" (*with a partner but still in a group setting*), was "identified with elegance and refinement" (*sophistication and nobility*), and was "an indispensable skill for...the elite classes" (*important for affluent Europeans*).

4) Square knot: 1, 5
    Bowline knot: 4, 6, 7
We can determine that the square knot "can join two ropes or cords" (*tying two ropes together*) and is used "to tie stitches that close up wounds" (*has a role...in medical surgeries*). The bowline knot "uses just the end of one rope" (*Only one rope is needed*), "can be used as a seat to lift someone" (*provides support*), and "can hold sailboats to a dock" (*secures a movable thing to a... dock*).

5) General reference map: 3, 4, 6
    Thematic map: 2, 5
According to the passage, a general reference map "may show the whole world or magnify a small area" (*show very large or very small areas*), helps "people find places" (*planning a route*

ahead of time), and "shows... natural and constructed (*man-made*) features." A thematic map "illustrates the distribution of population, rainfall, or a natural resource over an area (*a specific characteristic...spread over a location*)," and "may use colors" or symbols to depict distribution (*colors...reveal information*).

6) Earthenware: 2, 7
    Stoneware: 3, 4, 6
According to the passage, "the clay used to produce pieces [earthenware] is easier to work with" (*potters can mold this easily*). It also states that earthenware is "less expensive" but "easily chipped or broken" (*affordable but fragile*). Stoneware, on the other hand, "was invented in China" (*People in China originally developed it*), "is glass-like" (*resembles glass in some ways*), and is "able to hold liquids" (*is dense enough to hold water*).

7) Girder bridge: 2, 6
    Truss bridge: 3, 5, 7
The passage states that girder bridges "are flat beams supported...by massive posts" (*horizontal planks supported by vertical posts*) and are built from "steel and concrete" today (*concrete and durable metals*). A truss bridge uses "tall vertical triangular shapes" (*specially designed supports*), offers "great strength and can be built with simple materials" (*basic materials...can hold up tremendous weight*), and does not have "supporting posts underneath that can interfere with streams or traffic below them," so it *allows things to pass under it without obstruction*.

8) Incas: 3, 6
    Aztecs: 1, 2, 7
In the Inca Empire people had to "work on farms or public projects" (*provide labor to produce community goods*), and collected community resources to "prevent hunger in a challenging mountain environment" (*Food was challenging to grow*). Meanwhile, in the Aztec Empire, officials "collected tributes or taxes from their subjects" (*taxation was mandatory*), merchants could "travel freely in Aztec-controlled land and in foreign... lands" (*People could negotiate*

for goods in a central location or foreign territory), but "many merchants…were also employed as spies" (*traveling…had a hidden purpose*).

9) Holstein cow: 1, 6, 7
   Jersey cow: 4, 5

Holstein cows "produce the most milk" (*great quantities of milk*), "have a spotted black-and-white coat" (*looks…blotched with black ink*), and "tends to be the largest of the dairy breeds." The Jersey cow's "milk contains the most butterfat" (*milk that is denser in fats per liter*), and "is the smallest of the dairy breeds" (*the littlest in size*).

10) Description: 1, 3
    Imagery: 2, 5, 7

Description is a literary technique that "'paints' a scene (*constructs a picture*) piece by piece using adjectives." Thus, it describes objects using adjectives like *smooth, red, and a bit shiny*. Imagery "employs unexpected (*surprising*) comparisons to another object" and adds "an extra layer of meaning or feeling" (*extra associations*). Thus, imagery uses metaphor, and *may describe a city bus as a "whale."*

Exercises Ch. 9-10   p. 155

1) 1, 4, 5   The correct answers focus on the change or on "mixed results" of the changes. To bring about the population decline, "fewer than two babies per two adults (*per couple*)" are being born. Consequences include "economic burdens" because the young are "supporting…an aging population" (*A decline in youthful segments of the population…can create economic problems*), but conversely, the decline "will help ease environmental problems" so that *there may be more resources for everyone.*

2) Genderless languages: 1, 3, 6
   Gendered languages: 5, 7

The passage states that genderless languages "have more gender-neutral words." Therefore, *"sibling"* may be used *more often than "sister" or "brother"* and saying *"teacher" could mean either a male or female one.* However, "when a language is genderless, people tend to…think of everything as masculine" (*as-

sume that most things are masculine*). Gendered languages "divide words into feminine or masculine categories," so a word such as *plate* may be feminine while a *"cup" is masculine.* Thus, one has to memorize *masculine and feminine categories of words.*

3) 1, 3, 4   Reasoning helps "people think about…evaluate…and make a judgment" about information (*what facts or observations may mean*), but this process "may not always be accurate or true" (*is not always correct*). Since "Reasoning can be deductive or inductive," it uses *general or specific information to help draw conclusions.*

4) Crawler-mounted crane: 3, 7
   Tower crane: 1, 4, 6

The crawler-mounted crane "can 'crawl'…over all kinds of surfaces" (*moves over many different surfaces*), and has "Heavy weights on the back" *to keep it from falling over.* The tower crane "is shaped like a 'T'." It is "built temporarily in elevator shafts" *inside buildings that are being constructed*, and it "can also be increased in height" *to match the height of the building that it is serving.*

5) 1, 2, 6   The correct answers support the idea of the amendment's unintended effects and unpopularity. According to the passage, the results of the 18th Amendment included "criminal gangs [that] took over production and sales of alcohol" (*The law did not prevent crime*), "Political corruption rose" (*public servants became corrupted*), and eventually "voters…repealed (*overturned*) the 18th Amendment."

6) Type 1 diabetes: 4, 5, 6
   Type 2 diabetes: 1, 7

Type 1 diabetes will "develop over the course of weeks" (*rapid onset*), "commonly strikes a person during childhood" (*before they reach adulthood*), and because of Type 1, "the body's own immune system attacks part of the body" (*attacks the body's own cells*). Type 2 diabetes' "risk factors include obesity and lack of exercise," so *the chances of getting* it *may be reduced with good habits*, and *People with certain ethnic backgrounds,*

"African, Hispanic" *may be more susceptible* to Type 2.

7) 1, 4, 5   The correct answers focus on how swamps have affected U.S. history. The passage states that swamps *were an obstacle for…English settlers* because "colonists died of dysentery and typhoid," Americans organized "attacks from the swamps" *to frustrate the British army during the Revolutionary War*, and "slaves…lived in secret communities in swamplands" (*Swamps harbored runaway slaves*).

8) Thermal: 2, 3, 5
   Photovoltaic: 6, 7

Thermal systems "operate by gaining and storing heat" (*Heat energy is a key component*). The heat forms by "focusing a great deal of reflected light onto a single spot" (*reflect light on a single point*) which will then "focus light onto a central tube filled with water" (*concentrates…onto a container of liquid*). Photovoltaic power works "by exposing panels of materials to the Sun" (*Flat panels…create electricity*); these panels "absorb photons of light and release electrons" (*gives off electrons when exposed to light*).

Chapter 11
Actual Practice

Actual Practice 1   p. 164

1) Ⓒ   Generally, *immense* means great or large. However, using context we can determine that *immensely* describes the Gaia Hypothesis, which claims that many things affect each other; thus, the system is *immense*, or *extreme*, in its complexity.

2) Ⓑ   The use of the pronoun *it* and the mention of *Gaia* in the added sentence indicate that the sentence refers back to "The Gaia Hypothesis." Since the only time the hypothesis is fully named is in the first sentence, the added sentence must come directly after.

3) Ⓓ   The main idea of Paragraph 1 describes Earth as a system involving both living and non-living things. Thus, we can infer that without living organisms, a key component in the cycle, *the present world would be

unsustainable.*

4) Ⓐ   The highlighted sentence states that living things and their surrounding conditions sustain each other. Thus, we can simplify the statement to say that *organisms create and maintain the ecosystems that they need.*

5) Ⓑ   Paragraph 2 describes how trees in tropical rainforests absorb and release water in a cyclical fashion. Thus, the paragraph supports the Gaia Hypothesis by showing how it applies to *an environmental process.*

6) Ⓑ   Since the sentence is discussing how trees circulate water, replacing *it* with *rainwater* in the sentence makes sense because *rainwater* is the nearest possible referent and helps continue the discussion about water circulation to support the hypothesis.

7) Ⓒ   Since *transpiration* describes the process in which trees circulate rainwater, the author is showing how the Gaia Hypothesis applies to nature. Thus, *transpiration* is mentioned because it *supports the* [Gaia] *hypothesis.*

8) Ⓐ   The passage states that the Gaia Hypothesis was developed "In the late 1960s." Since the 1960s fall in the 20th century, we know that the hypothesis was not *popularized in the 19th century.*

9) Ⓑ   Lovelock claimed that life on other planets could be found "by looking for atmospheric chemicals, such as oxygen and methane." This quote can be restated as *analyzing the atmospheres for particular gases.*

10) Ⓐ   Lovelock developed the Gaia Hypothesis, and since "Lynn Margulis later collaborated with *him* to further expand the [Gaia] theory," we can determine that *him* must refer to *Lovelock* since he is the only male associated with the Gaia theory.

11) Ⓑ   The final sentence claims, "However…[the hypothesis] has been used in many… disciplines." Because of the use of "however," we can infer that it was not at first "used in many disciplines," likely because it was not an accepted theory. Thus, context tells us that *skepticism* means *doubt.*

12) Ⓑ   We can infer that if the hypothesis is "used in many aca-

demic disciplines," then scientists have spent time developing it and *have been working to improve* it.

13) 2, 4, 5 The correct answers explain details of the Gaia Hypothesis. The hypothesis claims that "living things…affect how their physical surroundings evolve" (*Organisms affect…the sea, land, and air*), "Tropical rainforests demonstrate the [Gaia] principle" (*rainforests help maintain their climate*), and researchers place an "emphasis on microbial interactions" within the system (*tiny microbial creatures support…conditions*).

Actual Practice 2   p. 166

1) Ⓐ A *monument* is regarded as structure with cultural significance. Only *house* and *landmark* could fit this definition, since both are structures, but *landmark* is the best choice because *landmark* denotes a structure that has historical or personal value, whereas a *house* is simply a residence.

2) Ⓐ It makes sense that *it* refers to *Stonehenge* since the mystery of Stonehenge's construction is a key point of the passage. Thus, "No one knows…why *Stonehenge* was constructed."

3) Ⓒ Though all the choices could indicate Stonehenge's use as a burial ground, the passage states that "the site *certainly* was used…." This certainty means there is persuasive archaeological evidence for burials, or *human remains*.

4) Ⓒ Paragraph 1 states that Stonehenge was "used for religious ceremonies (*religious observances*), a healing center (*a place for the sick and injured*), and an astrological observatory" (*watching the stars, Moon, and Sun*), but there is no mention of *studying…plants*.

5) Ⓒ Since the passage states that "Similar…sites [to Stonehenge] exist elsewhere in… Ireland," we can conclude that Ireland was included to locate *sites that share features with Stonehenge*.

6) Ⓑ The added sentence should be placed at [B] because it contains general information about *earthen and stone parts*, and the following sentences

elaborate on the uses of these earth and stone-based components of Stonehenge.

7) Ⓒ Paragraph 2 states that "around 2600 BCE, people began erecting stones," whereas before they seem to have used earth and wood.

8) Ⓒ Because the author begins the discussion of stone transportation with "Somehow," we can infer that *it is not known…how people transported the stones*. If the transportation method was known, the author likely would have mentioned it.

9) Ⓐ By giving us the precise dimensions of the stones, the author is emphasizing the impressive size of the stones that were mysteriously put into place. Thus, these measurements describe *something amazing about the monument*.

10) Ⓓ Though *discouraged* and *prohibited* work in context and have a similar meaning, *prohibited* is the better selection because *forbade* and *prohibit* mean to actively prevent something, whereas *discourage* means to disapprove, but not actively stop something.

11) Ⓑ Since the stones are arranged to "mark the Sun's rising on…the longest *day* of summer," we can conclude that the stones were arranged to *emphasize a particular day*.

12) Ⓑ Though the passage states that Romans "forbade local religious practices" at sites such as Stonehenge, no mention is made of the destruction of the site.

13) Uses that are certain:
     1, 7
     Uses that are theorized:
     3, 4, 6
According to the passage, Stonehenge "certainly was used as a burial ground" (*human remains were buried there*), and more recently "the British government began to restore the monument" (Britain *manages the site for tourists*). Theories about its use include that it seems to have "marked the Sun's rising on the summer solstice"; that ancient peoples used Stonehenge as "a healing center" (*people came to the site to heal injuries or*

illness); and that it was likely that Stonehenge was "employed for religious ceremonies."

Actual Practice 3   p. 168

1) Ⓒ Since aesthetics was considered "the study of what is beautiful," but now it has "developed into a much broader study," we can conclude that the study has changed. The introduction *contrasts* current aesthetic studies *with its earlier purpose*.

2) Ⓒ To *regard* something is to *consider* it a certain way. Therefore, the idiomatic phrase "regarded as" is closest in meaning to *considered as*.

3) Ⓐ The term *art* can refer to both a particular work and a larger field of study. Thus, the author uses the term "in general" to show that the "art" referred to in the passage is *all of the arts as a concept*.

4) Ⓒ Both [C] and [D] seem like reasonable places for the added sentence, but [C] is correct because the transition word, "Moreover," used before the final question helps indicate that the list of questions followed by only one question is coming to an end.

5) Ⓑ The art described in Paragraph 3 "emphasized the viewer's experience of art." This emphasis, plus the mention of exhibits that involved serving food and viewing human models, allows us to infer that RA *emphasized viewer participation*.

6) Ⓒ Paragraph 3 states that Bourriaud is an "art curator and critic." The duties of a curator and critic would include giving *evaluation of art exhibits* since critics evaluate exhibits.

7) Ⓐ An "odd situation" can be described as a peculiar or unfamiliar event. The answer choice with the closest meaning to this description states that visitors experienced *something that they had not encountered before*.

8) Ⓓ The referent *visitors* is the closest applicable referent to *them*. Also, earlier in the sentence, the author mentions "exhibits that showed *visitors*…." Therefore, it makes sense that "exhibits that invited *them*" means "exhibits that invited *visitors*…."

9) Ⓓ The highlighted portion presents a contrast between Bourriaud's view of RA exhibits and the views of RA critics. Thus, the best paraphrase of the highlighted segment will express this contrast, which only (D) accomplishes.

10) Ⓑ Examples of *fields* given later in Paragraph 4 include psychology, anthropology, and sociology. Since aestheticians use "concepts and research" from these fields, we can use context to determine that a *field* is an area of study, or a *discipline*.

11) Ⓒ The passage mentions that aestheticians "may look… to understand how creating art relates to…religion" (*discuss how religious themes are reflected in art*), write "about RA" and other aesthetics topics (*write about art trends*), and "look to anthropology" (*consult with an anthropologist*). However, no mention is made that they *set prices for works of art*.

12) Ⓒ The final sentence states that aestheticians hope to "shed light on how the idea of 'art' varies" based on the highlighted factors. Thus, the highlighted portion helps *explain why people have different concepts of… "art."*

13) 1, 3, 4 According to the passage, aestheticians ask questions like "what is art?" (*articulate what makes… "art"*), "how should art be judged and valued?" (*understand and evaluate art*), and they try to understand "how the idea of 'art' varies" (*explore the role of art in different societies*).

Actual Practice 4   p. 170

1) Ⓓ The passage states that the dam "provides flood control" (*protects…areas from floods*), gives "electric power" (*generates electricity*), and created "a lake for recreational use" (*boating and swimming*), but the passage does not state that the dam *protects canyon habitats*.

2) Ⓑ Often, to help a person reference an unfamiliar location, we can place the unfamiliar place relative to somewhere well known. Thus, Las Vegas is mentioned as *a location that readers* *may know* so that they can better imagine where the Hoover Dam is located.

3) Ⓐ Paragraph 2 states that the dam "was of a size that had never before been undertaken." Thus, we can infer that the dam was quite large, and "*imposing* height" refers to the *impressive size of the dam*.

4) Ⓐ The previous sentence discusses the difficulties *engineers* faced in constructing such a large structure. Therefore, the statement "*they* were successful" must refer to the success of the *engineers* in designing the dam.

5) Ⓓ The added sentence refers to the condition of the dam in its completed state (notice the use of the present tense verb "is"). Therefore, we must place this sentence after "in the end…."

6) Ⓒ Though the passage mentions that the dam's "costs were expensive at the time of construction," we have no indication of whether the project was finished within its budget or not.

7) Ⓑ The highlighted portion indicates that the population of the Southwest was increasing rapidly. The new "farms and towns" would need a consistent source of water. Thus, the arrival of "farms and towns" *explains a motivation for building Hoover Dam*.

8) Ⓐ The main idea within the highlighted portion is that a water cycle made it difficult to continually distribute water. The only choice that states this without adding unsupported or unnecessary information claims *variances in water flow…hindered redistribution*.

9) Ⓑ The passage states that the Southwest "could support a larger population if there was some kind of water project." This allows us to infer that the Southwest *has few water sources* of its own to sustain a large population.

10) Ⓒ Mentioning the Great Depression in the passage tells us why the public "blamed him [Hoover] for the economic woes." Therefore, the reference explains the *public disdain for naming the dam after Hoover*.

11) Ⓓ Since the "*presidential administration* called the structure the 'Boulder Dam'," we can eliminate *the president* and *the administration. Las Vegas residents* are not mentioned at all, so they are eliminated. Thus, we can deduce that *a legislative body*, also known as Congress, "made the name 'Hoover Dam' official."

12) Ⓑ Because the dam was originally named for Hoover, but then changed because "many Americans blamed Hoover for the economic woes," then changed back once more, we can infer that *People viewed him differently as time passed*.

13) 1, 5, 6 The correct answers focus on the dam's "beneficial consequences." The Hoover Dam "was of a size that had never before been undertaken" (*proved that dams of its size could be successful*). It provides "water for 20 million people" (*support population growth in a vast area*) and "provides flood control" (*prevents flooding in downstream communities*).

Actual Practice 5   p. 172

1) Ⓐ Paragraph 1 presents *rate of exchange* by explaining a simple process of swapping one thing for another. Since Paragraph 2 gives a much more detailed *rate of exchange* between dollars and quetzals, we can determine that the introduction is a *simplified example* of a process.

2) Ⓑ The highlighted sentence sums up the preceding example of butter's value "in terms of loaves of bread." The phrase *the value of one item versus another* accurately describes *rate of exchange* and provides the most accurate paraphrase.

3) Ⓒ Since Paragraph 2 gives an in-depth discussion about the *rate of exchange* of Guatemalan *coffee beans* when trading, we can determine that *coffee beans* serve as an *example of a commodity that is traded*.

4) Ⓓ In the sentence, *quetzal* is the nearest possible referent for *its*, and when *quetzal* replaces *its*, the sentence is coherent since "demand for the quetzal" is

likely to "drive up the *quetzal*'s value."

5) Ⓒ Paragraph 2 states that a *floating exchange rate* means "businesses know how to exchange it [currency] that day." From this information, we can infer that *Exchange rates are made public* so that "businesses know how to exchange" their money on a day-to-day basis.

6) Ⓓ Paragraph 2 states that "the market determines the ever-changing…value of each country's currency." Thus, *governments* do not *decide on… exchange rates*.

7) Ⓑ According to the passage, "floating currency" means its value changes regularly. Since Paragraph 3 presents a different exchange rate, we can infer that a "*fixed* currency" will not float. Hence, *fixed* must mean not changing, or *set*.

8) Ⓒ If each currency is backed by gold, then *redeeming* money for gold would be a process similar to exchanging, or trading, one for the other. The word closest in meaning to this process of exchange is *compensating*.

9) Ⓑ The added sentence elaborates upon the idea that "exchange rates [were] based on precious metals" and should be placed at [B] because it reiterates the meaning of "fixed exchange rates" mentioned in the previous sentence.

10) Ⓓ Once countries let their "currencies float," we can infer that they gained economic flexibility because prices were no longer fixed.

11) Ⓐ Since Paragraph 4 provides an example where a country may effectively trade with itself to stabilize its economy, we can determine that *intervene* means *step in* because governments have to *step in* to the floating system and play the roles of buyer and seller.

12) Ⓓ If governments have to sometimes disrupt the "floating exchange rate" by altering the value of their own currency "to keep their economies more stable," we can infer that floating currency *may cause internal economic instability*.

13) Gold standard:
1, 3
Floating exchange rate:
4, 5, 7
The Gold Standard forced countries to "convert…currency to a rigidly fixed amount of gold or silver" (*values decided by different countries,* and *governments…make promises about… money*). The floating exchange rate is based on the idea that "the market determines the ever-changing…value of each country's currency" (*it relies on supply and demand* and *changes on a daily basis*) and causes governments to buy and sell "huge amounts of their own currencies" (*governments…buy or sell their own money*).

Actual Practice 6   p. 174

1) Ⓓ The passage states that the supernova was named because it "appears to viewers on Earth to be a super-sized new star blazing into life." But the author then informs us that a supernova is a dying star. Thus, the supernova is introduced by *explaining why it was misnamed* as a "new star" instead of a dying one.

2) Ⓑ Since "a supernova might outshine its whole galaxy," it must give off *unbelievable* "amounts of light."

3) Ⓒ According to the passage, the supernova will explode, give off light, and then fade away. *It* must refer to *supernova* because *it* refers to the process by which the light from the supernova fades away "a few months or years later."

4) Ⓐ Paragraphs 1 and 2 emphasize that supernovas "create such a bright light," so it makes sense that the mention of "10 billion light years" serves to further emphasize *how powerful and how far away* the bright light from supernovas must be.

5) Ⓒ The prefix *ex-* often means "away from." Furthermore, the passage states that supernovas explode, so they would *force out* "elements that form new stars and planets."

6) Ⓑ Because a supernova creates the materials "that form new stars and planets," we can infer

that *without supernovas, fewer stars and planets would form*.

7) D The passage defines a *white dwarf* as "a star that…has shed its outer material" with a "dense and hot" interior. Thus, the white dwarf is *the hot core of a cooling star*.

8) A Because of *gravity*, "the white dwarf can attract matter… [which] creates pressure." Therefore, *gravity* is mentioned as *the force that attracts matter inward*.

9) A The process in the highlighted portion can be described as 1) *pressure leads to heat*, 2) heat leads to fusion (*joining of atoms*), 3) "fusion creates an explosion" (*releases enormous energy*).

10) B If a star's material is attracted to its center, as described in Paragraph 4, then we can infer that *collapse* describes this movement towards the center, which means the star's material on the outside *falls* towards the middle.

11) D The passage states that, during Type 2 supernovas, "iron atoms begin fusing [or joining] together." Since the atoms are joining, it is impossible that the same *iron atoms are split apart*.

12) B The transition word "However" indicates that the information in the added sentence contrasts previous information, and the sentence previous to [B] states that a neuron or white dwarf star may be left after a Type 2 supernova, which contrasts with the added sentence's claim that *no object…remains behind*.

13) Type 1 supernova: 3, 4
Type 2 supernova: 1, 6, 7
According to the passage, a star undergoing a Type 1 supernova "can attract matter…from another star," and *the pressure from hydrogen gas* "can lead to atomic fusion." A star undergoing a Type 2 supernova, on the other hand, will "collapse into its own center" (*can no longer resist its own gravity*), it "may leave behind a…white dwarf star" (*becomes a white dwarf*), or it *may become so big that it* "collapses into a black hole."

Actual Practice 7   p. 176

1) B The phrase "apocryphally attributed" means that often, but not always, people claim that Hemingway wrote the story. Thus, *the story is widely believed to have been written by* Hemingway.

2) D The qualities of short stories include "one setting… [and] a few characters" and these stories may "surprise the reader by the end." However, no mention is made of *complex plots*.

3) C The entirety of Paragraph 2 discusses the development of stories into modern short stories. Thus, the historical introduction to Paragraph 2 begins to *trace the origin of the modern short story*.

4) C Paragraph 2 indicates that "the earliest story to be written down was…recorded on 12 clay tablets." Since clay is made from hardened mud, it can be described as *earthen*, or from the earth. Thus, *earthen panels* is the best choice.

5) A Using the context of the passage, we can determine that *character*, *setting*, and *conflict* do not work because they are elements contained within a short story, and according to the passage, the "short stories connected to an overall *narrative*." By process of elimination, a short story must fit into an overall *story*, so *narrative* means *story*.

6) B Paragraph 2 states that the *Decameron* involves young people who "amuse each other with stories." Therefore, the book *is filled with entertaining tales* that the young people tell each other.

7) C Because 10 people telling stories for 10 *consecutive* night results in "100 tales," we can infer that the stories are told for 10 nights in a row. The answer choice with the closest meaning to "in a row" is *successive*.

8) B The pronouns "These" and "*they*" in the sentence both refer back to *gift books* because the sentence serves to define and describe the qualities of this type of publication.

9) C The added sentence presents the general information that *novelists turned to writing short stories*. Since the sentence following [C] gives a specific author who did so, we can determine that the added sentence should be placed at [C] as most information is presented using general statements followed by more specific examples

10) A Because Hawthorn's short story collection "pioneered a new literary trend," we can infer that *it inspired other authors to publish short story collections*.

11) D Since a "perfect vehicle" is the best way to express or accomplish something, we can conclude that *The short story was especially suited to magazines*.

12) B Because "modern short fiction found a perfect vehicle" in magazine publication, it makes sense that magazines devoted a reasonable amount of space for "short fiction." Hence, magazines likely did not *primarily* consist *of nonfiction stories*.

13) 2, 4, 5 Modern short stories were "molded" when "Long epic tales…may have been told first as short stories" (*Ancient tales were broken into segments*), "some writers framed short stories in a larger story" (*short stories as episodes of a larger plot*), and magazines provided "a perfect vehicle" for short fiction (*magazines created a demand for short fiction*).

Actual Practice 8   p. 178

1) C Because Firestone was the president of a tire company as well as a *promoter* of "car culture," we can determine that a *promoter* is someone who supports something. Of the answer choices, supporter is closest in meaning to *advocate*.

2) A Firestone was the "*founder* and president" of a company that has his name in it. Using this information, it makes sense that a *founder* is a *creator* since it is usually a *creator* that gets to choose the name for something.

3) C Paragraph 1 presents the information that "Firestone was one of the earliest promoters of America's 'car culture'" and that he was "founder and president" of "one of the leading tire manu-

facturers." Thus, we can put these pieces of information together to infer that he *promoted car culture to sell more tires*.

4) A Paragraph 2 never mentions other tire companies, never criticizes Firestone, and never states that his name influenced his business. Hence, the name was included simply to *explain the background* of the name.

5) B Paragraph 2 explains that Firestone "began working as a salesman." Since salespeople work in the field of retail, Firestone *worked as a carriage retailer*.

6) D According to the passage, Firestone began working with tires to gain "an advantage over his competition." Thus, *he tried improving them* [tires] *so that he could sell more*.

7) C Paragraph 3 states that Firestone made his own tires "Within a few years" of starting in Ohio. Hence, the company did not start *making its own tires immediately* since "a few years" it much longer that *immediately*.

8) B An *acquaintance* is someone known, but not well, by another. From this definition, we can conclude that *the two men had met*, but that they were not yet close friends or business partners since those events are explained later in Paragraph 4.

9) B Since the passage mentions "*collaborators* with each other" in Paragraph 4, only *partners* makes sense because the passage already implied that they were both *managers, manufacturers,* and *specialists* of their own companies.

10) C Because the passage points out that Edison was an inventor and previously mentioned the innovations of Ford and Firestone, we must assume that these men were brought together because of their *interest in technical innovations*.

11) A The final paragraph discusses major investments and innovations Firestone was involved within the automotive industry. The added sentence's general statement should come before these specific instances, to serve as the introduction to the final paragraph.

12) Ⓑ *It* refers to the *"Ship by Truck" campaign* because "urged delivering merchandise by truck" provides an exact definition of "Ship by Truck."

13) 2, 4, 5 The correct answers refer to recognizing business opportunities. Firestone changed the automotive industry with "air-filled tires, which provided an even smoother ride" (*an advantage to using air in rubber tires*); he "furnished half of the tires that Ford Motors used" (*provided parts for the first mass-produced automobiles*); and he "was one of the earliest promoters of…'car culture'" (*encouraging drivers would increase demand for tires*).

Actual Practice 9   p. 180

1) Ⓒ The two main ideas in the highlighted portion are that 1) polystyrene is economical and 2) it "creates environmental hazards." The only choice that mentions both these factors without adding unsupported information mentions *its danger to the Earth* and that it *is strong and cheap*.

2) Ⓓ The passage states that polystyrene "makes up many of the *hard* plastic everyday objects that people use." Thus, it is not *used in soft products*.

3) Ⓐ Though it is unlikely that many readers are familiar with polystyrene insulating foam, *Styrofoam* is a common term, so the author likely mentioned the brand name as *a more familiar name*.

4) Ⓑ Paragraph 2 identifies styrene as "consisting of eight carbon atoms and eight hydrogen atoms." Since the word "and" denotes addition in mathematics, we can determine that *8 carbon atoms + 8 hydrogen atoms* make *styrene*.

5) Ⓑ Polystyrene was discovered "by accidentally isolating it from a tree's resin," and *resin* is a sticky substance in trees. Thus, polystyrene was *found in the thick liquid of a tree*.

6) Ⓓ "Chains of atoms" are only mentioned in reference to polystyrene, so the referent for *its* must be *polystyrene* because *its* shows ownership over "chains of atoms."

7) Ⓒ When explaining a complex process, such as the molecular structure of polystyrene, one should start with general information and then mention specifics. Thus, the added sentence should be placed at [C] because it gives a general impression of what happens to polystyrene when heated whereas the following sentence presents more specific information.

8) Ⓓ Though [A] and [D] both present answers resembling inferences, [D] is the stronger choice because we have no evidence to support that the atomic arrangement is more complex than in other materials. Moreover, [D] is relevant to the main idea of the passage and supported by the statement that "the atoms make the material moldable (*useful*)…[but] more durable than people may want (*problematic*)."

9) Ⓓ Polystyrene litter creates "special hazards in oceans and rivers," and we can infer that some of these "hazards" are threats to "Earth's ocean species."

10) Ⓐ A *mold* is generally described as a hollow form to shape substances. Thus, a mold provides an outline, or a *frame*, that substances can fill in to give something its desired shape.

11) Ⓓ Something that is *hollow* has an *empty space* or cavity. This can be determined from context since the liquid plastic is forced "to the edges of the mold," meaning the inside would be an *empty space*.

12) Ⓐ Polystyrene products are formed by mixing "*heated* liquid polystyrene," and by applying "*pressure* to trap nonreactive gas bubbles," but no mention is made of using *flexibility*.

13) Hard plastic molding:
3, 6
Plastic foam molding:
1, 2, 7
During hard plastic molding, "melted polystyrene [*is forced*] into a mold," and sometimes "vacuum molding draws it in" (*uses suction to pull liquid plastic into a mold*). Also, blow molding *uses a blast of air*,

"forcing the liquid plastic out to the edges of the mold." The process of plastic foam molding includes using "gases that contribute to global warming" (*atmosphere-harming gases*), using "a compound that will… release gas bubbles" (*uses the breakdown of a compound*), using "pressure to trap nonreactive gas bubbles" (*forces a gas into liquid plastic*).

Actual Practice 10   p. 182

1) Ⓓ Though the word *stoic* has come to mean not showing much emotion, the author uses the first paragraph to differentiate the modern meaning of *stoic* from *Stoic philosophy*.

2) Ⓒ We can infer that Justinian I suppressed Stoicism "in favor of Christianity" because he didn't want people studying belief systems that *conflicted with Christian beliefs*.

3) Ⓐ When something is *divine*, it pertains to a god or is *godlike*. This godliness makes sense considering the Stoic "divine essence" is universal and actively changes the physical world.

4) Ⓓ Paragraph 3 states that natural matter remains inactive unless acted upon by logos. Thus, *matter is the passive part of the divine*.

5) Ⓓ The pronoun *they* refers to the closest preceding referent, *Individuals*. It makes sense to substitute it: "*Individuals* are virtuous if *individuals* humbly accept…."

6) Ⓒ The *He* that begins the added sentence indicates that the previous sentence included a singular male, and the only mention of a male in Paragraph 4 is the "Stoic philosopher Epictetus." Thus, the added sentence must be placed at [C].

7) Ⓒ Paragraph 4 states that *cognitive-behavioral therapy* is a "current therapy," and because Stoicism was popular nearly 2,000 years ago, this therapy was included to bridge this time gap and to show how *Stoic philosophy has influenced today's society*.

8) Ⓐ Paragraph 4 claims that "a person could judge what is

true…and then accept it in a selfless way." Thus, Stoics believe that one should make the best of, or accept, all the *lemons* in life and *make lemonade* from them.

9) Ⓒ Since Stoics believe that "a person can judge what is true about the natural order," we can determine that in stoicism, the statement *people cannot make sense of* [the universe] is false.

10) Ⓑ If "all people come from the same" spirit and material, then we can infer that, despite "apparent differences," *people are not fundamentally different*.

11) Ⓐ The final paragraph discusses Stoics' views on slaves; "them" refers to people who did not speak "about ending slavery," so "they" must refer to *Stoics*.

12) Ⓒ Stoics claimed that "slaves can be free in their minds," but they also never "spoke about abolishing slavery," which greatly restricts physical freedom. Thus, we can infer that Stoics likely *believed that mental and physical freedom were different*.

13) 1, 5, 6 The correct answers describe how Stoics believed one should live. Stoicism states: a person should "accept reality as it is" (*accept whatever happens*), "that any person can become wise (*Perfection*)…and free of destructive emotions," and that all people, including "slaves can be free in their minds," so *all people can attain freedom through their mental states*.

Actual Practice 11   p. 184

1) Ⓓ Because Paragraph 1 states that Wounded Knee Creek "has a tragic history filled with death and violence," we can determine that a *massacre* is an event related to this "death and violence." The only choice mentioning death is *slaughtered*, which is a synonym of *massacred*.

2) Ⓒ Since the passage focuses on two conflict-filled events that occurred near Wounded Knee, we can infer that the protesters chose Wounded Knee *to focus national attention on wrongdoings of the past* and link them to the *present*.

3) B The highlighted sentence focuses on Native American "mistreatment, including forced removal from their lands." The only answer choice that mentions these two major points without adding false or unsupported information is [B], which mentions Native Americans *suffered* and *the seizure of...land.*

4) A Since the Ghost Dance focused on "bringing about peace," we can determine that the dance did not *encourage followers to attack others.*

5) D Paragraph 3 mentions interactions only between the U.S. cavalry and the Ghost Dancers. Since "the soldiers required *them...*" we know that the soldiers are not them, so "them" must be the only other group in the paragraph, *a Lakota leader and his followers.*

6) D Paragraph 3 opens with the statement that "U.S. military leaders...set out to arrest (*take into custody*) their [Ghost Dancer's] leaders (*leaders of a spiritual movement*)."

7) C According to Paragraph 3, shortly before "the military began shooting at the Lakota," there was a "tense" atmosphere because the soldiers "tried to take away the Lakota's guns."

8) A To *ensue* means to come after, or to *follow*. This can be determined from context since the sentence describes an order of events: first "A shot rang out," then (*followed by*) chaos.

9) B Because some Native Americans believed that the ceremony "would lead to the end of the U.S.," it is likely that *the U.S. military felt threatened.*

10) D Paragraph 4 mentions that the 1973 Wounded Knee incident took place between "200 armed people" and "heavily armed law enforcement." Because the passage mentions that both sides of the conflict were armed, we can infer that "exchanged fire" means the two sides *shot at each other.*

11) A The circumstances of an event are usually mentioned before their consequences, and since the added sentence describes the circumstances of the Wounded Knee incident, it

should be placed towards the beginning of the paragraph at [A].

12) B Whereas the 1890 conflict ended in many deaths, the 1973 demonstration ended in "the death of a U.S. Marshal... [and] a young man." From this information we can conclude that the 1973 incident resulted in two deaths, not hundreds of deaths.

13) 1890 Wounded Knee
Massacre: 2, 3, 7
1973 Wounded Knee
Incident: 1, 6

The 1890 massacre began after "a shot rang out" (*unfolded... after a mysterious gun shot*), during the conflict "women and children...tried to flee" (*people attempted to escape* and *women and children were killed and injured*). In the 1973 incident, "there was a crush of media attention" (*photographers witnessed the event*) and "two sides exchanged fire" (*a standoff between two sides*).

Actual Practice 12   p. 186

1) D Paragraph 1 describes a Social Darwinist as someone who "wants to cut government support," so the term is introduced *by giving an example of how it might be used.*

2) C A "disparaging term" can also be an *uncomplimentary label*, and "if it is not something one would call himself" we know *no one seeks to be associated* with the term.

3) D Paragraph 2 claims that 1) competition is part of survival, 2) survival leads to reproduction, and 3) *reproduction leads to adaptation*, which in turns leads to survival. Since the added sentence summarizes the process, it should be placed at [D].

4) D Since successful species pass traits to their offspring, we can infer that passing these traits helps *the offspring survive.* Therefore, *them* refers back to the *offspring* of successful species.

5) A Natural selection can be summarized as the process by which species "pass on their winning traits to their offspring, helping them [offspring] survive." Because some species

have these "winning traits," they will survive longer and produce *more young.*

6) A Though his theory later became associated with social hierarchies, Paragraph 2 indicates that Darwin applied his theories to nature, and therefore *was concerned primarily with biological processes.*

7) B Social Darwinists describe "the economy as a competitive arena," so having money (a *big house, powerful friends,* and *plentiful leisure*) makes you a winner, not having a *rigid moral code.*

8) C Since, according to Social Darwinism, "Those who are rich have 'won'," human society is primarily a *competition for wealth.*

9) A Because "winning traits" help one become rich, we can determine that *poverty comes from not having* certain *qualities,* or "winning traits."

10) B Social Darwinists may believe that social progress comes from having wealth, and therefore helping the poor would decrease wealth for those with "winning traits." Thus, helping the poor *delays,* or *impedes,* the goal of getting rich.

11) A To *revive* something means to restore it to life, so *revive* is used to show how Social Darwinist *came back into use* in the 20th century.

12) D Since Social Darwinism was used by Hofstadter to refer to fascism, brutality, and violence," we can infer that the term that was once associated with wealth *was increasingly seen as a very negative term* in the 20th century.

13) 1, 4, 5 According to the passage, Social Darwinism was based on natural selection (*adapted from a theory*), it "ignores circumstances that are beyond an individual's control" (*equal circumstances to begin with*), and stated "helping them [the poor] would impede society's overall progress" (*helping poor would be bad for society*).

Chapter 12 Actual Test

Reading 1   p. 189

1) C Although the Spanish "forced native Californian and Mexican tribes to work at the missions" that "served as... farms," Paragraph 1 does not mention anything about the Native Americans learning *farming skills* from the Spanish that would help the Native Americans *sustain their own communities.*

2) C The added sentence introduces the conflict between the Mexican colonists and the Spanish empire, so it must be placed before the results of the conflict. Thus, the most reasonable place for the added sentence is at [C].

3) D The passage states that the "Mexican government began closing the missions" (*old institutions built by the Spanish*).

4) C To *culminate* is to arrive at a final stage, or to *result* in something. In this case, closing missions *resulted* in "property being granted" to rich Mexicans.

5) A To *grant* something is to formally give it away. Thus, *grant* does not imply an exchange of money, so *granted* means *awarded.*

6) D The highlighted sentence states that "natives' fate changed again" (*changing the native people's lives again*) after the U.S. "won the Mexican-American War and took over the region" (*after winning the Mexican-American War, the U.S. assumed control of California*).

7) D Since "many natives lost their ranch jobs," as well as traditional lands, we can infer that they were unable to find more work or gather food and therefore *had no way to earn a living.*

8) A The passage states the Jackson wanted to "draw attention to the mistreatment of California native people" (*publicize an injustice*).

9) D Because Ramona and her lover "run away to get married," we can infer that her aunt would have disapproved of the marriage so they had to elope.

10) B The prefix *melo-* means emotional or sentimental, so melo + dramatic means very

dramatic and emotional, so the *characters and actions are exaggerated*.

11) Ⓑ The final paragraph discusses the impact *Ramona* had on California, so "*its* immediate effect" refers to the effect *Ramona* had on creating "a tourist craze."

12) Ⓐ Paragraph 5 states that "Ramona's world was "*enthusiastically* marketed." Because marketing involves advertising something to make money, we can determine that California hoteliers were eager *to profit from tourists' interest in California*.

13) 1, 2, 4 The correct answers describe consequences of colonization on native California tribes. The passage states that the "native Californian...tribes" were disrupted by missions (*mission system started the process of dislodging Native Californians*), they had to "find work on the ranchos" (*worked as laborers on ranchos*), and they "lost most of their hunting and gathering territory" (*immigrants settled in... tribal territories*).

Reading 2   p. 194

14) Ⓓ Paragraph 1 ends with the statement "the term [Yankee] probably came about in relation to Dutch settlers," which provides *one theory about its origin*.

15) Ⓒ The prefix *dis-* means apart or away, so a *dispute* is something that moves people away from each other, like a *debate*.

16) Ⓓ Paragraph 2 states that "'Yankee' may have originated from a derisive term for Dutch (*non-English*) people" who settled in the U.S.

17) Ⓐ Since "Yankee" comes from an unknown Dutch source, but now is part of everyday English, we can infer that *anglicized* refers to the process of a word being *made English*, or suitable for English language.

18) Ⓓ In Paragraph 2, *colonists* is the nearest applicable referent for *ones*, and it works in context since the sentence is discussing the use of "Yankee" for "all (including English) *colonists*."

19) Ⓑ The first two sentences of Paragraph 2 show how *Jan*

may be the origin of "Yankee." Since the added sentence also mentions *Jan*, we can infer that it should follow these similar discussions.

20) Ⓑ The highlighted sentence emphasizes that "Yankee" was used negatively by the British, and only choice [B] places this emphasis on "Yankee" being negative.

21) Ⓐ The British song describes the Americans as "fools" who think a feather in a hat is enough to make one stylish. Thus, the Americans were *overconfident* (in their fashion, at least) and *undersupplied* (since all they had was a feather to make themselves look good).

22) Ⓐ The entire passage discusses the underlying meanings, or *connotations*, of the word "Yankee." Something that is underlying, or connoted, can also be *implied*.

23) Ⓑ The highlighted sentence emphasizes that some people didn't want the U.S. involved in others' conflicts. Only [B] states a similar main idea.

24) Ⓒ Paragraph 4 states that "northern troops were called 'Yankees'" during the Civil War, but it does not state that this *use became problematic* at that time.

25) Ⓒ Because the Civil War was between the northern and southern states of America, we can infer that Southerners used the term "Yankee" as an *insult* to their enemies, the *Northerners*.

26) Yankee – Positive tone:
    1, 4
    Yankee – Negative tone:
    2, 5, 7
"Yankee" was used positively "during World War...II...as a friendly nickname for American soldiers" (*Allied forces used* "Yankee" and *fighters became proud of the name*). It was used negatively "for Dutch people, who famously made good cheese" (*deride 'cheesemakers'*); when "the British tried to suppress the rising colonial revolt" (*during the Revolutionary War*); and when "the U.S. became involved in conflicts abroad" (*used to criticize U.S. activity in foreign conflicts*).

Reading 3   p. 199

27) Ⓒ Paragraph 1 primarily discusses hummingbirds' flight by describing their flight control, speed, and maneuverability.

28) Ⓓ Hummingbirds can "fly...upside down," "hover in one place," and "zoom and dart," but the author does not mention that hummingbirds *soar on drafts of air*.

29) Ⓒ Since hummingbird wings beat "so fast that the motion is a blur to human eyes," we can infer that the markings on their wings would be indistinguishable if a hummingbird were in flight.

30) Ⓒ The mention of *Another beneficial sense* indicates that the added sentence should come after the mention of a hummingbird senses (like sight or smell). Since the only other sense mentioned is "sight," in the sentence preceding [C], we can determine that the added sentence should come immediately after the sentence on sight.

31) Ⓐ Because "the hummingbird is the smallest warm-blooded *vertebrate*," *miniscule* weight must refer to the hummingbird's small size. Moreover, since the prefix *dim-* refers to something become smaller or harder to see, *diminutive* must be a synonym for small or diminishing.

32) Ⓑ The "hummingbird's eyes can see a wider spectrum of hues" than human eyes, so a hummingbird is able to *see more colors in its habitat*.

33) Ⓑ Something is *relative* when it is placed in comparison to something else. Thus, *relative* to its body size, a hummingbird's brain is quite large.

34) Ⓐ The highlighted sentence mentions that the flowers became "tube-shaped" (*adapted to be tubular*), allowing "pollination" (*exchanging pollen*) by hummingbirds.

35) Ⓓ The passage states that "hummingbirds chose red flowers for *a practical reason*," which is that "bees do not see red very well"; by choosing red flowers, hummingbirds are able to have red flowers "all to themselves."The *practical reason* is that red flowers are *less*

distinct to bees.

36) Ⓓ The passage mentions that hummingbirds prefer red flowers to avoid competition with bees, so the mention of *Bees* serves to *explain why hummingbirds* choose red flowers.

37) Ⓑ Nectar is hummingbirds' primary food source, and they consume massive quantities daily. Thus, without this nectar, we can infer that they *cannot survive for long*.

38) Ⓒ Since Central and South America are equatorial climates, and hummingbirds travel during the warm seasons (spring and summer), we can infer that *they thrive in warmer climates*.

39) 1, 2, 3 The correct answers focus on hummingbird adaptations. The passage states that hummingbirds can "zoom and dart at other birds...and chase them away" or *protect "their" territories* with *their flying abilities*. Moreover, a hummingbird's miniscule size...allow[s] the bird to hover...while it sips nectar," so we can tell that *Their small size allows them to hover while the feed*. Finally, the hummingbirds "see a wider spectrum of hues" (*eyes*), have "long, thin beaks" (*narrow beaks*), and have "relatively large" brains that help them "remember which ones [flowers] provide the most nectar" (*good memories help them access good nectar sources*).

SIMPLE ANSWERS

Chapter 1
Warm Up
1-5: metropolis, solitude, intercept, satisfying, abstain
6-10: extraordinary, monologue, benefactor, equidistant, microscope
11-15: thermometer, antislavery, supervise, suggest, propel
16-20: multilingual, minor, manuscript, uniforms, megaphone

Quick Practice
Practice #1 (1-4):
A C B C
Practice #2 (5-8):
D B A C
Practice #3 (9-12):
B C C A
Practice #4 (13-16):
B A D A
Practice #5 (17-20):
D C A B
Practice #6 (21-24):
D C B A
Practice #7 (25-28):
D A D C
Practice #8 (29-32):
C B B A
Practice #9 (33-36):
D B D C
Practice #10 (37-40):
A B B C

Chapter 2
Warm Up
1-10: neither, it, one, it, both / its, it, a few, it, their
11-20: our, your, the first, one, others / her, the latter, he, their, a little

Quick Practice
Practice #1 (1-2): D C
Practice #2 (3-4): C D
Practice #3 (5-6): B D
Practice #4 (7-8): D A
Practice #5 (9-10): C C
Practice #6 (11-12): C C
Practice #7 (13-14): D C
Practice #8 (15-16): D C
Practice #9 (17-18): A C
Practice #10 (19-20): C B

Exercises (Ch. 1, 2)
Exercise #1 (1-10):
C A A B C / C D B A D
Exercise #2 (11-20):
C A C C B / D D A C C
Exercise #3 (21-30):
A C D A A / D D B C C
Exercise #4 (31-40):
A B B A A / D A D C A

Chapter 3
Warm Up
1-10:
F F O O F / O O F O O
11-20:
F O F F F / O O O F F

Quick Practice
Practice #1 (1-4):
A B C D
Practice #2 (5-8):
B A C B
Practice #3 (9-12):
C D A B
Practice #4 (13-16):
B C B A
Practice #5 (17-20):
B D C B
Practice #6 (21-24):
A C A D
Practice #7 (25-28):
D C C B
Practice #8 (29-32):
C C C B
Practice #9 (33-36):
C C A B
Practice #10 (37-40):
D D C C

Chapter 4
Warm Up
1-10:
C D E B E / D E B A C
11-20:
E D E E C / A A D C C

Quick Practice
Practice #1 (1-2): B B
Practice #2 (3-4): C A
Practice #3 (5-6): C D
Practice #4 (7-8): B A
Practice #5 (9-10): D A
Practice #6 (11-12): A B
Practice #7 (13-14): B C
Practice #8 (15-16): C A
Practice #9 (17-18): B D
Practice #10 (19-20): C A

Exercises (Ch. 3, 4)
Exercise #1 (1-4):
B B C D
Exercise #2 (5-8):
B C D B
Exercise #3 (9-12):
C D A C
Exercise #4 (13-16):
D C B A

Chapter 5
Warm Up
1-5:
3-1-2 / 2-1-3 / 3-1-2 /
3-1-2 / 1-2-3
6-10:
2-1-3 / 1-2-3 / 1-2-3 /
2-1-3 / 2-3-1

Quick Practice
Practice #1: B
Practice #2: A
Practice #3: C
Practice #4: B
Practice #5: B
Practice #6: C
Practice #7: A
Practice #8: C
Practice #9: B
Practice #10: D

Chapter 6
Warm Up
1-10:
A A B B A / A B A A B

Quick Practice
Practice #1 (1-2): B C
Practice #2 (3-4): D A
Practice #3 (5-6): B B
Practice #4 (7-8): D B
Practice #5 (9-10): B A
Practice #6 (11-12): D C
Practice #7 (13-14): D B
Practice #8 (15-16): B A
Practice #9 (17-18): C D
Practice #10 (19-20): A B

Exercises (Ch. 5, 6)
Exercise #1 (1-2): A D
Exercise #2 (3-4): B B
Exercise #3 (5-6): A C
Exercise #4 (7-8): B B
Exercise #5 (9-10): A C
Exercise #6 (11-12): B D
Exercise #7 (13-14): C D
Exercise #8 (15-16): B D

Chapter 7
Warm Up
1-10:
DES, CR, PER, DES, DES /
CR, DES, PER, DES CR

Quick Practice
Practice #1 (1-2): B D
Practice #2 (3-4): D A
Practice #3 (5-6): C B
Practice #4 (7-8): D C
Practice #5 (9-10): C A
Practice #6 (11-12): C A
Practice #7 (13-14): D C
Practice #8 (15-16): D B
Practice #9 (17-18): A C
Practice #10 (19-20): B C

Chapter 8
Warm Up
1-10:
A B B A B / B A A B B

Quick Practice

Practice #1 (1-2): C D
Practice #2 (3-4): D C
Practice #3 (5-6): A B
Practice #4 (7-8): B C
Practice #5 (9-10): D A
Practice #6 (11-12): C A
Practice #7 (13-14): B C
Practice #8 (15-16): A D
Practice #9 (17-18): D A
Practice #10 (19-20): C B

Exercises (Ch. 7, 8)

Exercise #1 (1-4): B A C C
Exercise #2 (5-6): D D
Exercise #3 (7-10): D C D B
Exercise #4 (11-12): B C
Exercise #5 (13-16): B A D B
Exercise #6 (17-18): D A
Exercise #7 (19-22): B A C C
Exercise #8 (23-24): A C

Chapter 9
Warm Up

1-10:
2, 3, 1, 3, 2 / 1, 2, 2, 1, 3

Quick Practice

Practice #1: 1, 4, 6
Practice #2: 1, 4, 6
Practice #3: 2, 5, 6
Practice #4: 2, 3, 4
Practice #5: 1, 5, 6
Practice #6: 1, 2, 4
Practice #7: 1, 4, 5
Practice #8: 2, 3, 4
Practice #9: 2, 4, 5
Practice #10: 2, 3, 6

Chapter 10
Warm Up

1) Train: 1, 4, 5
   Plane: 3, 6, 8
2) Play: 1, 5, 6
   Movie: 2, 3, 7

3) Whale: 1, 7, 8
   Shark: 3, 5, 6
4) Brain: 2, 5, 6
   Computer: 1, 3, 8
5) Golf: 1, 7, 8
   Tennis: 3, 5, 6
6) Italy: 2, 4, 7
   Egypt: 1, 5, 8
7) Ocean: 1, 7, 8
   Lake: 2, 4, 6
8) Comedy: 2, 4, 7
   Tragedy: 1, 5, 6
9) Chemist: 1, 5, 8
   Psychologist: 2, 3, 6
10) Energy: 2, 6, 8
    Fatigue: 3, 4, 5

Quick Practice

1) Adolescent brain: 3, 6
   Adult brain: 2, 4, 7
2) Shield volcanos: 4, 7
   Stratovolcanos: 2, 3, 6
3) Folk dances: 1, 3
   Social dances: 4, 6, 7
4) Square knot: 1, 5
   Bowline knot: 4, 6, 7
5) General reference map:
   3, 4, 6
   Thematic map:
   2, 5
6) Earthenware: 2, 7
   Stoneware: 3, 4, 6
7) Girder bridge: 2, 6
   Truss bridge: 3, 5, 7
8) Inca: 3, 6
   Aztecs: 1, 2, 7
9) Holstein cow: 1, 6, 7
   Jersey cow: 4, 5
10) Description: 1, 3
    Imagery: 2, 5, 7

Exercises (Ch. 9, 10)

1) 1, 4, 5
2) Genderless languages:
   1, 3, 6
   Gendered languages:
   5, 7
3) 1, 3, 4
4) Crawler-mounted crane: 3, 7
   Tower crane: 1, 4, 6

5) 1, 2, 6
6) Type 1 diabetes: 4, 5, 6
   Type 2 diabetes: 1, 7
7) 1, 4, 5
8) Thermal: 2, 3, 5
   Photovoltaic: 6, 7

Actual Practice
Actual Practice 1

1-5: C B D A B
6-12: B C A B A / B B
13: 2, 4, 5

Actual Practice 2

1-5: A A C C C
6-12: B C C A D / B B
13: Uses that are certain:
   1, 7
   Uses that are theorized:
   3, 4, 6

Actual Practice 3

1-5: C C A C B
6-12: C A D D B / C C
13: 1, 3, 4

Actual Practice 4

1-5: D B A A D
6-12: C B A B C / D B
13: 1, 5, 6

Actual Practice 5

1-5: A B C D C
6-12: D B C B D / A D
13: Gold standard:
   1, 3
   Floating exchange rate:
   4, 5, 7

Actual Practice 6

1-5: D B C A C
6-12: B D A A B / D B
13: Type 1 supernova:
   3, 4
   Type 2 supernova:
   1, 6, 7

Actual Practice 7

1-5: B D C C A
6-12: B C B C A / D B
13: 2, 4, 5

Actual Practice 8

1-5: C A C A B
6-12: D C B B C / A B
13: 2, 4, 5

Actual Practice 9

1-5: C D A B B
6-12: D C D D A / D A
13: Hard plastic molding:
   3, 6
   Plastic foam molding:
   1, 2, 7

Actual Practice 10

1-5: D C A D D
6-12: C C A C B / A C
13: 1, 5, 6

Actual Practice 11

1-5: D C B A D
6-12: D C A B D / A B
13: 1890 Wounded Knee
   Massacre: 2, 3, 7
   1973 Wounded Knee
   Incident: 1, 6

Actual Practice 12

1-5: D C D D A
6-12: A B C A B / A D
13: 1, 4, 5

Actual Test
Reading 1

1-5: C C D C A
6-12: D D A D B / B A
13: 1, 2, 4

Reading 2

14-18: D C D A D
19-25: B B A A B / C C
26: Yankee – Positive tone:
   1, 4
   Yankee – Negative tone:
   2, 5, 7

Reading 3

27-31: C D C C A
32-38: B B A D D / B C
39: 1, 2, 3